[BR]OTHER

OATWAY & SKUY

Photographs by James Oatway and Alon Skuy
Texts by Jan Bornman, Justice Edwin Cameron,
Justice Malala, Professor Achille Mbembe,
Dr Jean Pierre Misago, Koketso Moeti,
James Oatway and Joao Silva
Designed by Gabrielle Guy
Published by Jacana

[BR]OTHER

OATWAY & SKUY

This book is dedicated to all those who have been affected by violence, intolerance and hatred.

Whenever fresh violence erupts, my stomach begins to knot with tension. Whenever I hear rumours of attacks, or see a new flyer on my phone stating that 'foreigners must go', I get heart palpitations and panic attacks. I become absent-minded and feel suffocated by dread as I remember the brutality of previous attacks. I feel angry and frustrated that we have allowed these attacks to continue.

It's no coincidence that the most brutal xenophobic attacks take place in areas where poverty and unemployment are worst. Ramaphosa settlement, Makause settlement, Zandspruit, Diepsloot, Alexandra, Jeppe Hostel, Khayelitsha. These are places where it's not easy to live. Places where poor South Africans feel let down and forgotten.

In 2008, seven years before I photographed the attack on Emmanuel Sithole, I spent many hours working in the same area – ironically nicknamed 'Pan' after nearby Pan Africa Shopping Centre – photographing xenophobic attacks.

In 2015, not much had changed; and even today, sewerage leaks into the streets from rows of plastic bucket toilets. Residents must queue at communal taps for water. We see the same violent scenes, in the same depressing areas.

But even in these unacceptable conditions, can anybody justify violent attacks and murder?

We hope this book will serve as both a historical record and a call to action. We want the debate to continue. We want people to think before they act.

James Oatway, Johannesburg, March 2020

The xenophobic violence that occurred in South Africa in May 2008 was the start of what some might call the most troubled era to grip South Africa since the dawn of democracy in 1994.

Twelve years later, intermittent attacks and chaos continue to shake the foundations of this fragile state.

In documenting this violence, I – alongside many other photographers – have tried to make sense of the inexplicable torment and cycles of unrest that migrants, as well as South Africans, have been thrust into with no real intervention by the state.

When I think back on these darkest days and nights, it stirs in me things I've long suppressed. I cannot imagine what those on the receiving end of such attacks must live with.

During the process of looking at these photographs so closely again now, years later, I am reminded of how unprepared South Africa was for such waves of violence.

With this collection of images – a worryingly unfinished story – we wish to create deeper dialogue around the issues at stake; and to honour those so deeply affected by intolerance, whose resilience we hope will outlast this tragic period in our history.

Alon Skuy, Johannesburg, March 2020

'No African is a foreigner in Africa!
No African is a migrant in Africa!
Africa is where we all belong!'

Professor Achille Mbembe
Philosopher, political theorist and public intellectual

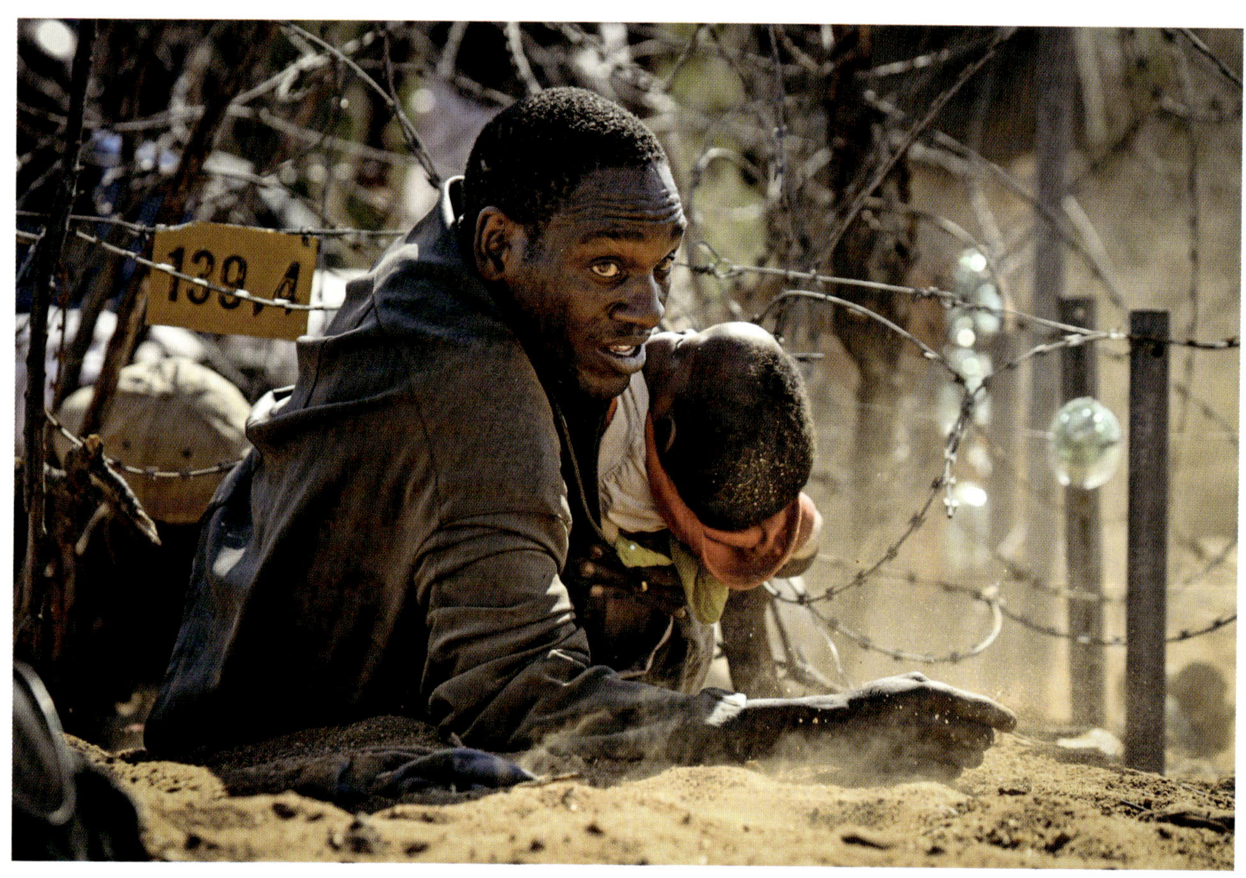

A man and child cross under the border fence between Zimbabwe and South Africa on 27 June 2008; the same day Zimbabwe was holding what was widely viewed as a sham run-off election. JO

Foreword

Justice Edwin Cameron

Whose stories are told – and whose are
obscured? Who is allowed to be visible – and
who is erased? Photography entails more than
record-keeping. It engages processes of world-
making that organise how we understand our
worlds, and ourselves, and how we engage with
our communities. By engaging our attention on
certain sites and away from others, it frames
what and who are worth seeing. In this way,
the photographer helps produce a public
knowledge about who should be made visible.

South Africans know this acutely, for
photographers, some of them heroic, some at
cost to their own lives, made apartheid visible.

Targets of xenophobia are subjected to the
violence of estrangement. *Xenos*: the stranger,
the outsider, the 'alien'. To be called *xenos*,

to be made *xenos*, is to be categorised as
illegitimate – to be pushed beyond the bounds,
beyond citizenship, beyond moral concern.

These categories accrue. They come to
justify enactments of violence against bodies
that are present, that are real, that are living,
but do not belong.

South Africa has experienced brutal cycles of
xenophobic violence. These have led to horrific
murders, and to displacement of thousands of
cross-border migrants, mostly from our own
continent, Africa. Worse, they have led to fear
and suspicion and terror. They have torn at
the cloth of our constitutional inclusiveness,
shredding and tattering it.

The most recent wave began in late August
2019. There was a resurgence of anti-migrant
protests, looting of foreign businesses and
assaults: bodies stoned, beaten, burned
and killed.[1]

There is a conspicuous race and class
edge to this. The white cross-border migrant
in an affluent haven like Sandton will fear no
criminality beyond the ordinary. Five kilometres
away, in Alexandra township, the black African
cross-border migrant may be in fearful peril
of her life, her livelihood.

Our leaders have responded by
predominantly labelling xenophobia a crime.
This is true. In an obvious sense. But also only
partly true. The bigger, more horrendous truth
is that it is crime with an edge – an anti-migrant
crime, an anti-African-migrant crime. The
typology evidences denialism. As with our AIDS
epidemic, denialism springs from shame. There,
the shame of the virus, of infection, of its mode

of transmission, was unwarranted. Here, the shame is rightful. Shame that we turn against our own, our African own.

Of course there is a problem – here, in Europe, in the Middle East, in Asia, in the Americas. The problem is resources and their allocation in conditions of scarcity. Across party lines leaders have urged tighter border controls. They contend that cross-border migrants undermine South Africa's socio-economic development. Some have openly campaigned for undocumented migrants to be detained, in camps.[2]

Why? Fear. Fear of the Other, the intruder. Fear that African migrants will eventually take control, *take our country*.[3] Yet, allegations that migrants are disproportionately responsible for crime and that they drain public resources by claiming undue government support lack evidence. Still, the words lawlessness, human traffickers, drug dealers, thieves become metonyms for 'migrant'; our words shift between vocabularies of migration and criminality as though there is no boundary between the two.

The cross-border migrant is not a politically neutral figure. She bears the marks of our country's colonial and apartheid past. Yet, xenophobic violence seems reserved for poor black immigrants from Africa.

Our country's official policy on international migration[4] catalogues immigrants into categories. These distinguish between those who can and cannot contribute to our economy. These classifications designate only the exceptional, privileged and productive bodies as worthy of welcome. The inerasable fact that we are regionally and continentally interdependent is somehow erased.

Faced with inequality and unemployment, many seek to claim resources through the regime of citizenship. This is understandable. But it positions foreign nationals as undeserving of the rights owed to South Africans. Rather than constituting a direct physical harm, the mere presence of the migrant is imagined as the greatest danger since it threatens economic security and access to scarce resources. The African migrant is dangerous simply because she exists.

Yet, our Bill of Rights knows the difference between migrant and non-migrant. And it categorises them carefully, and respectfully. Apart from its entrenchment of citizenship itself (sections 3 and 20), the Constitution requires citizenship only for the vote (political rights, section 19), freedom of movement and residence (section 20(3)), a passport (section 20(4)) and freedom of trade, occupation and profession (section 22).

Beyond these, the rights in the Bill of Rights protect everyone within our borders equally. It is on this granite that the architecture of the Constitutional Court decisions on migrants is founded.[5]

Despite pleas from local civil society organisations, international and regional bodies, and other African governments, we continue to hush xenophobia with denialism. The migrant becomes a hyper-visible substitute for our failure to respond effectively to our history of subjugation. Yet, simultaneously, we erase the migrant from our understanding of violence, as xenophobia is subsumed into a narrative of rising crime.

Rather than a danger posed to particular, individual persons, xenophobia becomes lost in growing statistics of assaults, murders and robberies.

Dismissing xenophobic violence as mere criminality obscures the hard fact that we have failed adequately to address our country's structural legacies of Othering and, with this, the socio-economic conditions that provide the seedbed for violence.

Migrants are blamed for the daily hardships experienced by poor South Africans. By refusing to articulate what they experience as xenophobic, we are left without the reflective means to question the colonial histories and political failure that reinforce anti-immigrant attitudes, and that continue to structure our engagement with the Other within our country.

What we choose to frame shapes the personal and political responses available to us. Photography retrieves these bodies. It documents how our own Othering heightens the precarious status of certain groups. This book, by two distinguished, award-winning South Africans, makes the Other present and visible to us. Poignantly and often troublingly so. Sometimes magnificently so. This work by James Oatway and Alon Skuy instigates us to reflection, and discussion, and ultimately to action. This starts by positioning the cross-border migrant as central to a meaningful response to xenophobia. Most importantly,

it dignifies imperilled bodies by allowing them to be seen. From there, we challenge ourselves to seek new, more practical ways of embracing the other in our midst. In that way, we may find, begin to find, our own humanity.

I am grateful to my researcher at the Judicial Inspectorate for Correctional Services, Alexia Katsiginis, for providing a rich and full first draft of this Foreword.

1   https://www.hrw.org/news/2019/09/13/south-africa-punish-xenophobic-violence.

2   Particularly, the DA, FF Plus and COPE: see https://mg.co.za/article/2019-09-03-00-xenophobia-and-party-politics-in-south-africa/.

3   This was explicitly articulated by then-Deputy Minister of Police and ANC member, Mr Bongani Mkongi, in 2017. He warned that 'the whole of South Africa could be 80% dominated by foreign national and the future president of South Africa could be a foreign national': https://ewn.co.za/2017/07/14/deputy-police-minister-accuses-hillbrow-foreign-nationals-of-economic-sabotage.

4   2017 White Paper on International Migration: http://www.dha.gov.za/WhitePaperonInternationalMigration-20170602.pdf.

5   See, most recently, *Ruta v Minister of Home Affairs* [2018] ZACC 52; 2019 (2) SA 329 (CC); 2019 (3) BCLR 383 (CC) (20 December 2018) and *Nandutu v Minister of Home Affairs* [2019] ZACC 24; 2019 (8) BCLR 938 (CC); 2019 (5) SA 325 (CC) (28 June 2019).

Justice Edwin Cameron is the head of the Judicial Inspectorate of Correctional Services and Chancellor of Stellenbosch Univorcity. Ho retired from the Constitutional Court, South Africa's highest court, in August 2019, after serving as a judge since 1994.

2008

In May 2008, a series of xenophobic attacks accompanied by widespread looting and vandalism left at least 62 people dead,[1] 700 injured and 100 000 displaced. The violence began in Alexandra in Johannesburg after a local community meeting at which migrants were blamed for crime and for 'stealing' jobs. Within days the attacks had spread around the country, with Ramaphosa settlement on the East Rand becoming one of the areas that witnessed inhumanity on an unthinkable level. On 18 May, 35-year-old Ernesto Alfabeto Nhamuave was beaten, stabbed, covered with his own blankets and set alight. The following day, a 16-year-old migrant was hacked, burnt and left for dead on a refuse dump. Miraculously, he survived. Across the land, tens of thousands fled their homes, crowding into community centres and police stations for protection until they could be moved to makeshift camps. In the years that followed, prosecution of perpetrators was slow, socio-economic change was negligible, and the anger of poor South Africans, who have yet to see the promised fruits of their 1994 liberation, was left to simmer...

1   Of the 62 people killed, 21 were South African. In 2010, Loren B. Landau, director of the African Centre for Migration & Society at Wits University, offered this explanation in *African Affairs*, Volume 109, Issue 345: 'Most victims were from beyond South Africa's borders, but a third were South Africans who had married foreigners, refused to participate in the violent orgy, or had the misfortune to belong to groups that were evidently not South African enough.'

A crowd gathers in Alexandra before raiding nearby
government-subsidised houses and demanding to see
ID documents. Residents who were not South African
were beaten and forced out of their homes. JO

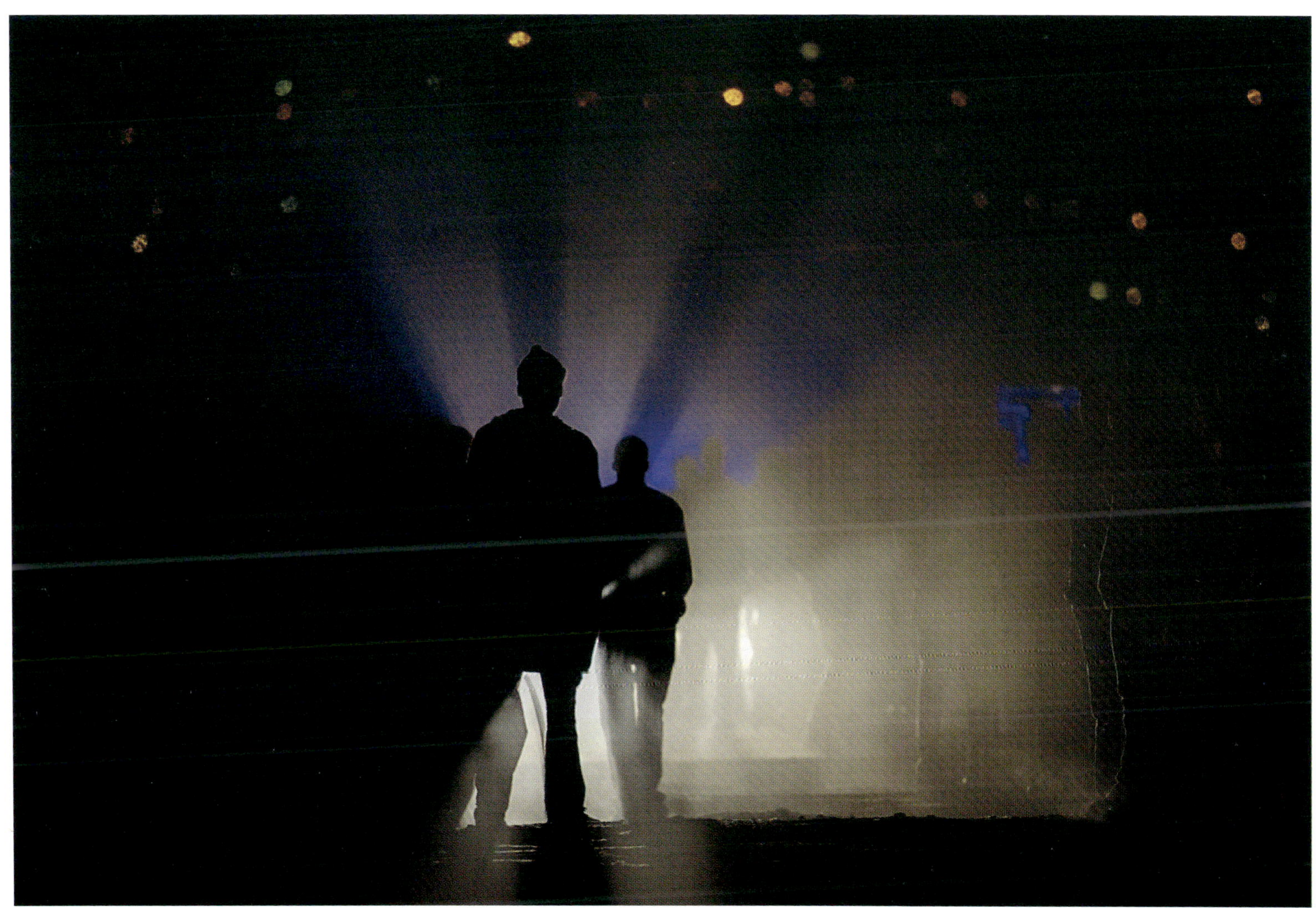

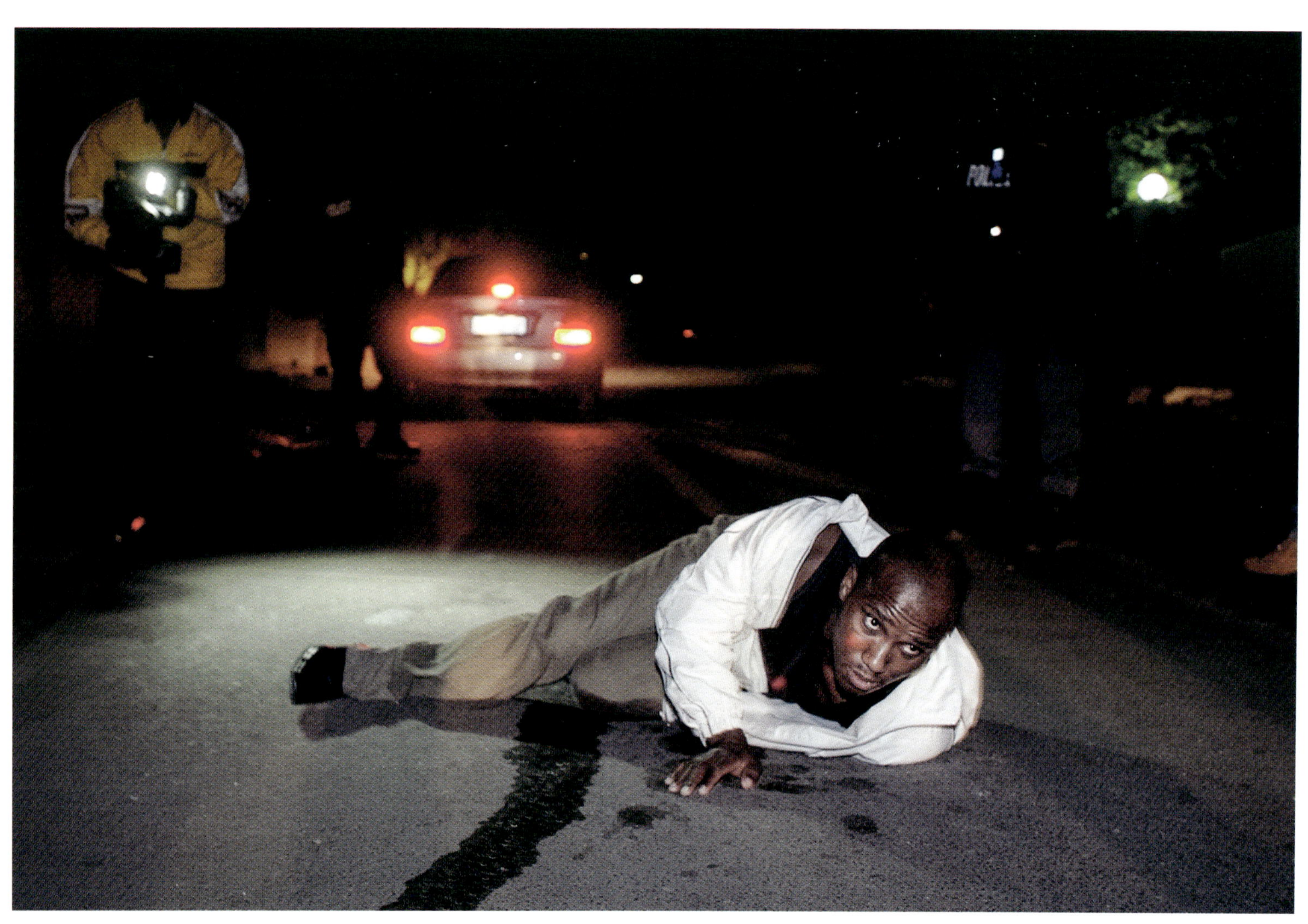

A man awaits help after being shot in Alexandra. The violence began in the Beirut
section and spread into the government-subsidised section of Extension 7,
where it is believed that some houses had been rented out to migrants. JO

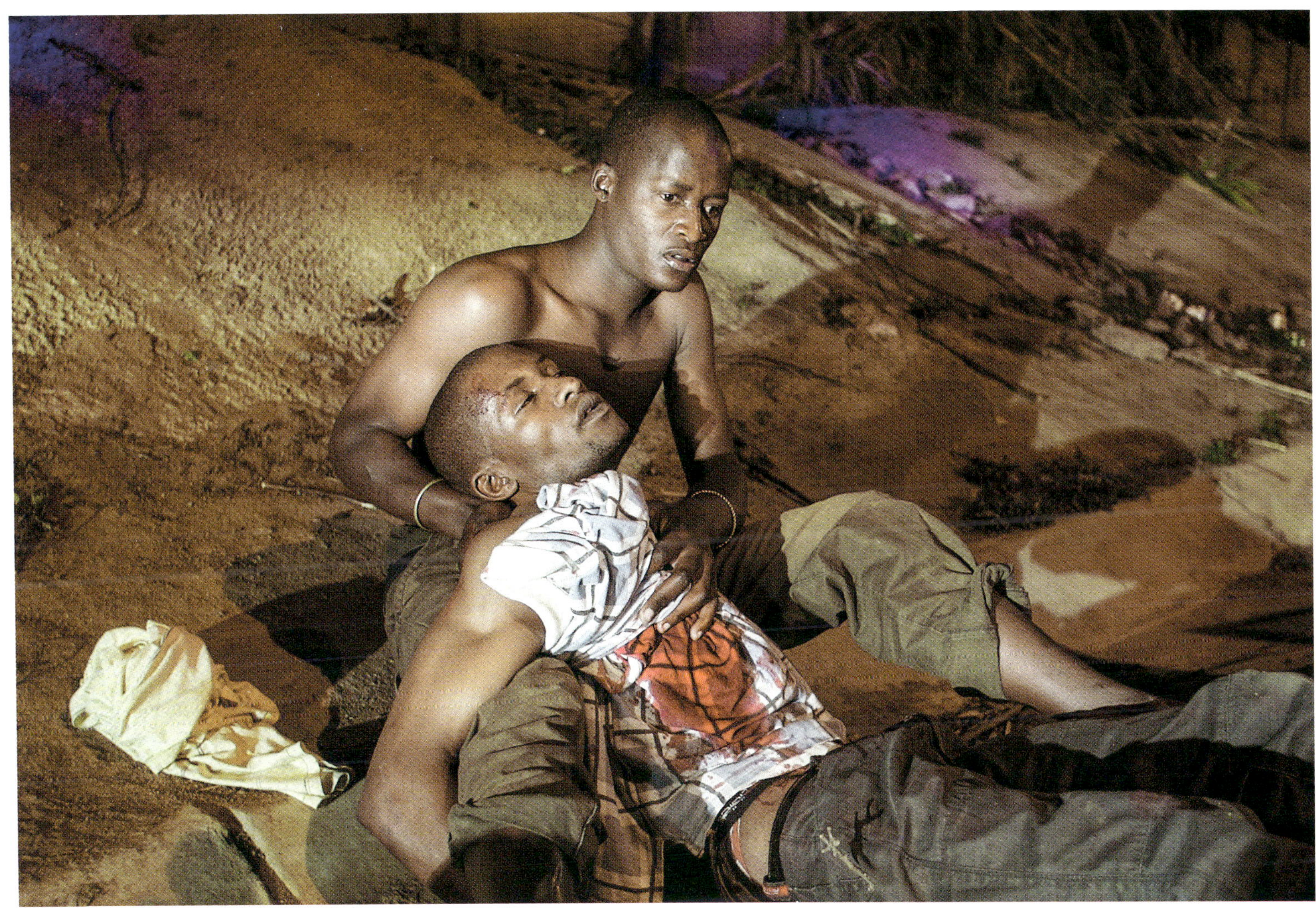

Michael Sambo cradles his seriously wounded brother Amos, who has been stabbed in Alexandra. Michael said they were local and that their family home was in Limpopo. JO

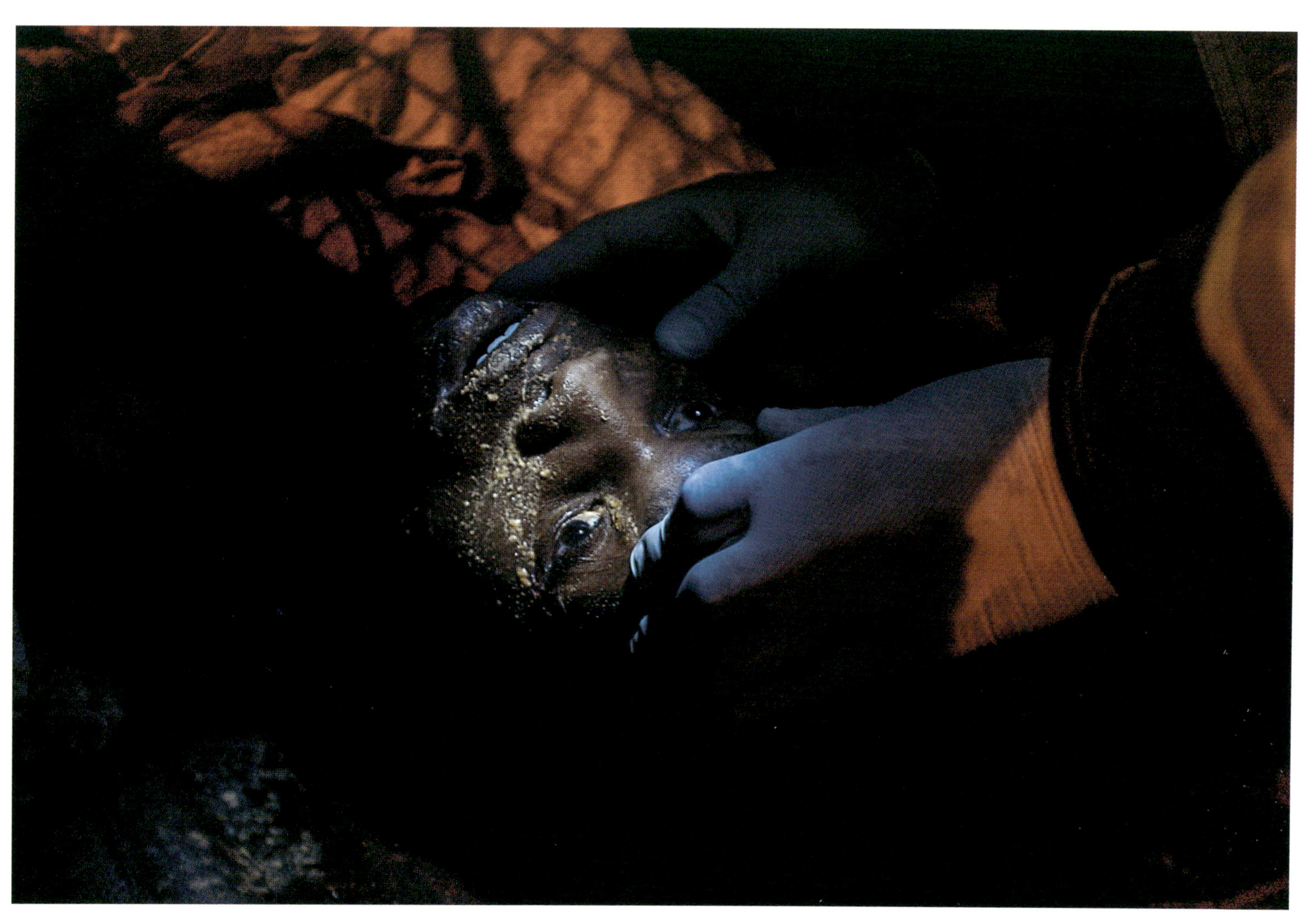

A paramedic finds no sign of life in a man who has been attacked in Primrose on the East Rand. JO

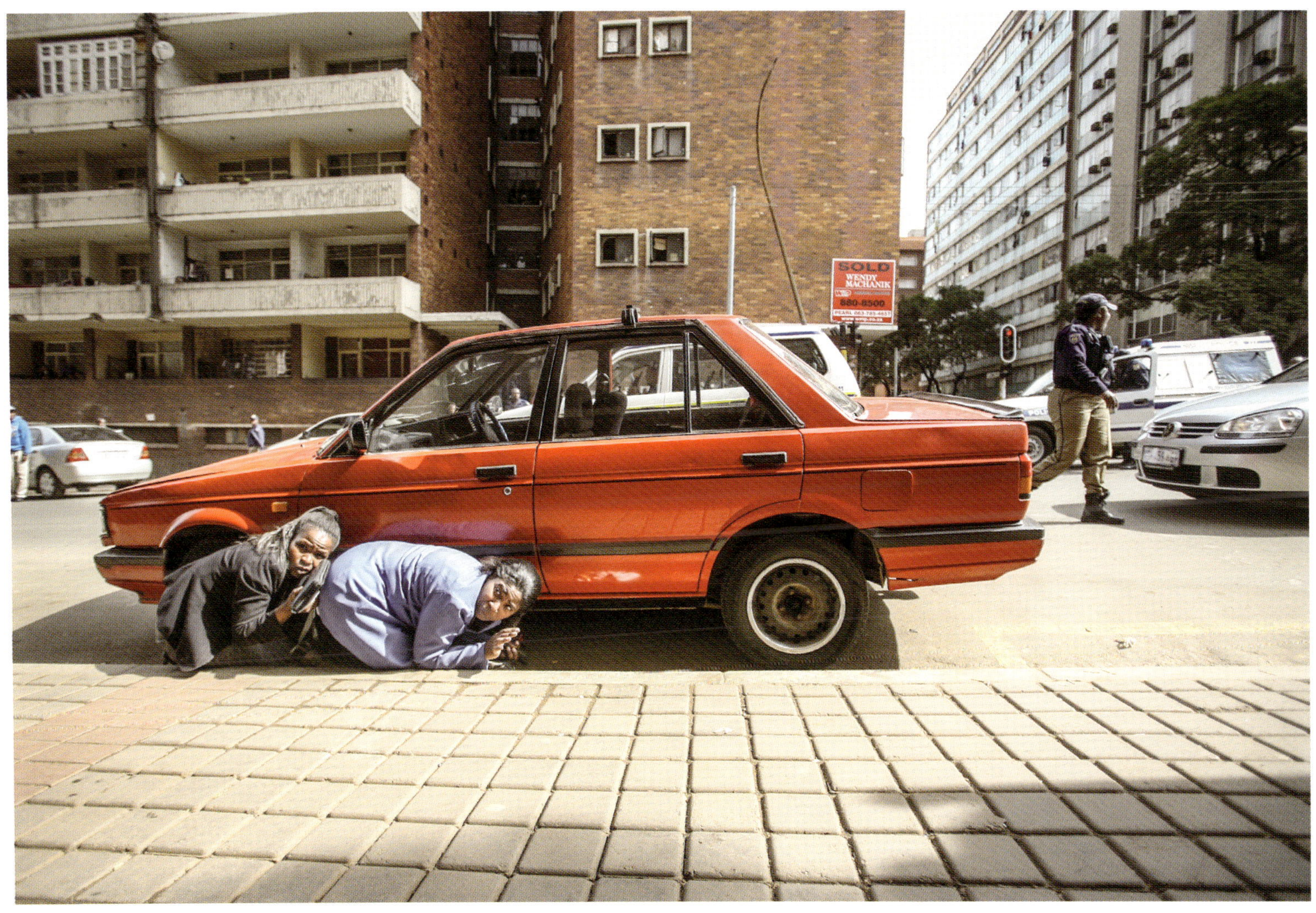

Pedestrians duck for cover as police attempt to control
unrest in the Johannesburg inner city. AS

Men lie injured after police intervention during an outbreak
of violence in central Johannesburg. AS

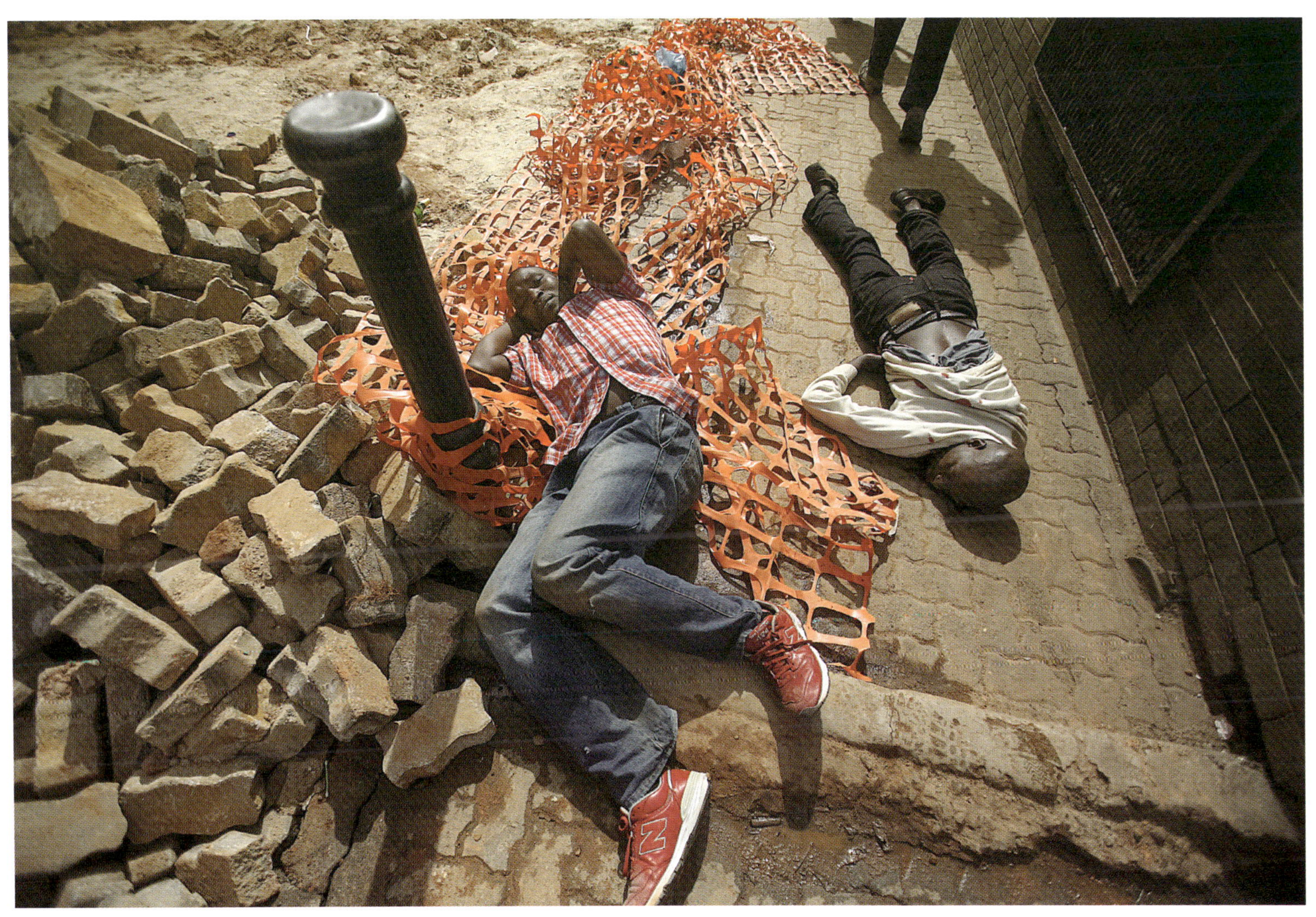

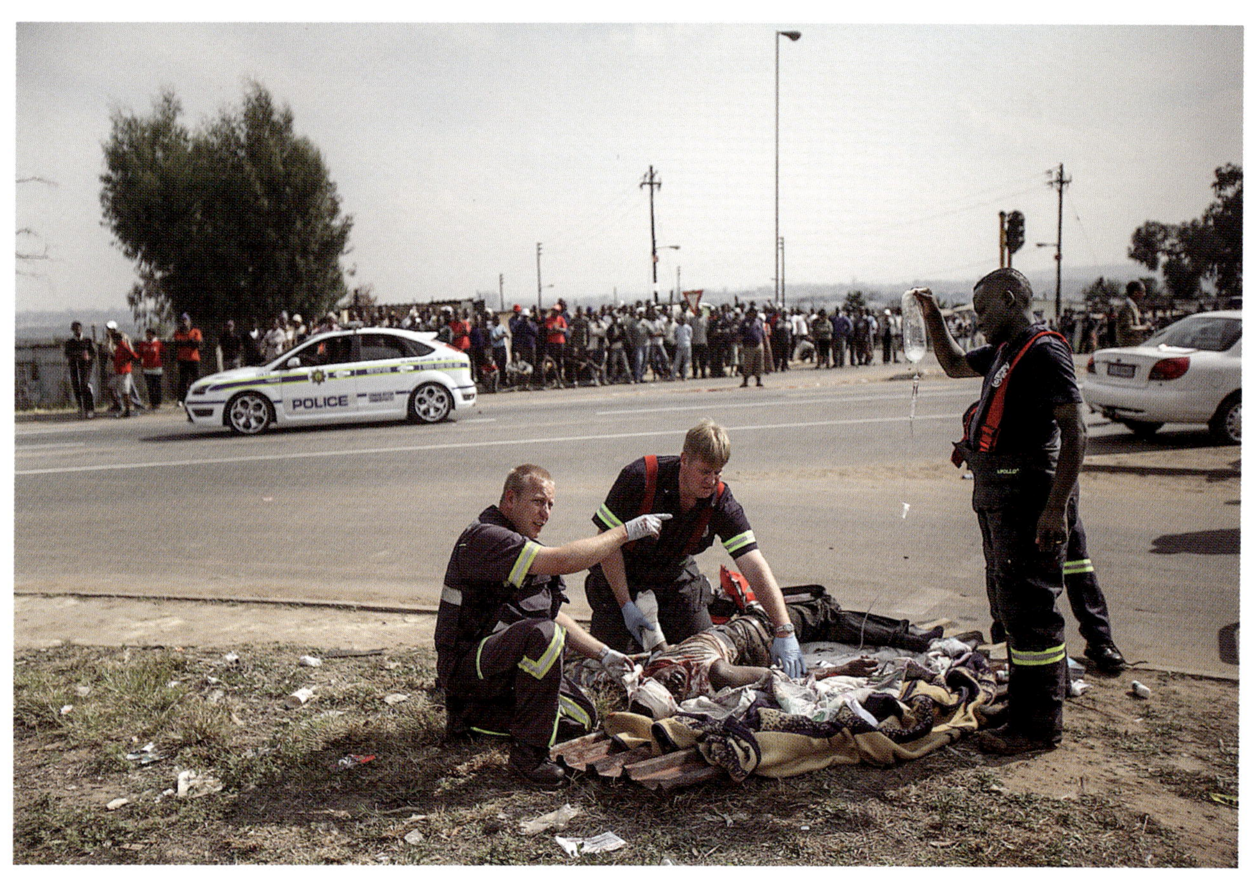

Paramedics treat a severely injured man on the outskirts
of Ramaphosa settlement near Germiston. AS

Extract from
Go Home or Die Here

My parents came from Mozambique, but I was born here in South Africa. I lost my mother in June 2004 and my father in October the same year. They left me a stand … and I was sustaining myself from the money tenants paid. I was too young to look for employment then but at least with the shacks I could survive. I tried to send myself to school for about one year but then I dropped out.

When all this violence took place I was at work, where I repair radios and TVs. I returned to my place and found it in a chaotic state, as people were being attacked and trying to flee. It was dark. While I stood with friends outside my house, a group of about 12 youths came armed with knives, iron bars, hammers, spears and all sorts of weapons. They said, 'We want this guy who fixes radios and TVs' and they meant myself. I said, 'I don't know this guy you are talking about.' They found my shack locked and went their way. But then this other woman they met advised them that the person they were looking for was the one they had just left alone.

That's when I jumped the fence and fled and joined the other people running away. We spent Sunday at the police station. On Monday I decided to go back to check my place and I was astonished to find it razed down. There was nothing remaining. They looted all my belongings and then removed the zinc sheets. There had been four shacks and they had looted all of them.

These guys who were the attackers moved as a group. There were nine people who came in the afternoon and had a meeting with the local committee. These people had regalia that they tied around their heads as a mark of identification. Without it you would be attacked. If you heard them shouting 'Hey comrade', you had to return the greeting by the same 'Hola comrade', and if you failed you would get attacked. They attacked you so that they could remove your shack and accommodate their relatives…

There was this boy who was coming home in the afternoon during the violence and he met a group of Zulu youths who were on standby, waiting to pounce on such people. When they attacked him, a lady who is also Zulu lay on top of the victim and said, 'It will be better if you kill me but let this innocent boy go.' So they couldn't continue. They said to him, 'You tell your dad that we don't want to see him here and he must leave.'

The lady escorted the boy away and he was so grateful for the lady who saved his life…

I did think of going back to Mozambique, but I am staying with a lady, a South African, and I could not just let her go like that. She is pregnant. My fiancée was also ejected from the shacks – they told her to follow her Shangaan man.

Another man told me that they came to evict his lady from the shacks. They wanted to hack off the head of their nine-month-old baby. The lady cried until they ordered her to follow her Shangaan boyfriend.

It is hard to believe that it was the people we know who attacked us and not strangers. The man who was burnt: what happened is that he went to the police and asked them to assist him after he had been chased from his place by attackers. The police just said, 'Go back, we are behind you and we will find you still on the way.'

The attackers waited for him and when they realised that he was not under police escort they captured him just as he left the station, tied him up, poured paraffin on his body and set him alight. The police did nothing.

This is an edited version of a survivor's* story that was recorded by Phefumula Nyoni as part of the Wits Forced Migration Studies Programme's Documenting Experiences of Xenophobic Violence Study at the African Centre for Migration & Society, and which appears in *Go Home or Die Here: Violence, Xenophobia and the Reinvention of Difference in South Africa*, edited by Shireen Hassim, Tawana Kupe and Eric Worby and published by Wits University Press. www.migration.org.za

* Survivor's name withheld

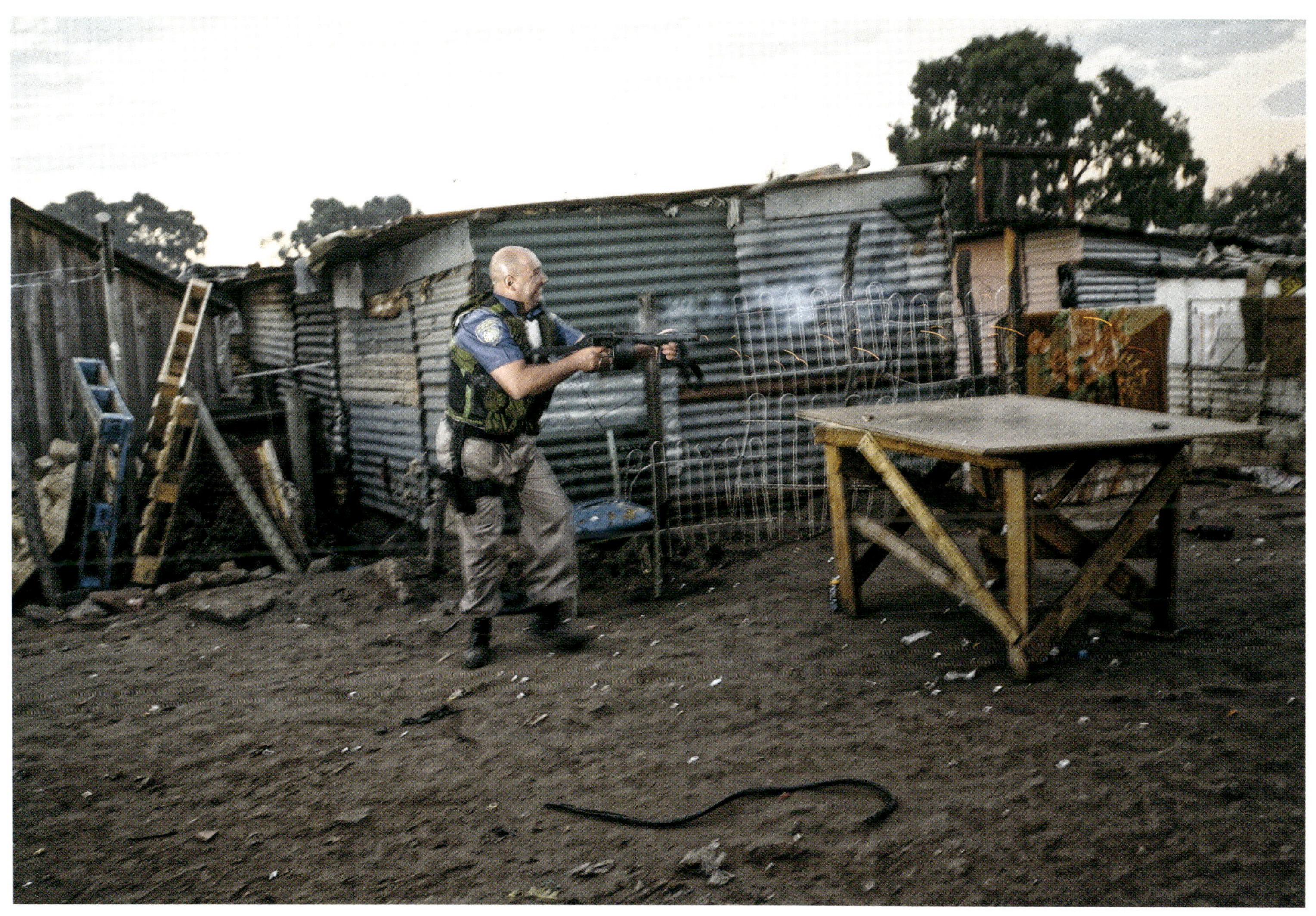

A law enforcement officer disperses crowds during
ongoing turbulence on the East Rand. AC

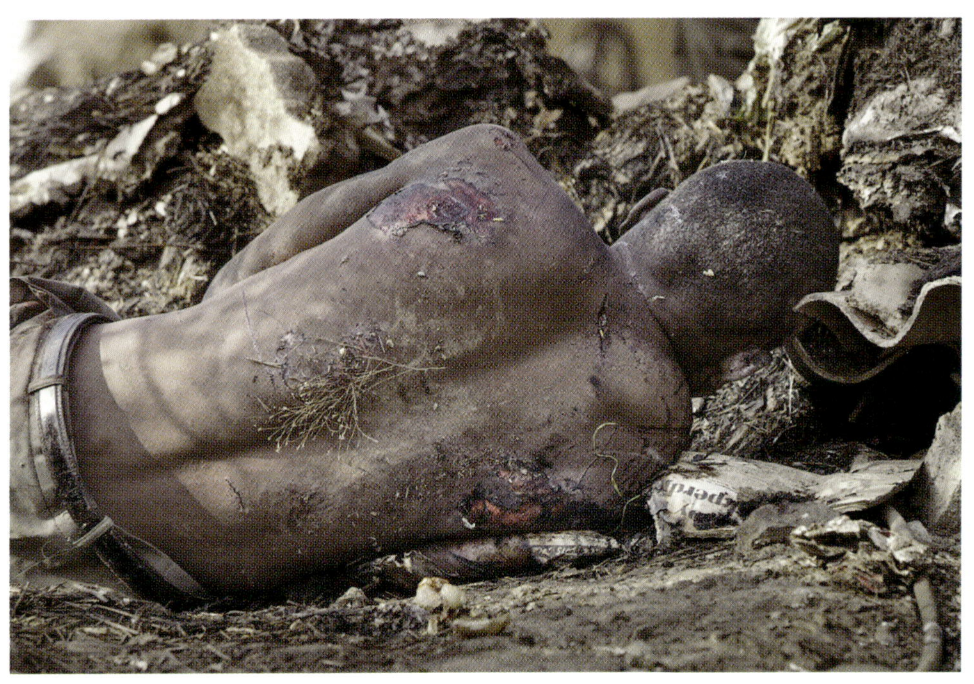

[This page] A sixteen-year-old youth lies in agony on a pile of debris in Ramaphosa after being hacked, set alight and left for dead on a bitterly cold Highveld winter night. [Facing page] Passersby look on before the injured youth was taken by ambulance to hospital. He survived the attack. JO

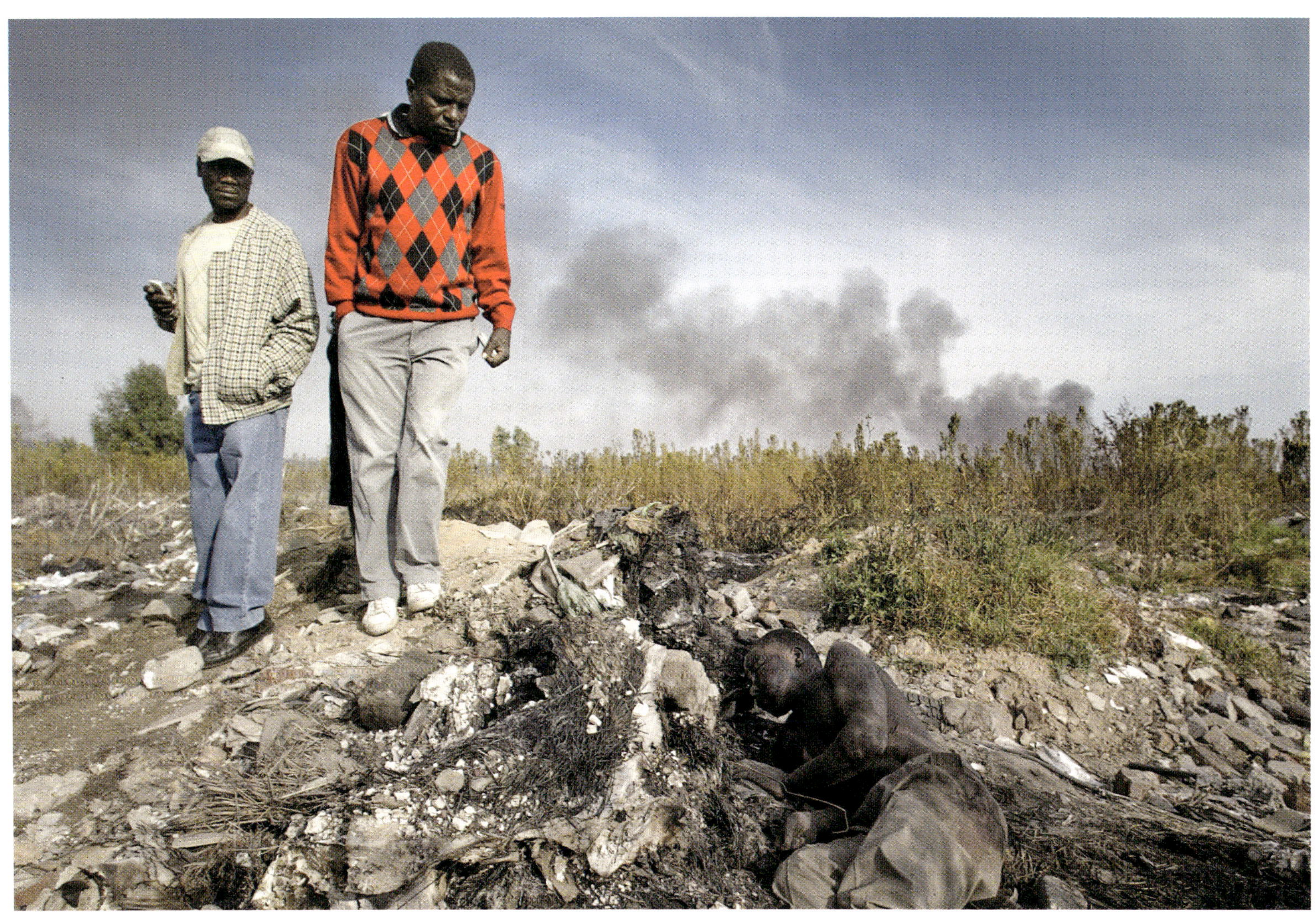

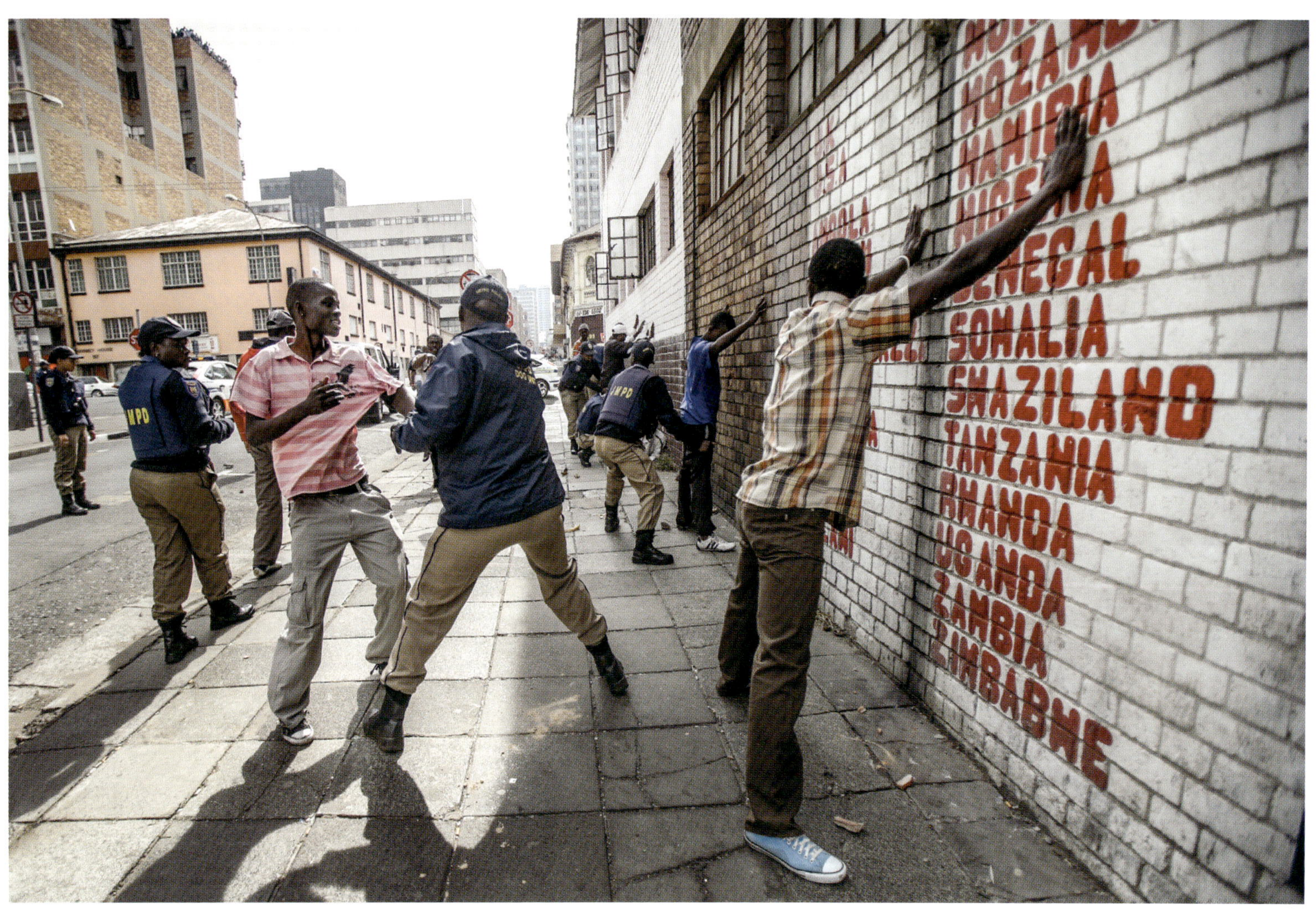

Law enforcement officers conduct random searches
of pedestrians at a time when xenophobic unrest was
sweeping through central Johannesburg. AS

No African is a foreigner in Africa

Professor Achille Mbembe

'Afrophobia'? 'Xenophobia'? 'Black-on-black racism'? A 'darker' as you can get is hacking a 'foreigner' under the pretext that the latter is 'too dark' – self-hate par excellence? Of course, all of that at once and much more!

Yesterday I asked a taxi driver: 'Why do they need to kill "blacks from elsewhere" in this manner? Why do they need to set them on fire?'

His response: 'Because under apartheid, fire was the only weapon we blacks had … With fire we could make petrol bombs and throw them at the enemy from a safe distance.

'Today there is no need for a safe distance between self and the new enemy. To kill "these foreigners", we [the killers] need to be as close as possible to their body. We can then set in flames or dissect it, each blow opening a huge wound that can never be healed. Or if it is healed … it must leave … the kinds of scars that can never be erased.'

I was here during the [2008] outbreak of violence against 'foreigners' or, as we prefer to say these days, 'foreign nationals', by which we basically mean 'blacks from elsewhere'.

Since then, the cancer has metastasized. The current hunt for 'foreigners' is the result of a complex chain of complicities. The South African government has recently taken a harsh stance on immigration. Anti-blacks-from-elsewhere sentiments are not the preserve of the poor amongst us. They are widely shared through society and the state. New draconian measures have been passed into law, with devastating effects on people already here legally. Work permits not renewed. Visas refused to family members. Children in limbo in schools. A Kafkian situation that extends to 'foreign' students or professionals from the rest of Africa who entered the country legally had their visas renewed all those years, but who now find themselves in a legal limbo. Through its new anti-immigration measures, the government is busy turning previously legal migrants into illegal ones.

Chains of complicity go further. South African big business is expanding across the continent, at times reproducing in those places the worse forms of racism that were tolerated here under apartheid. While big business is 'de-nationalising' and 'Africanising', poor black South Africa and sections of the middle class are being socialised into something we should call 'national chauvinism'.

National chauvinism is rearing its ugly head in almost every sector of South African society. Typical of national chauvinism is its permanent need of scapegoats. It starts with those who are not our kin, but very quickly turns 'ethnic', fratricidal.

I was here during the last 'hunting season'. The difference, this time, is the emergence of the rudiments of an 'ideology'. We now have a discourse aimed at justifying the atrocities, the creeping pogroms. The discourse starts with the usual stereotypes – they are darker than us; they steal our jobs and our women; they dabble in crime; they do not respect us; they are used by whites who prefer to exploit them as a cheap labour reserve army rather than employing us.

Furthermore, South Africa does not owe any moral debt to Africa. Evoke the years of exile? No, there were less than 30 000 South Africans in exile (I have no idea where this figure comes from) and they were scattered throughout Africa – four in Ghana, three in Ethiopia, a few in Zambia, and many more in Russia and Eastern Europe! So we will not be morally blackmailed by 'those foreigners'. As any other power in the world of realpolitik, we should simply pursue our 'national interests'.

Well, let's ask the difficult questions: Why is South Africa turning into a killing field for non-national Africans – to whom we have to add the Bengalis, Pakistanis, and who knows whom next? Why is this country so eager to turn into a 'circle of death' for anybody 'African'?

When we say 'South Africa', what does 'Africa' mean? An idea, or simply a geographical accident?

Should we be putting a price tag to everything that was sacrificed by Angola, Mozambique, Zimbabwe, Namibia, Tanzania, Zambia and others during the liberation struggle? How much money did the Liberation Committee of the Organisation of African Unity (OAU) provide to the South African liberation movements? Where did it come from? How many dollars did the Nigerian or Ethiopian states pay for South Africa's struggle? If we were to put a price tag on the destruction meted out by the apartheid regime on the economy and infrastructure of the Frontline states, what would this amount to? And shouldn't we give the bill to the ANC government and ask the South African state to pay back what was spent on behalf of the black oppressed in South Africa during those long years? Let's indeed open the negotiations on reparations and compensation.

Wouldn't we be entitled to add to these damages and losses the number of people killed by apartheid armies retaliating against our hosting South African combatants? The number of people maimed, the long chain of misery and destitution suffered in the name of our solidarity with South Africa? If black South Africans do not want to hear about moral debt, maybe it is time to agree with them, give them the bill, and return to the good old days of isolation and boycott.

Of course we all see the absurdity of this logic of insularity that is turning this country into yet another killing field for blacks in this world. We all see the absurdity of asking South Africa to carry, alone, the weight of our collective failures. Many poor Africans are here because they are running away from countries wracked by corruption and tyranny, brutality and disasters. It doesn't make sense to ask South Africa to atone for our own self-inflicted wounds.

But it is right to forcefully demand that the government of South Africa protect those who are here legally. South Africa has signed most international conventions, including the convention establishing the International Penal Tribunal in The Hague. Some of the instigators of the hunt against foreigners are known. Some have been making public statements inciting hate. Is there any way we could bring them to account for their actions? Impunity breeds impunity – and atrocities. If these perpetrators cannot be brought to book by the South African state, isn't it time to get a higher jurisdiction to deal with them?

Finally, one word about the people of this old continent and anyone else who is willing to tie his or her fate with the fate of Africa. No African is a foreigner in Africa! No African is a migrant in Africa! Africa is where we all belong, notwithstanding the absurdity of our official borders. No level of national chauvinism will erase this. No number of deportations will erase this. Instead of spilling black blood on the streets of South Africa, we should all be making sure that we rebuild this continent and bring to an end a long and painful history – that which, for too long, has dictated that to be black is a liability.

This article was previously published in *Africa is a Country*: https://africasacountry.com/2015/04/achille-mbembe-writes-about-xenophobic-south-africa

Professor Achille Mbembe is a philosopher, political theorist and public intellectual.

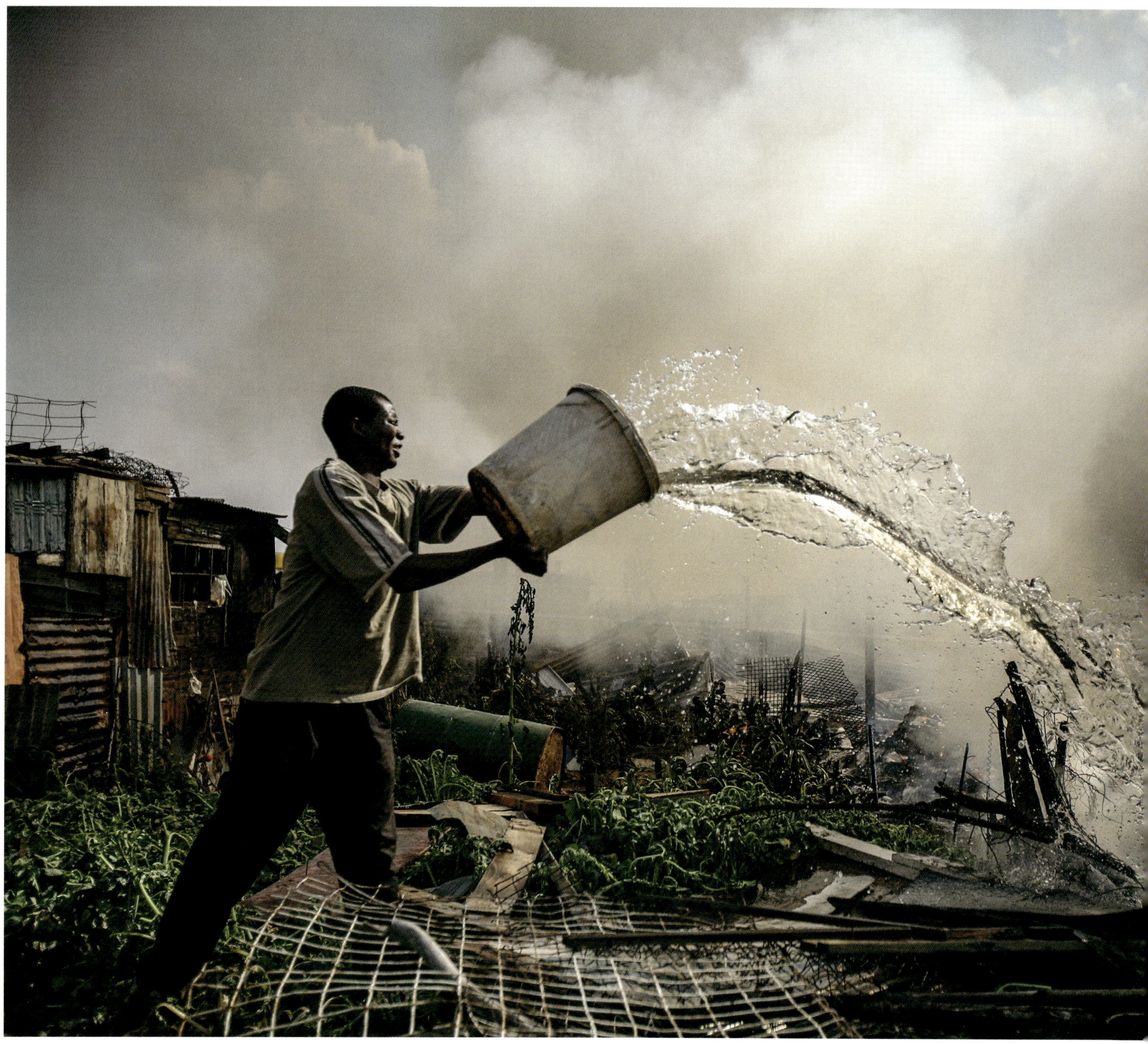

A man fights the flames engulfing a shack in Ramaphosa. Tens of thousands of people were displaced, more than 342 shops looted and 213 burnt down in the weeks of violence that swept the country in May and June 2008. AS

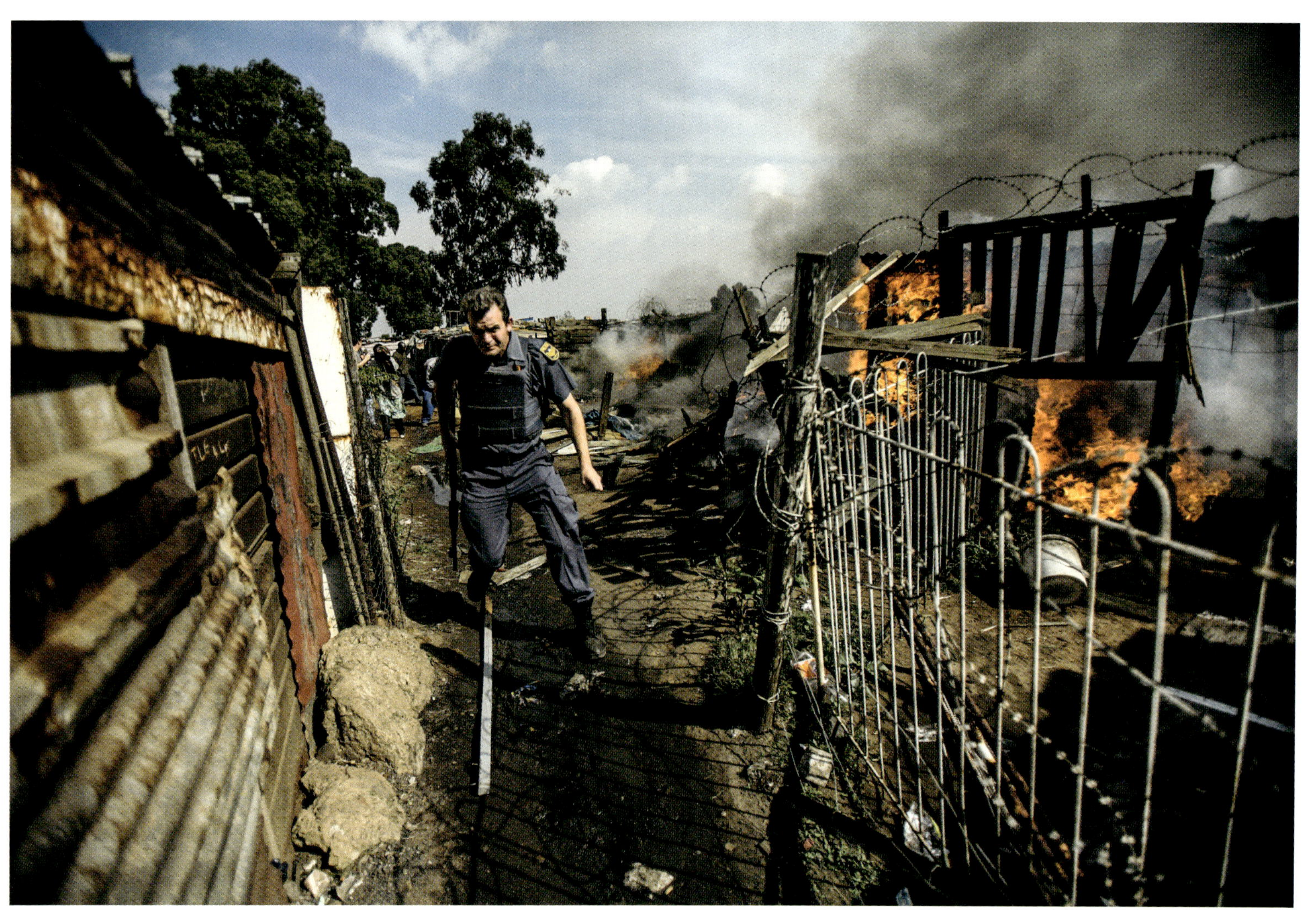

A member of the South African Police Service (SAPS)
hotfoots it through Ramaphosa where officers often met
with retaliation by rock-wielding rioters. AS

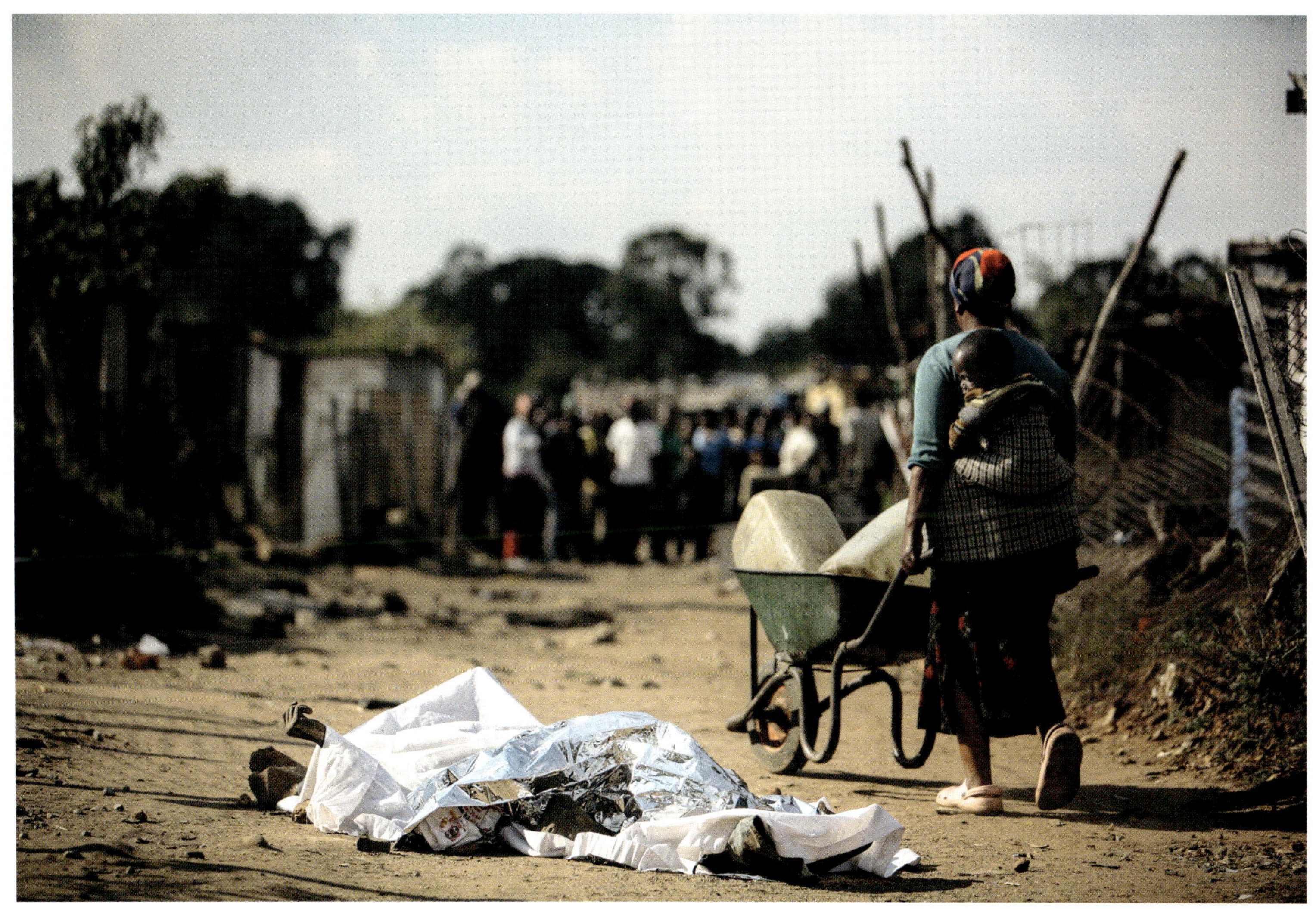

A woman and child pass the body of a man killed in overnight violence on the
East Rand. Many residents appear inured to the death around them, and in some
instances shield the identity of the killers out of fear for their own safety. AS

A shack roof becomes a vantage point at the height of anti-migrant
sentiment in various areas around Ramaphosa, Johannesburg. AS

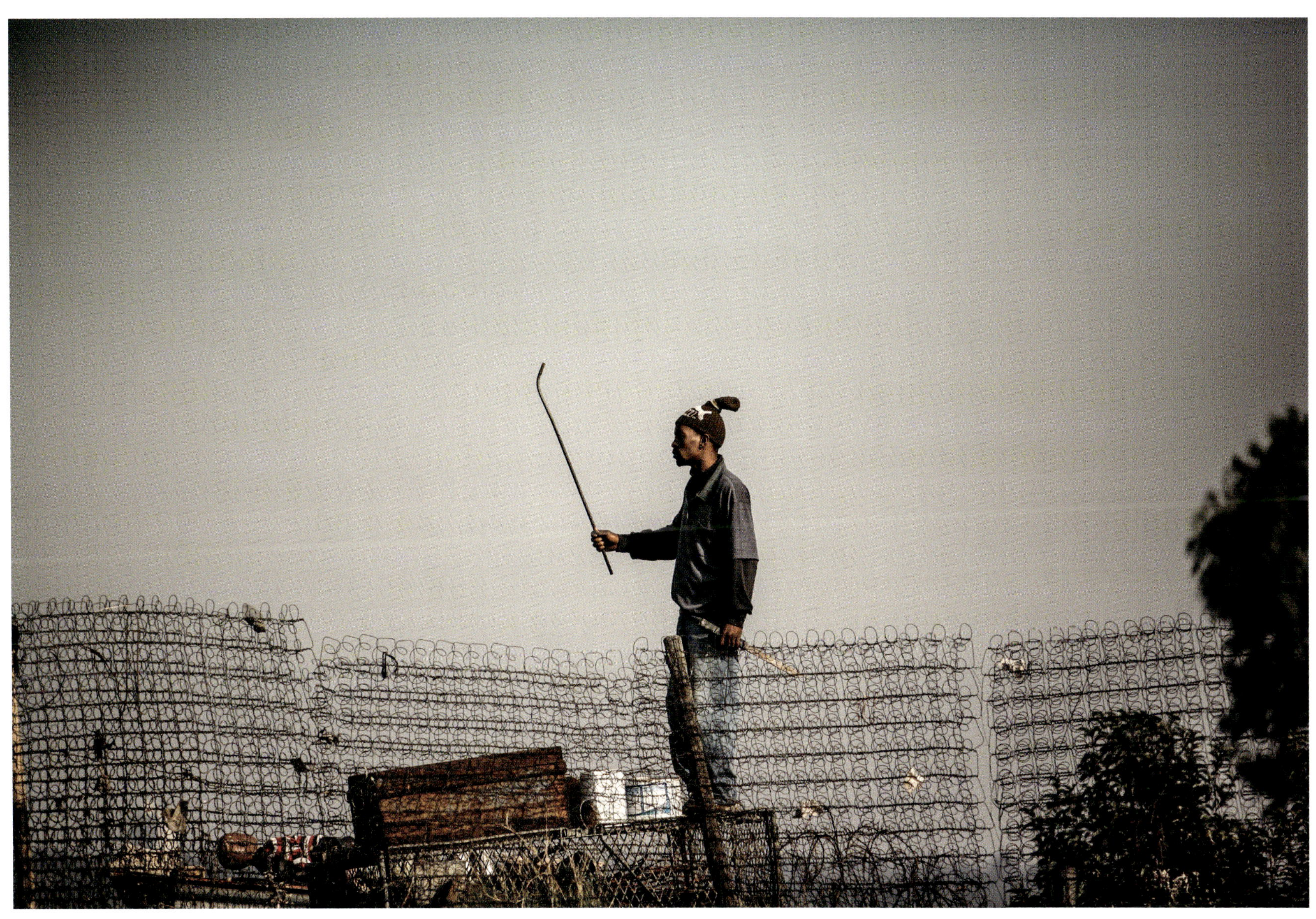

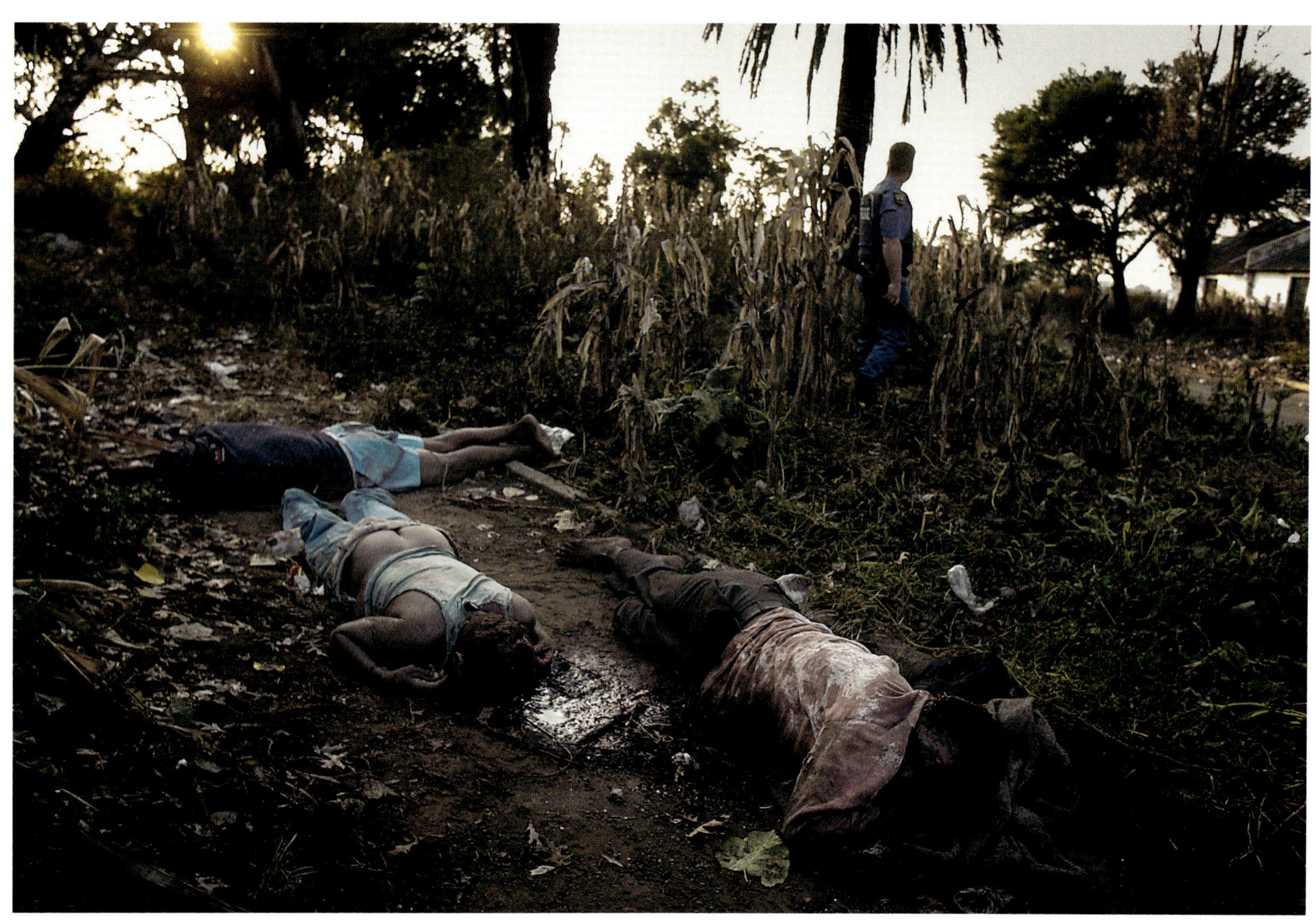

As the winter sun rises over Reiger Park on the East Rand, one man lies dead (centre) and two others dying – one of them Jose Eduardo Manguambe. The men worked at nearby East Rand Proprietary Mines and were attacked during the night of 19 May when a group raided Central Village Hostel looking for 'Shangaans' – a word often used generically to describe migrants. The gang dragged the men outside, beat them with steel pipes, stabbed and shot them, then left them for dead. JO

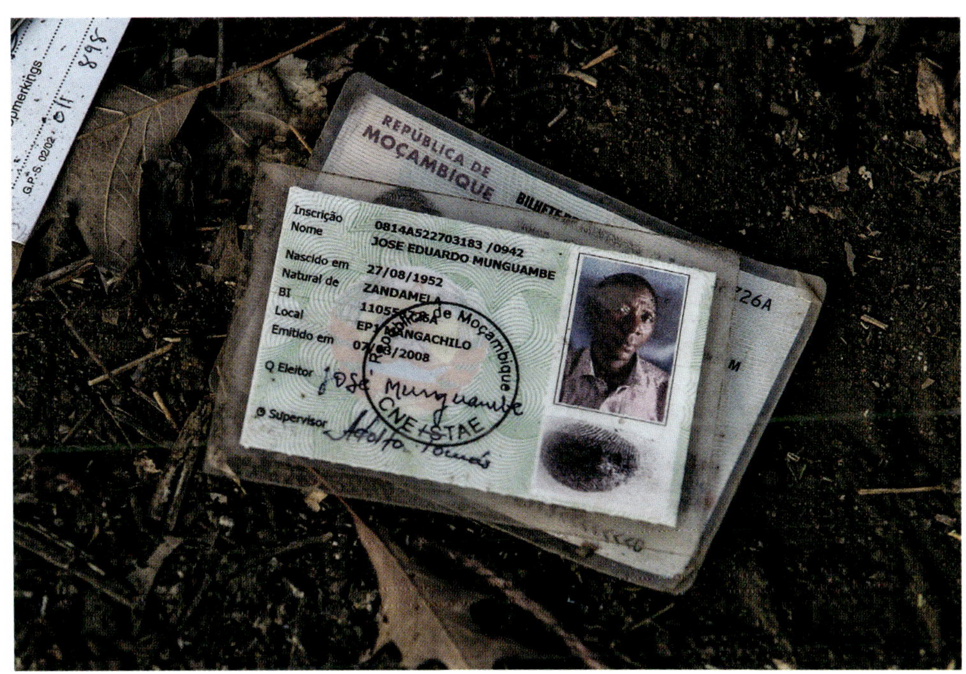

Jose Manguambe's identity card lies near the men's bodies. In a room back at the hostel, Arone Madombe, a 76-year-old who carried a South African identity card, lay slumped against his bed, beaten to death. Frantic hostel dwellers and mine officials had called SAPS while the attacks were underway, but police officers only arrived at daybreak. A fellow resident later named the other two men killed as Raimundo Mboane and William Chauke, but police were unable to confirm this, or the numbers of those killed and injured. JO

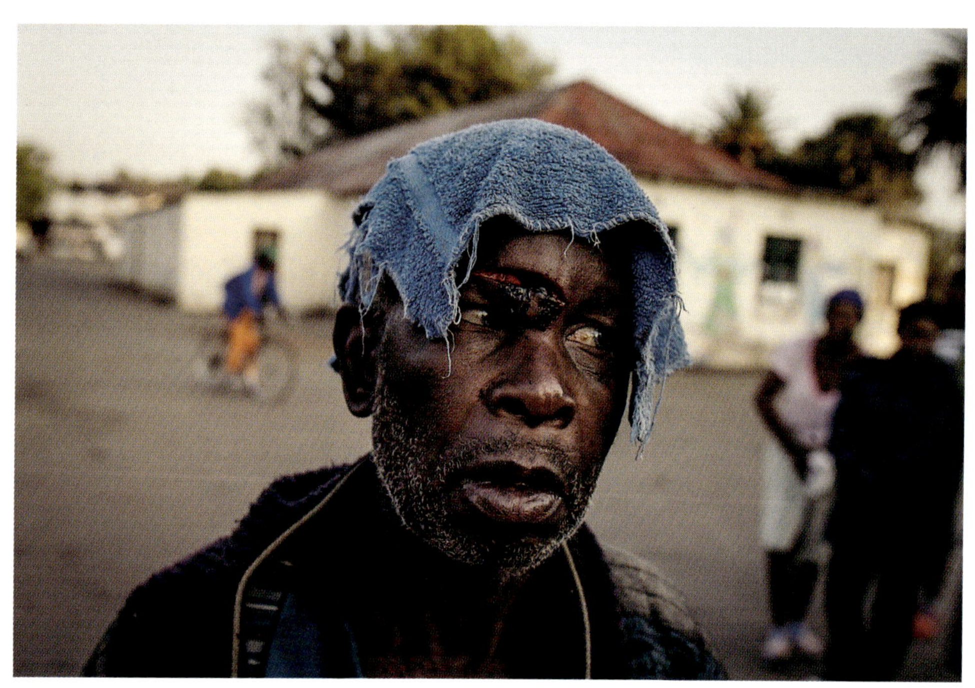

An elderly man was one of the survivors of a brutal attack on Central Village Hostel in Reiger Park. At least four men died after a group of attackers entered the hostel during the night searching for migrants. JO

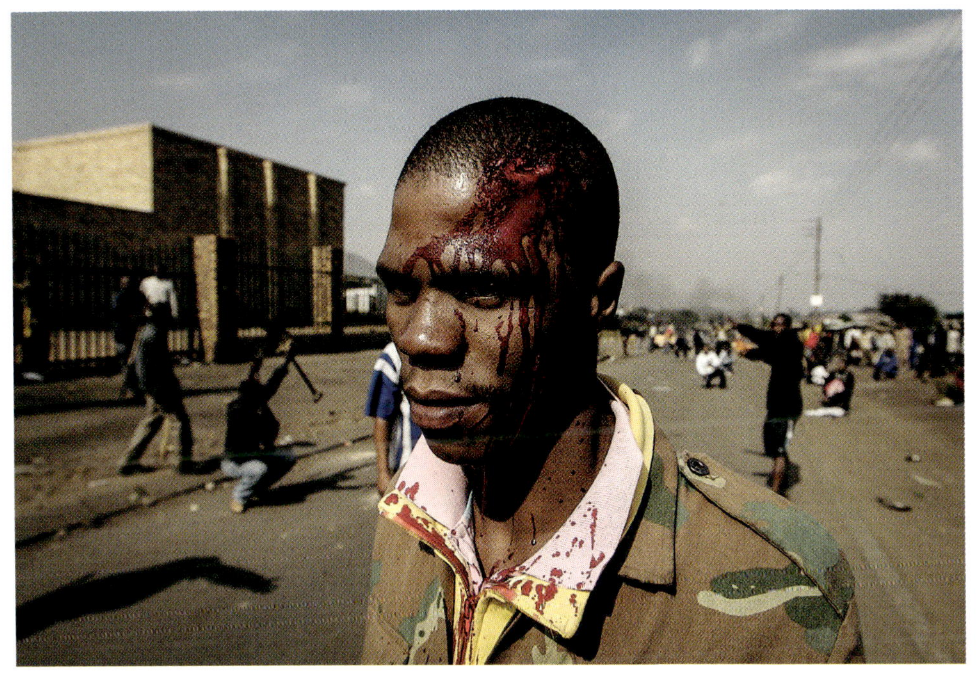

A leader of a group of alleged attackers, moments
after being shot by police in Ramaphosa. JO

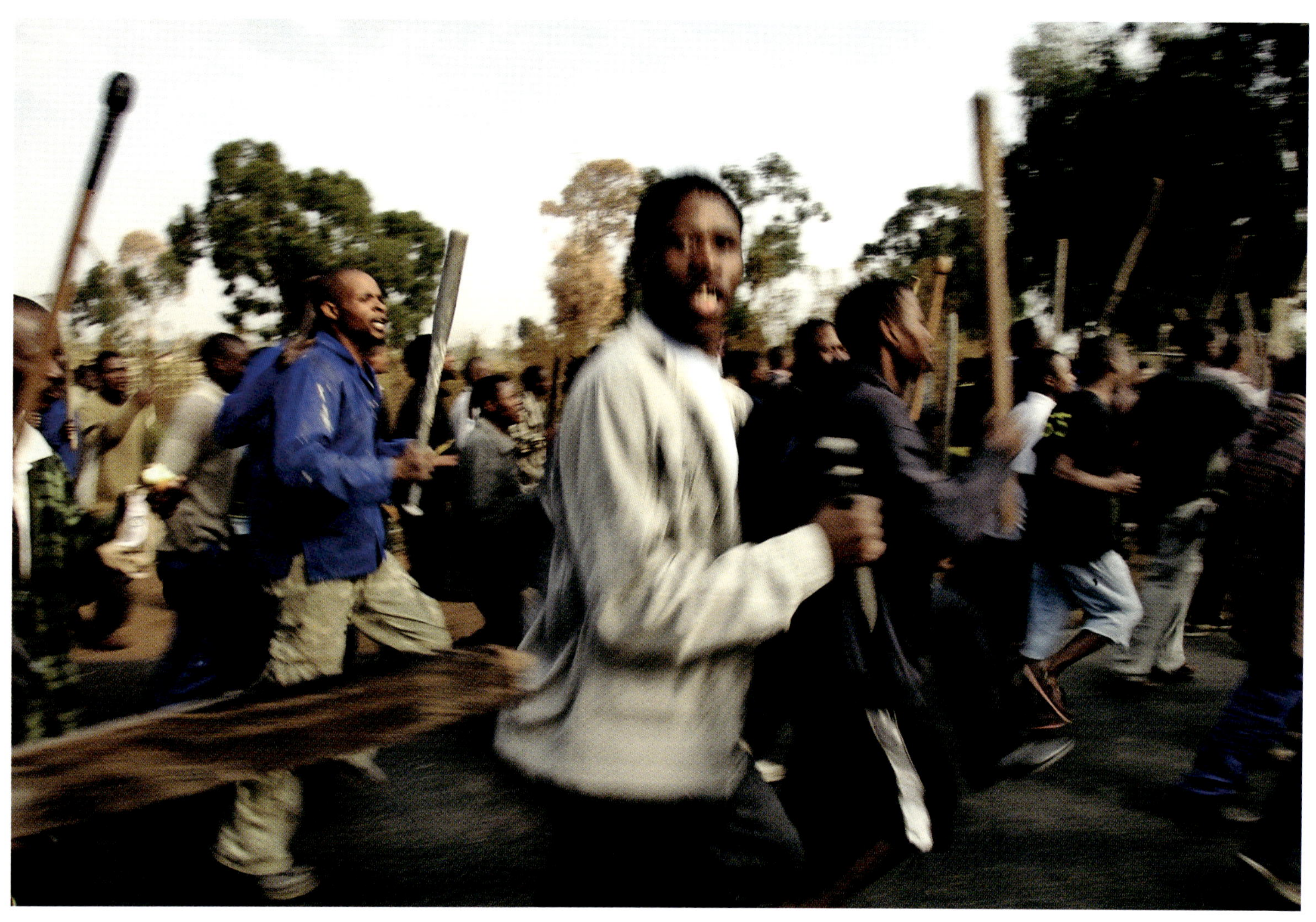

A group armed with crude weapons on the outskirts of Ramaphosa,
shortly before they gave chase to several men who appeared to
evade attack by hiding among nearby mine dumps. JO

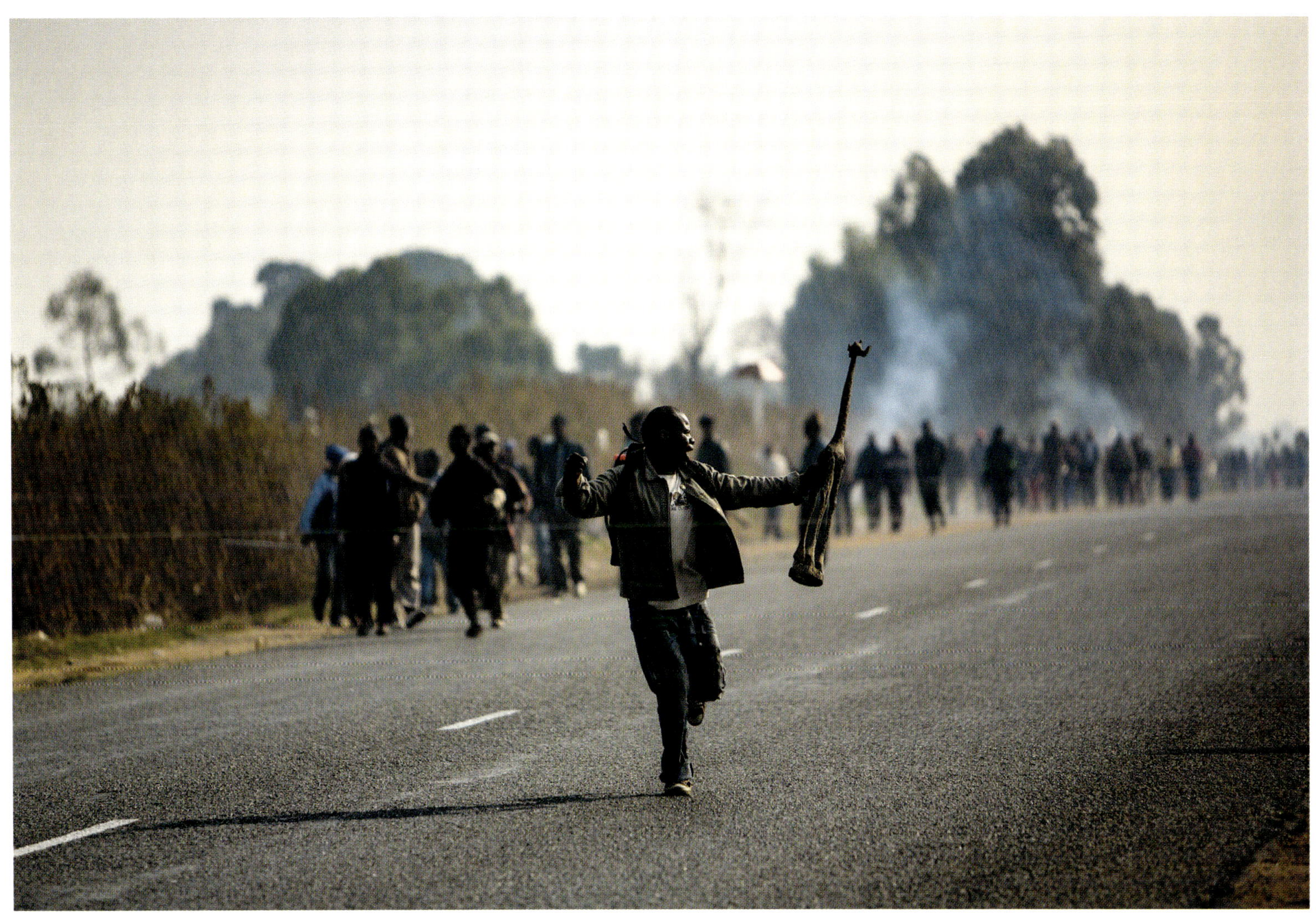

A man brandishes a wooden carving as a crowd
looking for people they say are 'migrants' heads
out of Ramaphosa. AS

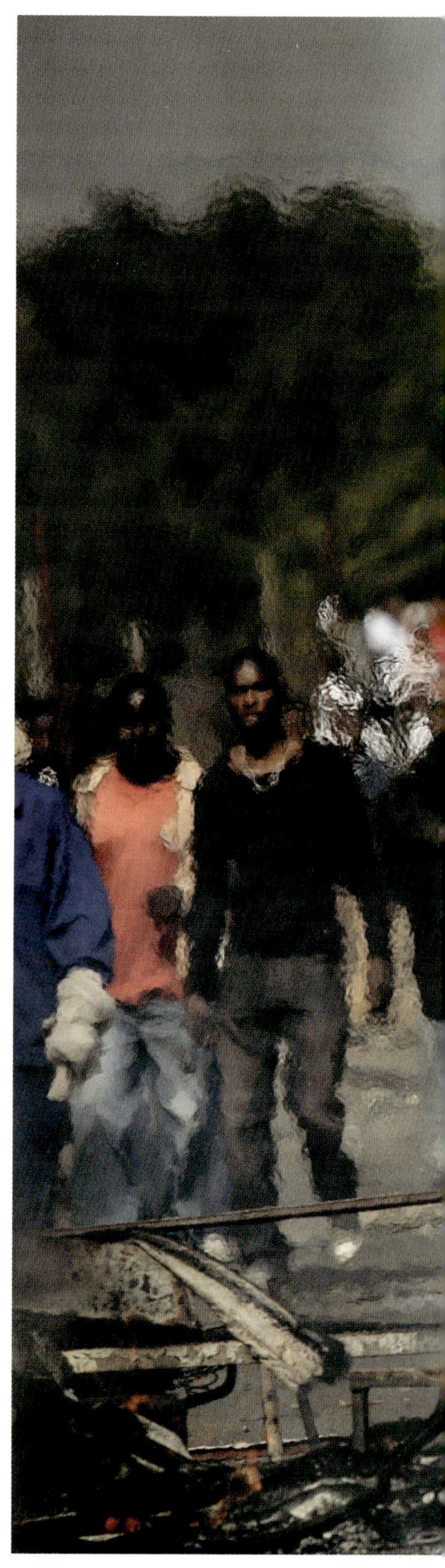

South Africans blockade a road in Ramaphosa. The root causes of local
residents' anger point to government failure to address crime, unemployment,
lack of housing and poor service delivery in impoverished areas. AS

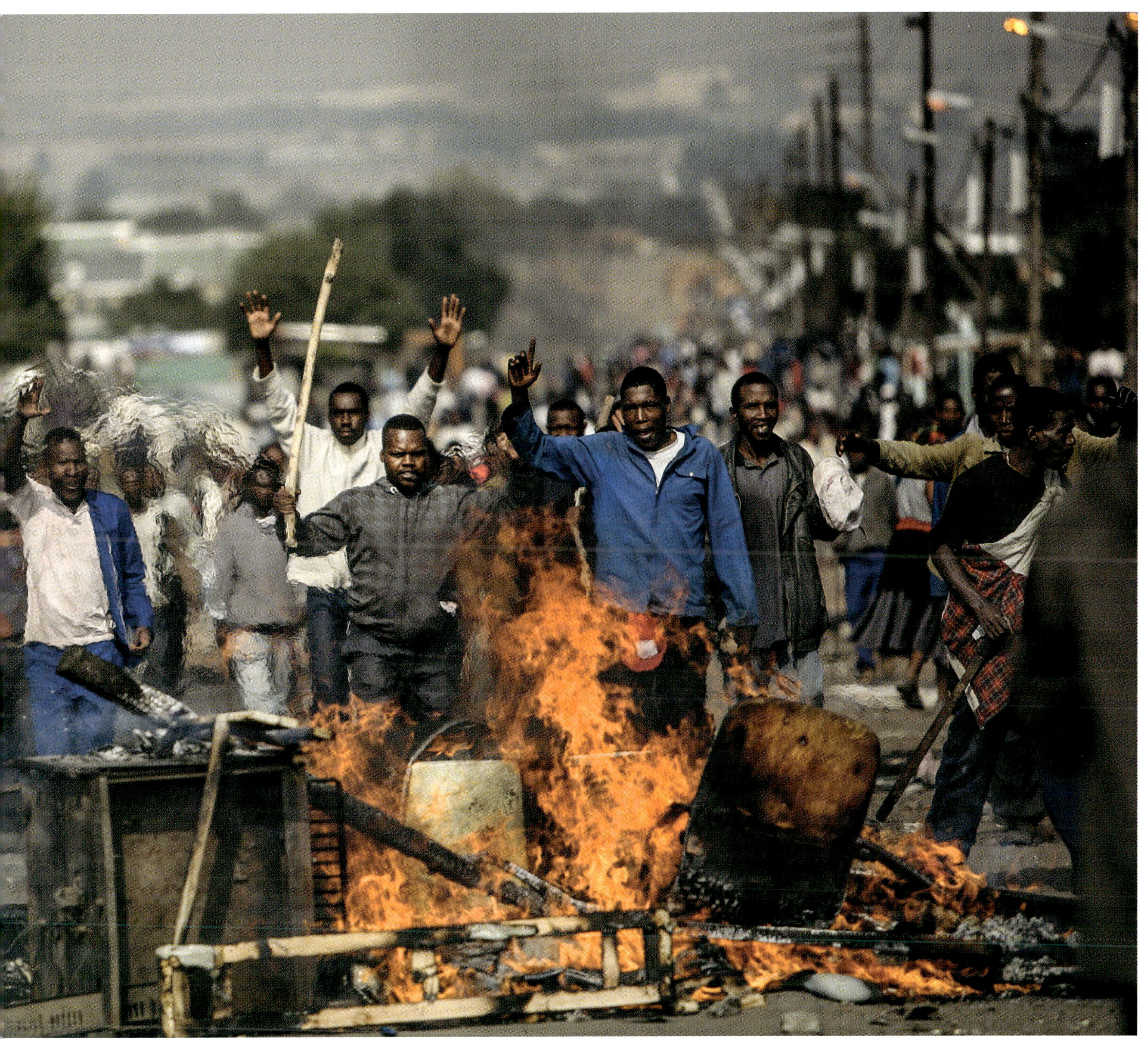

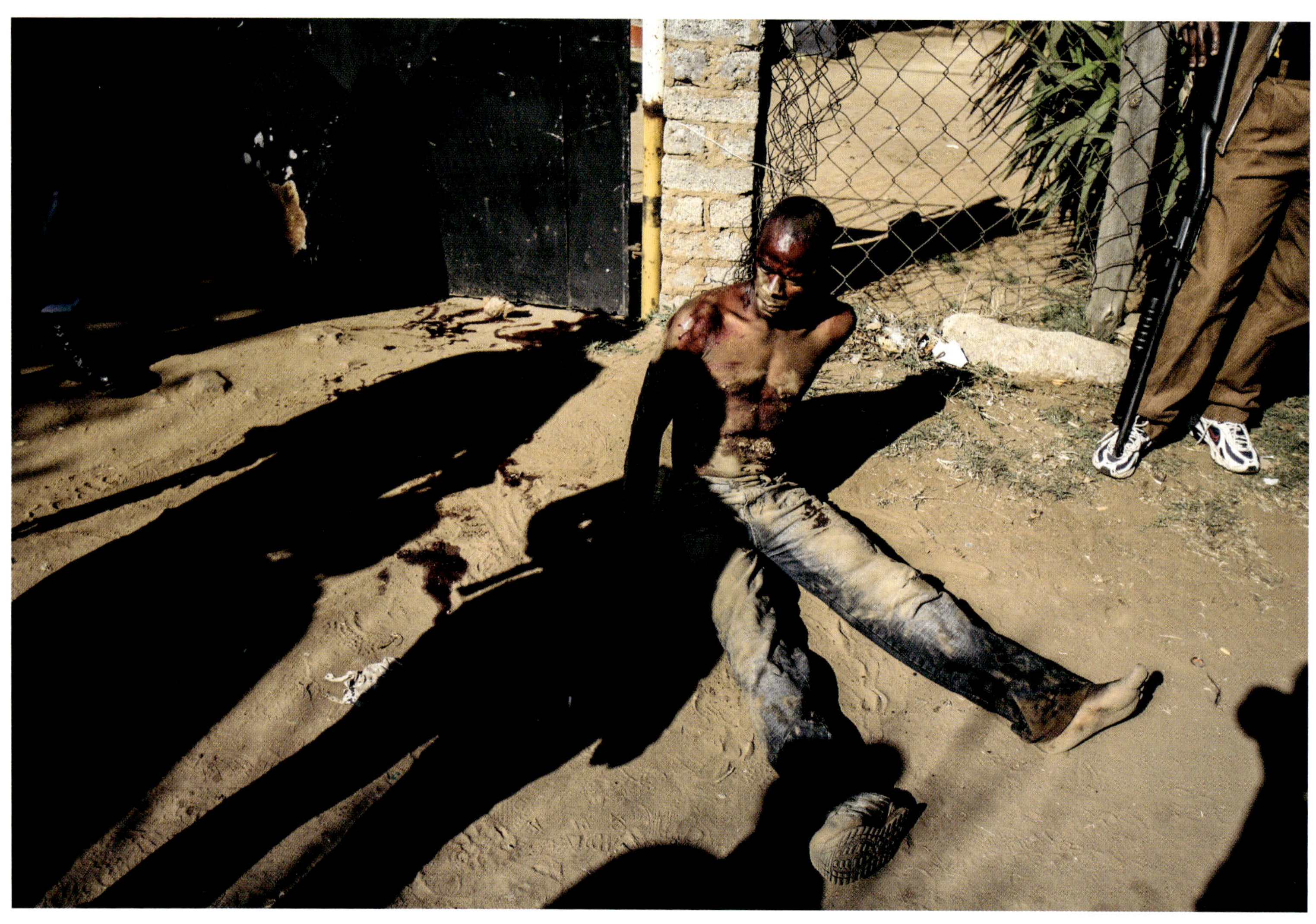

An injured man sits flanked by policemen in Ramaphosa.
Some in government blame unidentified 'third force'
elements for the violence that left dozens dead. AS

'The duty of a photojournalist is to bear witness; to show the world what is happening … and to hope that society will act.'

Greg Marinovich
Filmmaker, author and Pulitzer Prize-winning photographer

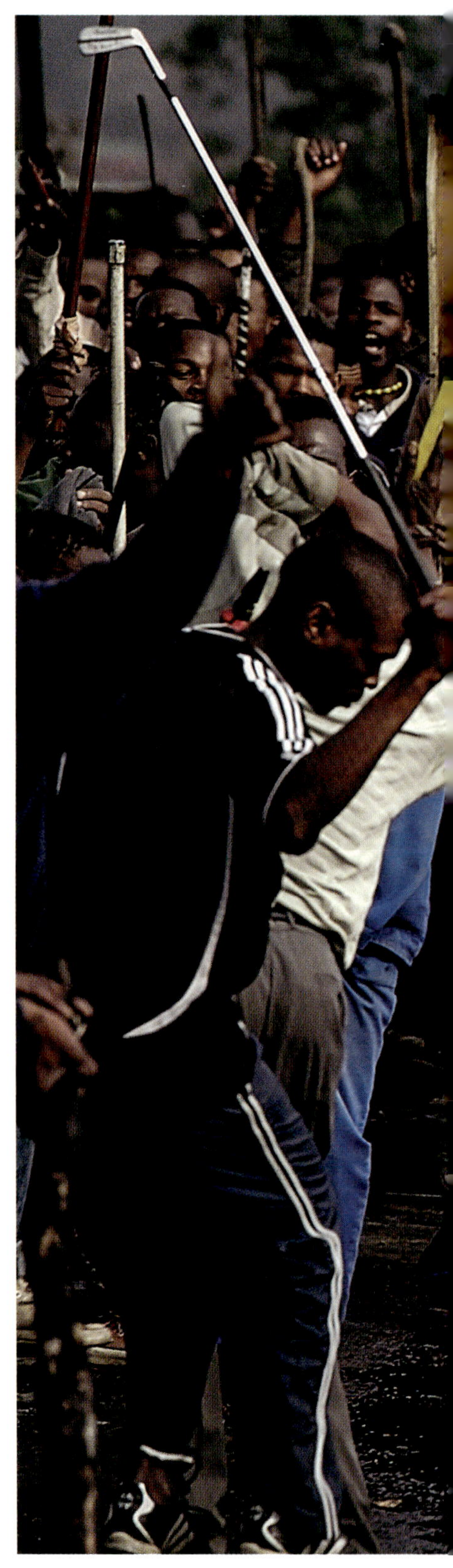

An inflamed crowd gathers before setting off in search of migrants in Ramaphosa. Similar scenes were playing out in low income areas across the country. JO

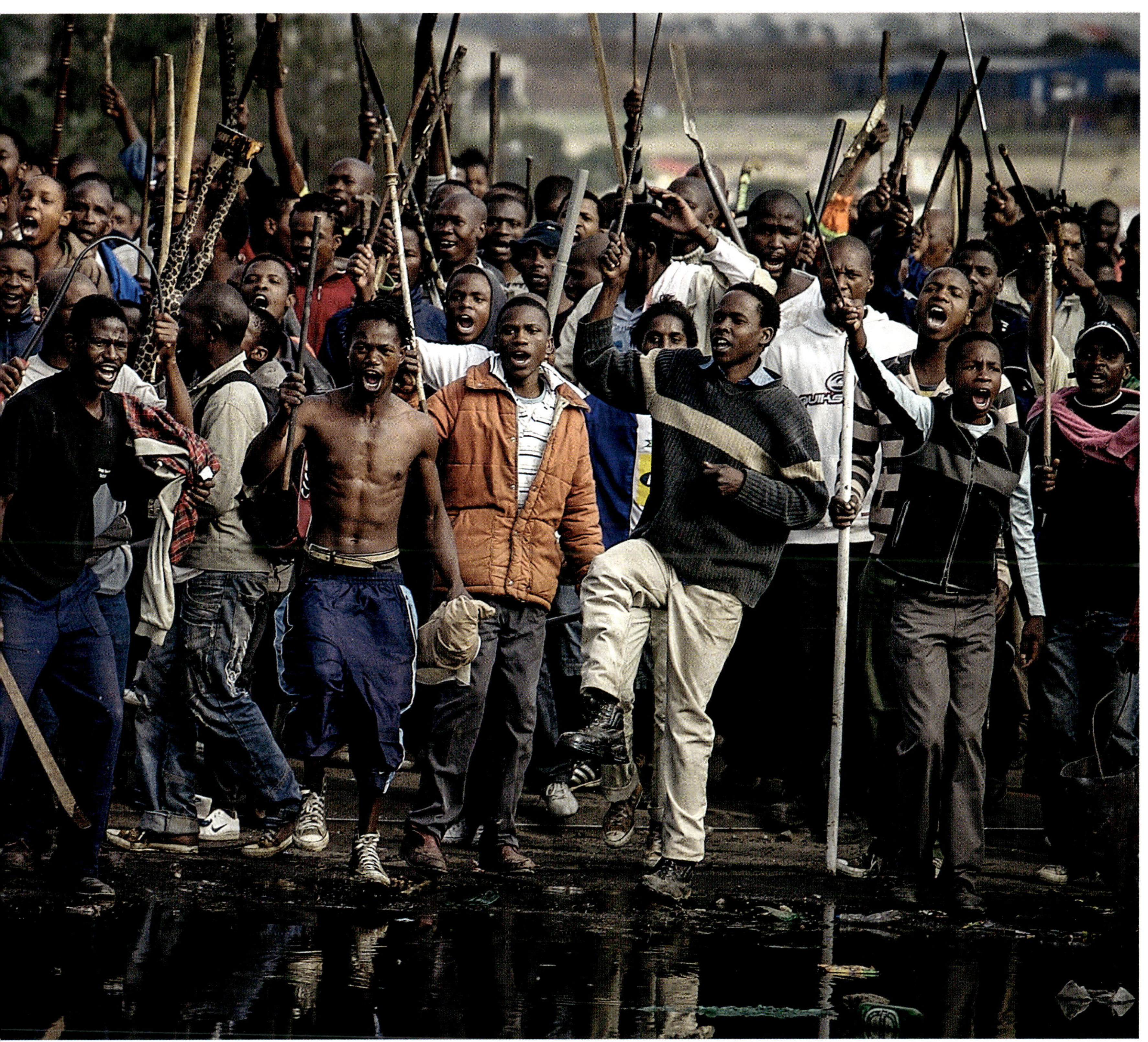

A shack-dweller in Ramaphosa tries in vain to save his possessions as his home burns to the ground. JO

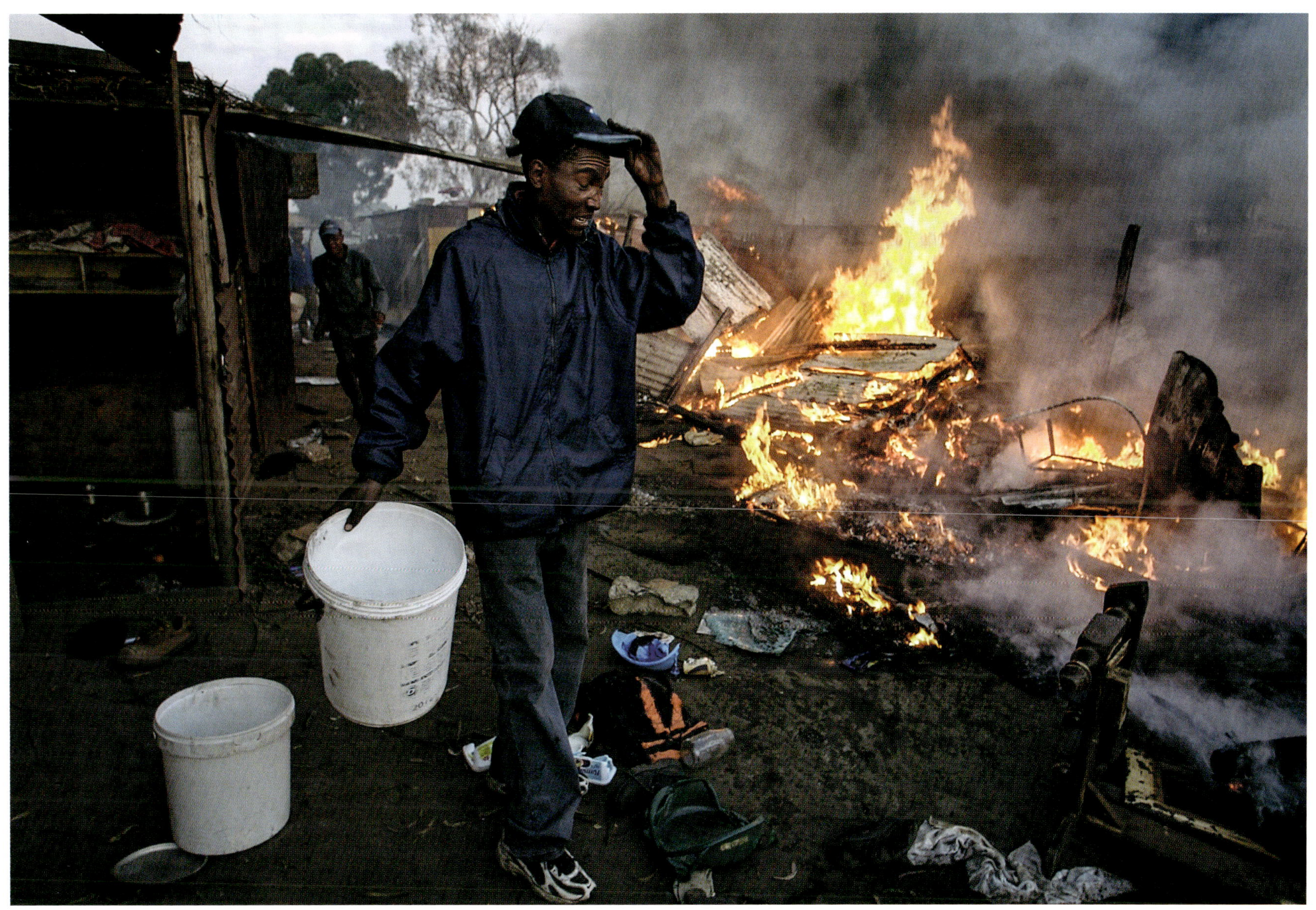

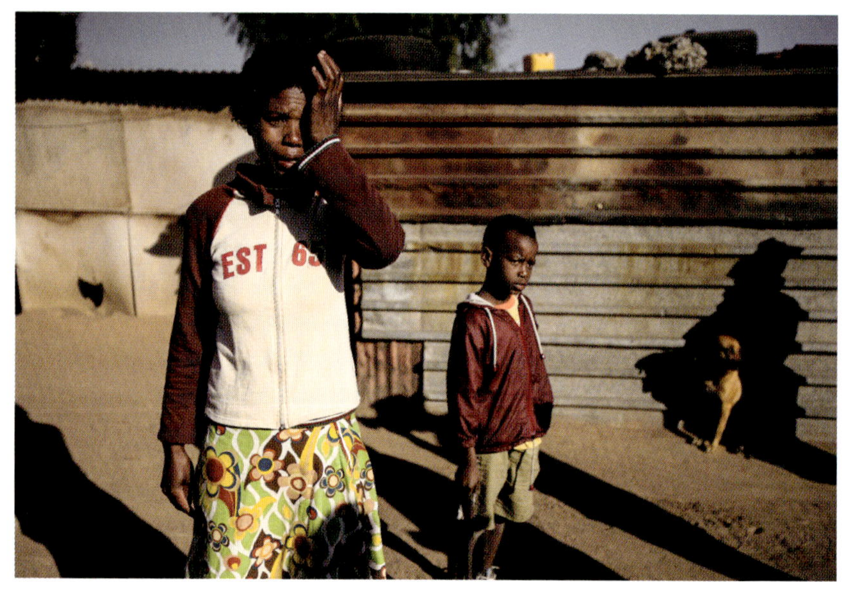

A woman weeps in the wake of an overnight attack in Ramaphosa. Post-traumatic stress disorder is extensive in communities affected by xenophobic violence. AS

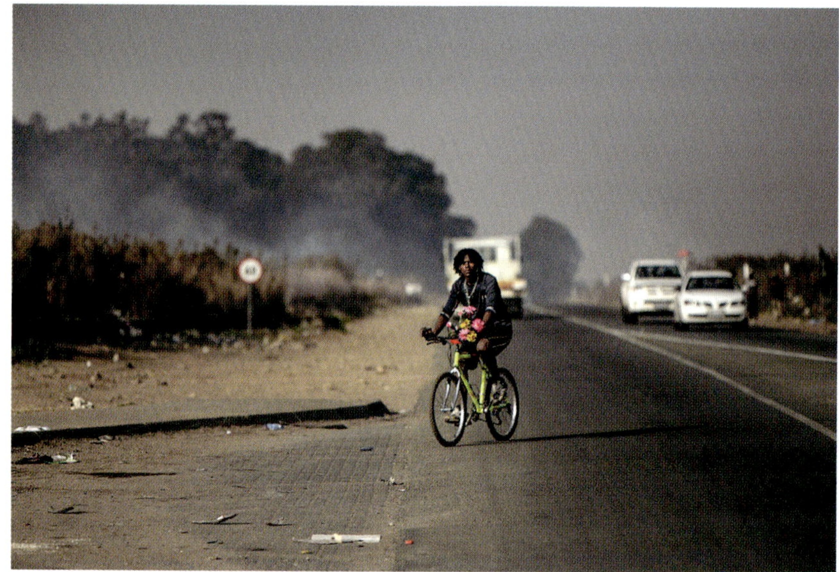

A quieter moment on a day when xenophobic attacks were shattering many lives in poor communities across the country. AS

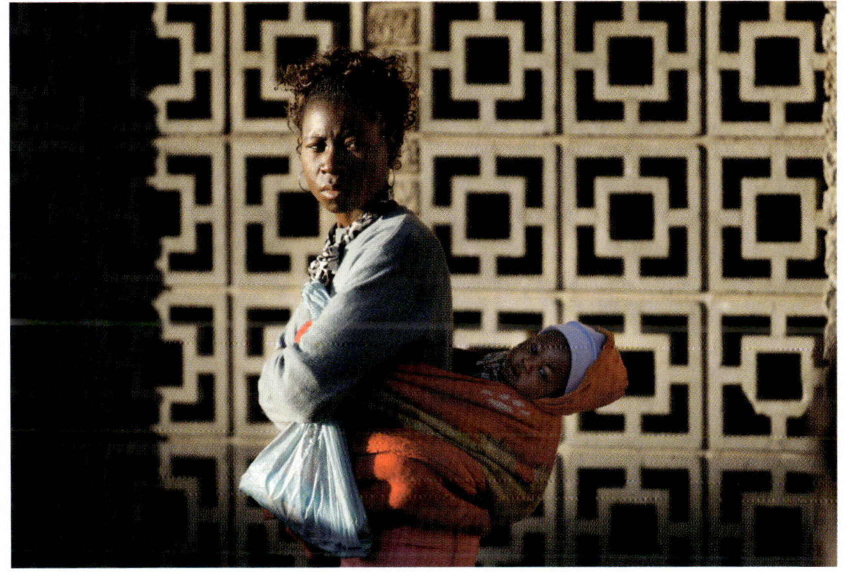

A young mother and child find refuge at a community
shelter after fleeing the violence in Ramaphosa. AS

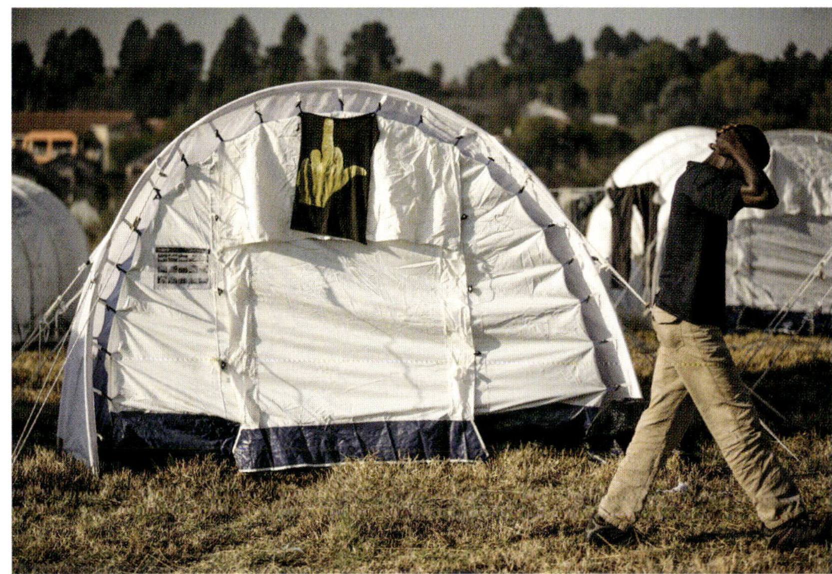

Many of the camps provided for displaced people by government authorities and aid
agencies failed to meet the basic standards set out by humanitarian organisations. AS

A refugee reads his bible at a temporary shelter in a field outside a police station
on the East Rand. Makeshift camps and shelters had to be hastily erected and
some migrants requested repatriation to their home countries. JO

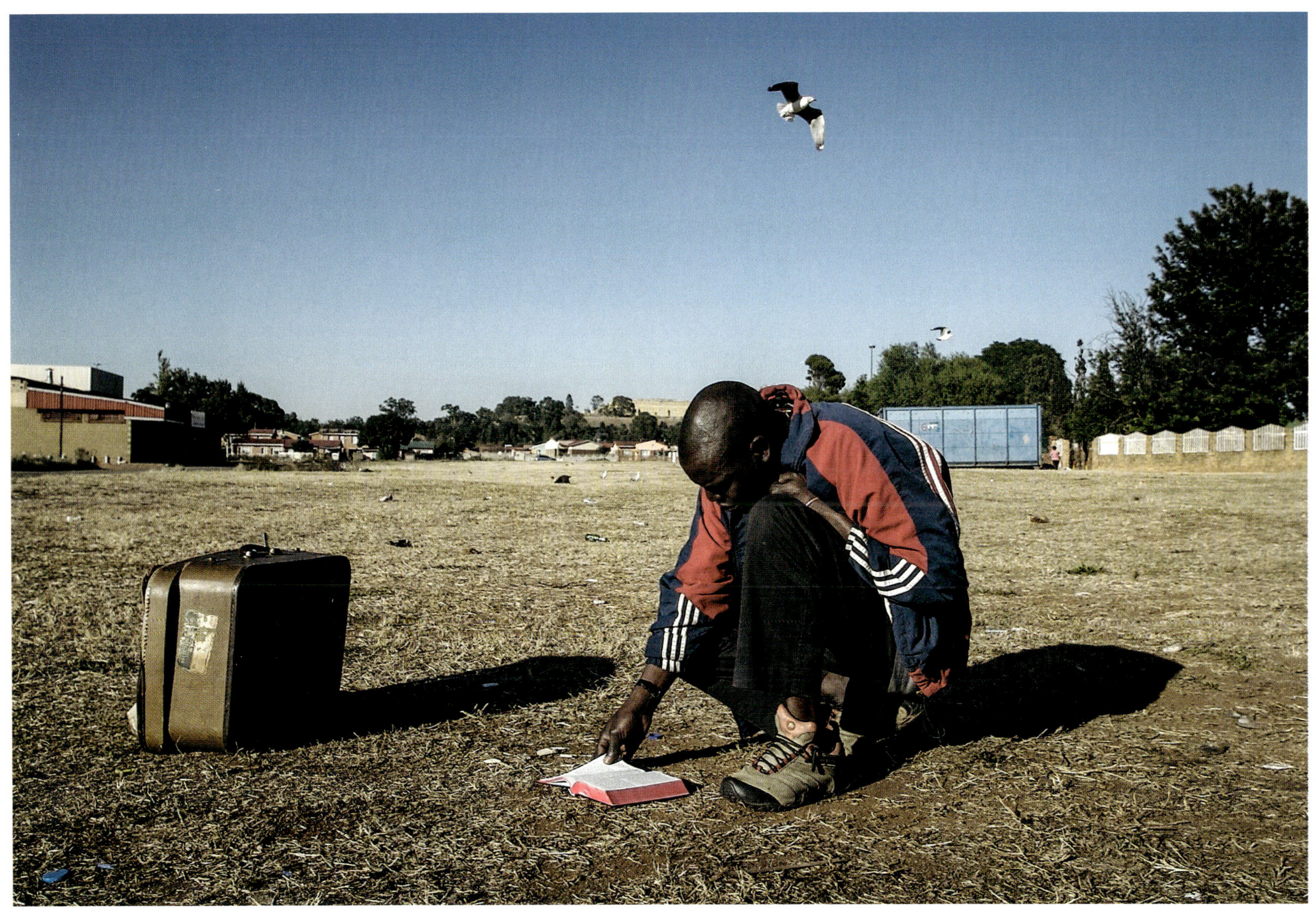

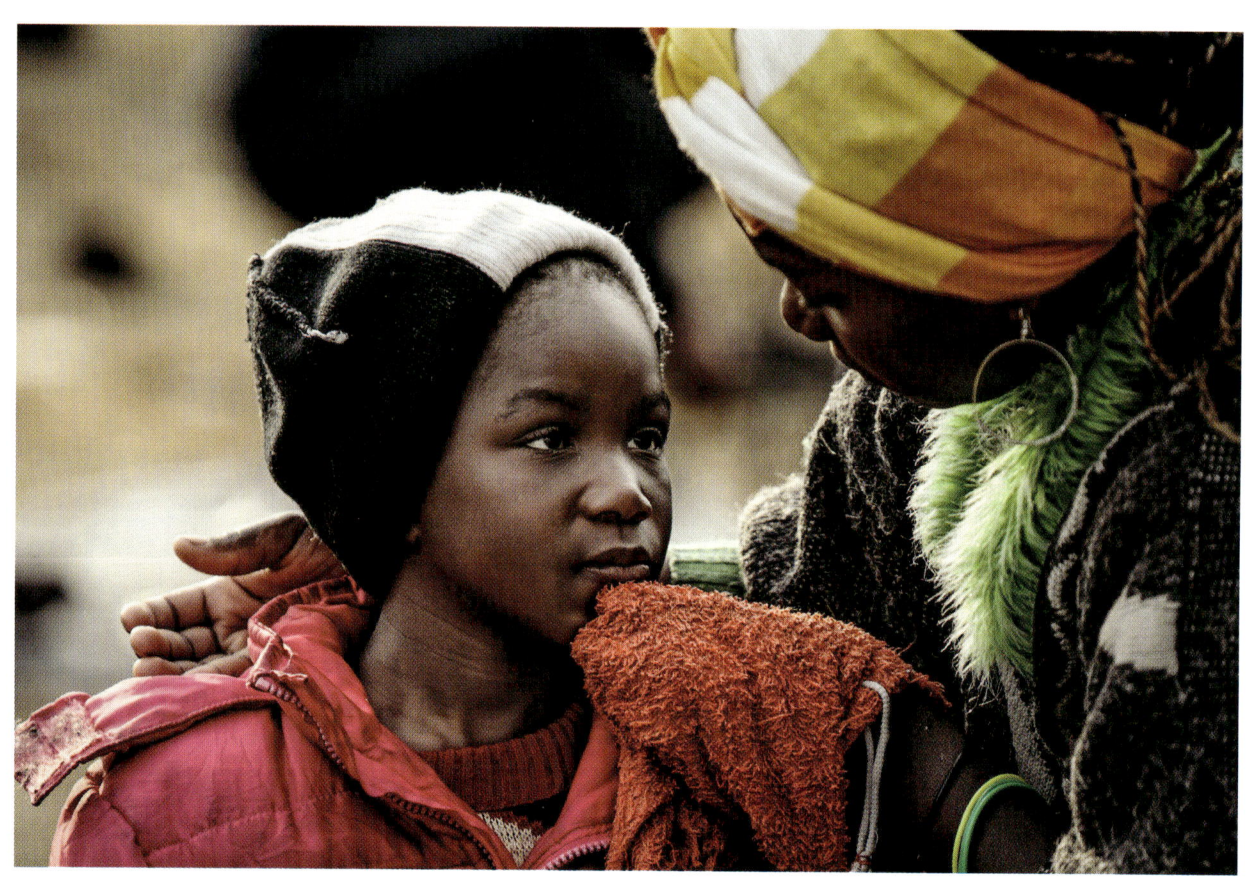

A mother bathes her daughter at an unsheltered roadside camp after being evicted from Lindela Repatriation Centre on the West Rand. Several hundred refugees were living alongside a busy thoroughfare. JO

Giving voice to those unheard

Joao Silva

This book documents a dark chapter in our country's history and these images serve as a reminder of how little it takes for human beings to turn into beasts. Hopefully, future generations can learn from these moments that have been captured for eternity. But more importantly, this body of work gives voice to those who would otherwise not be heard, and they put a human face on events that are difficult to comprehend for people who are not living that reality.

The camera as a tool in our passionate pursuit for justice gives us reason to explore humanity, and be a witness on behalf of victims who would certainly remain voiceless and faceless. And to a lesser extent, the final product serves to educate those who are fortunate enough not to live in a war zone.

It is a privilege to see history unfold before our eyes, and to be allowed into people's lives – too often, at the worst possible moments. But with this privilege comes huge responsibility. For us photojournalists, it is important to understand, when making images, that the people captured within them are living their worst nightmare. To be able to communicate the suffering of others effectively, we have to be true to our profession, true to ourselves, but most importantly, true to the people in the images whose lives we share – even only for a brief moment. For they are the true heroes.

In order to evoke emotion in a viewer, and to perhaps motivate political change, first, the photojournalist has to have empathy for fellow humans in need.

The body of work in this book, by two of South Africa's most dedicated and consummate professionals, is evidence of this ethos in practice. American photographer Irving Penn said: 'A good photograph is one that communicates a fact, touches the heart, and leaves a viewer a changed person for having seen it.' In this case, Alon and James, mission accomplished.

Joao Silva is a staff photographer at *New York Times*, an author and an award-winning war photographer.

2015–2018

In April 2015, an upsurge in xenophobic attacks began in Durban and soon spread to Johannesburg. Zulu King Goodwill Zwelethini was accused of fuelling the violence with his comments which were reported as: 'Let us pop our head lice. We must remove ticks and place them outside in the sun. We ask foreign nationals to pack their belongings and be sent back.' Zwelethini claimed the media had misrepresented his remarks.[1] In that month alone, at least eight people were killed and hundreds displaced. Perhaps most brutal of all was the murder of Emmanuel Sithole in Alexandra, which was captured on camera by James Oatway. These images brought home to millions around the world the true horror of xenophobia, and despite government denial that the killing was xenophobic, the army was deployed the day after their publication. In the following three years, violence continued around the country, and some African governments began repatriating their citizens.

1   The SA Human Rights Commission, responding to complaints about Zwelethini's remarks, criticised the Zulu monarch saying he had, by making multiple reference to migrants as 'criminals, which insinuates nefarious motive to their presence in South Africa', attacked a vulnerability minority; but this did not 'amount to hate speech'. Neither could his comments be interpreted as 'instigating violence' against migrants, the commission said. www.sahrc.org.za.

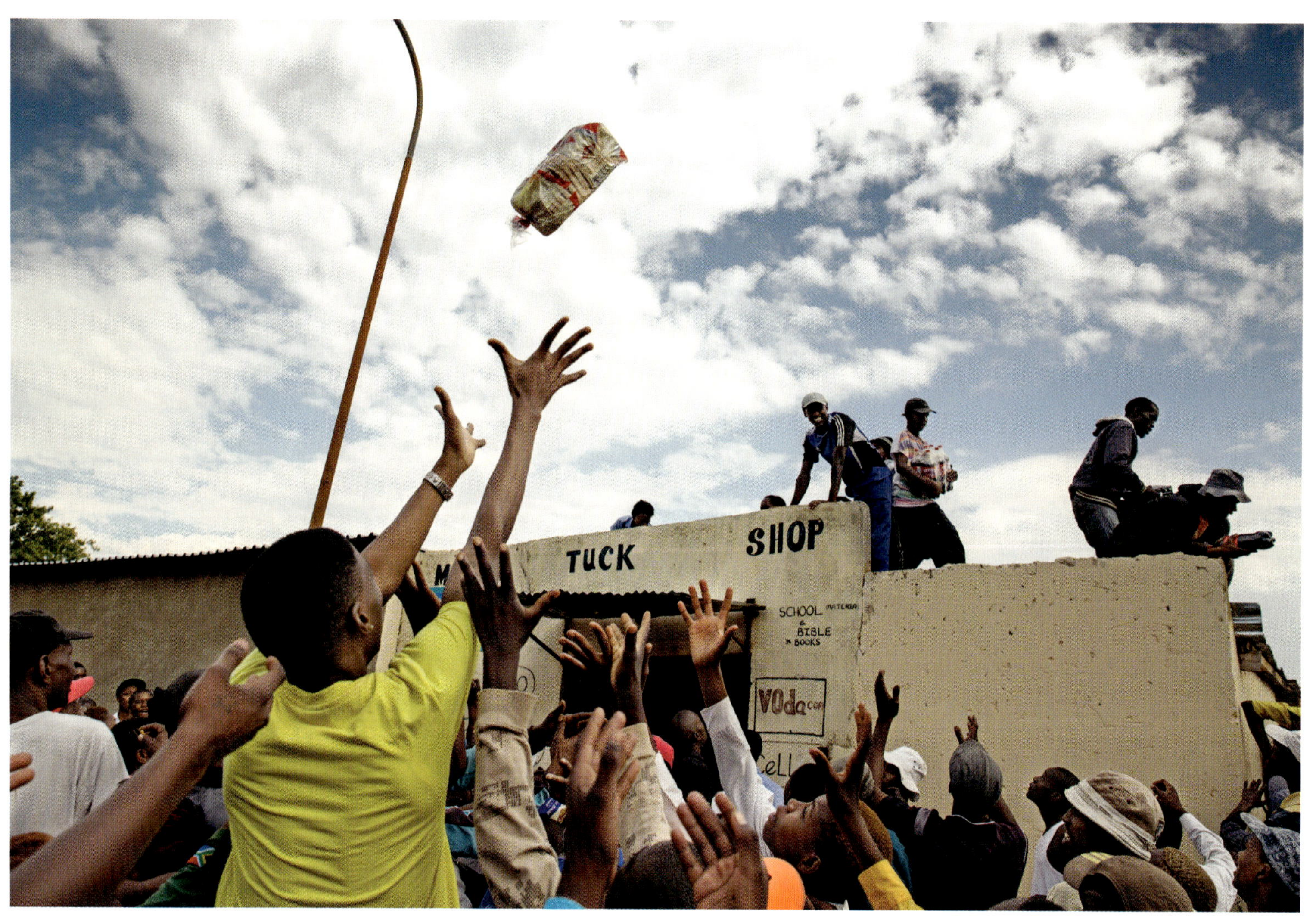

A group of young people ransacks a spaza shop in Meadowlands, Soweto, as anti-migrant sentiment sweeps the area. JO

'[These] actions are pure criminality …
for now we won't declare it
xenophobic attacks.'

Sizakele Nkosi-Malobane
Gauteng Community Safety MEC

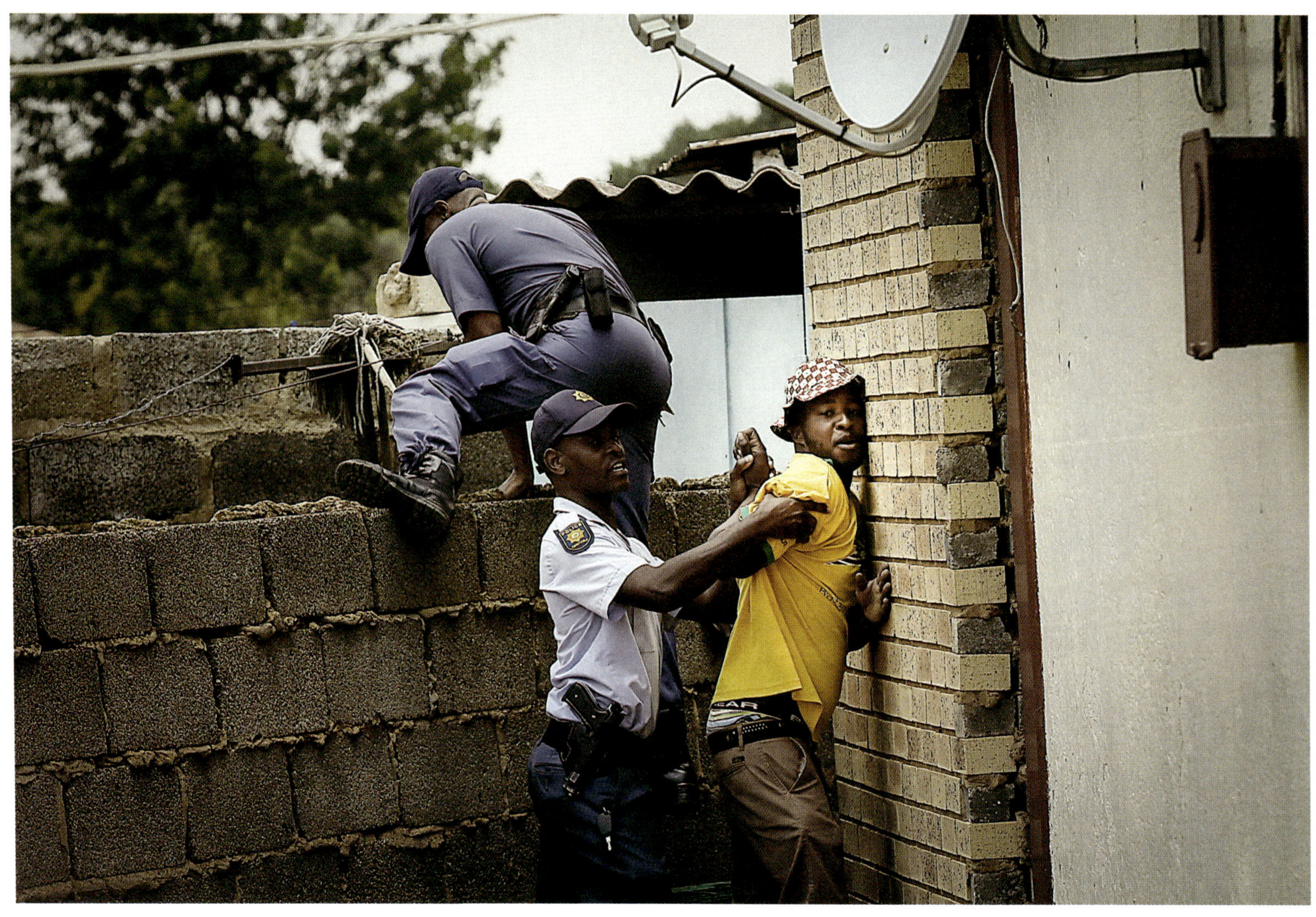

Police apprehend a man outside a shop in Meadowlands where
unruly crowds were plundering small businesses. AS

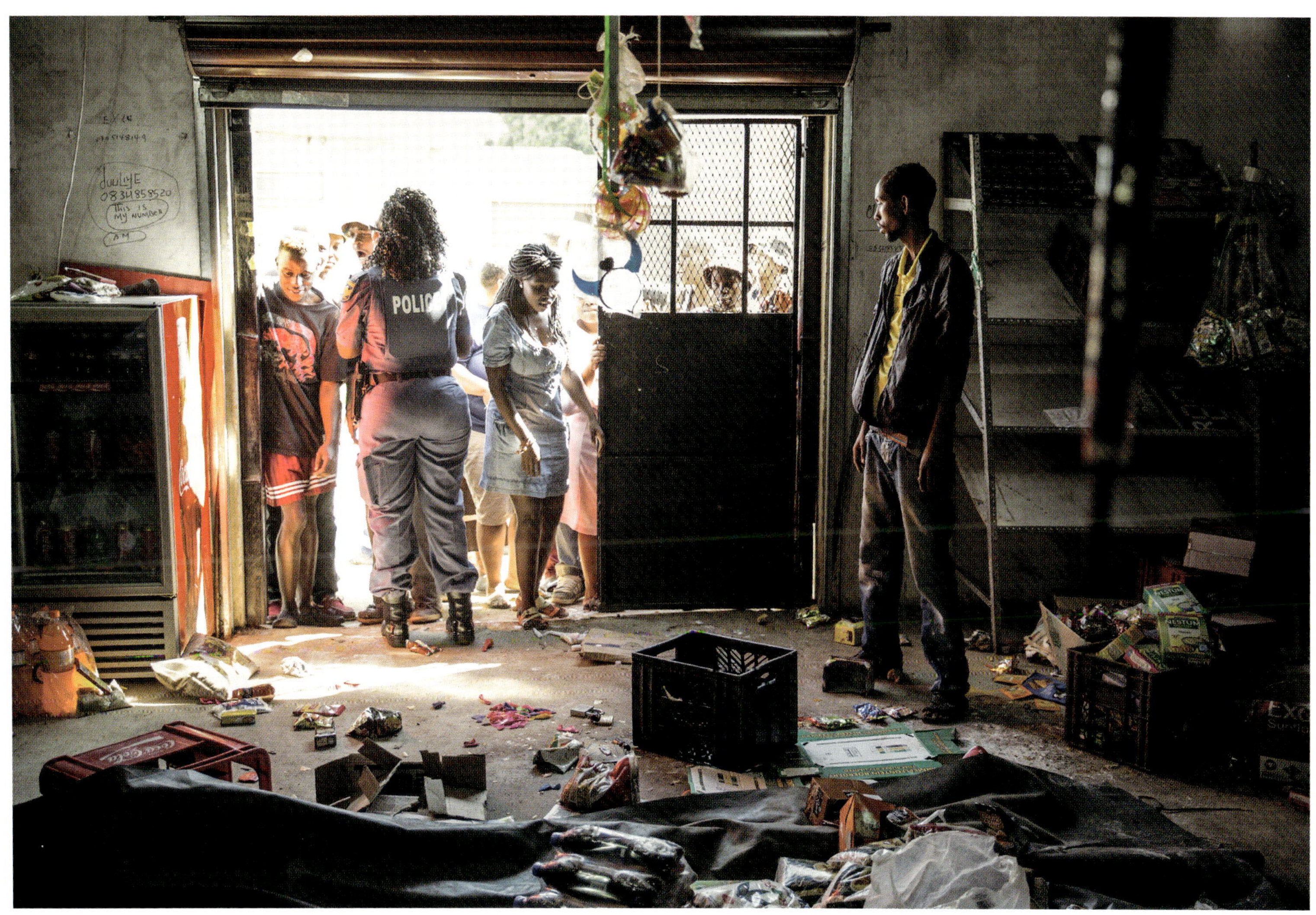

Temporarily protected by a police officer, a man checks the damage to
his store in Kagiso, west of Johannesburg. He removed what he could
before looters forced their way back in.

On 18 April 2015, Emmanuel Sithole was selling goods at
a small table in Alexandra in Johannesburg, when three
men and a minor approached his stand. At least two of
them were fresh from a night of drinking and looting. They
stole a packet of cigarettes and Sithole called after them,
demanding payment. Minutes later, he lay bleeding on
the pavement. Photographer James Oatway and reporter
Beauregard Tromp rushed Sithole to hospital, but it was
too late. He died from a stab wound to the heart. The
following year, Mthinta Bhengu and Sifundo Mzimela were
sentenced to 17 and 10 years respectively for the murder;
Sizwe Mngomezulu was released on set conditions; and
a minor, who could not be named, was given a suspended
sentence. Meanwhile, *Sunday Times* readers and members
of the public donated over R100 000 to a fund for Sithole's
mother, two wives and three young children. It was used to
build them a brick home in their village of Nhachunga in
Mozambique, and to buy a water tank, a water purifier,
a solar panel, four goats and a bicycle.

Mthinta Bhengu moves in to stab Emmanuel Sithole. JO

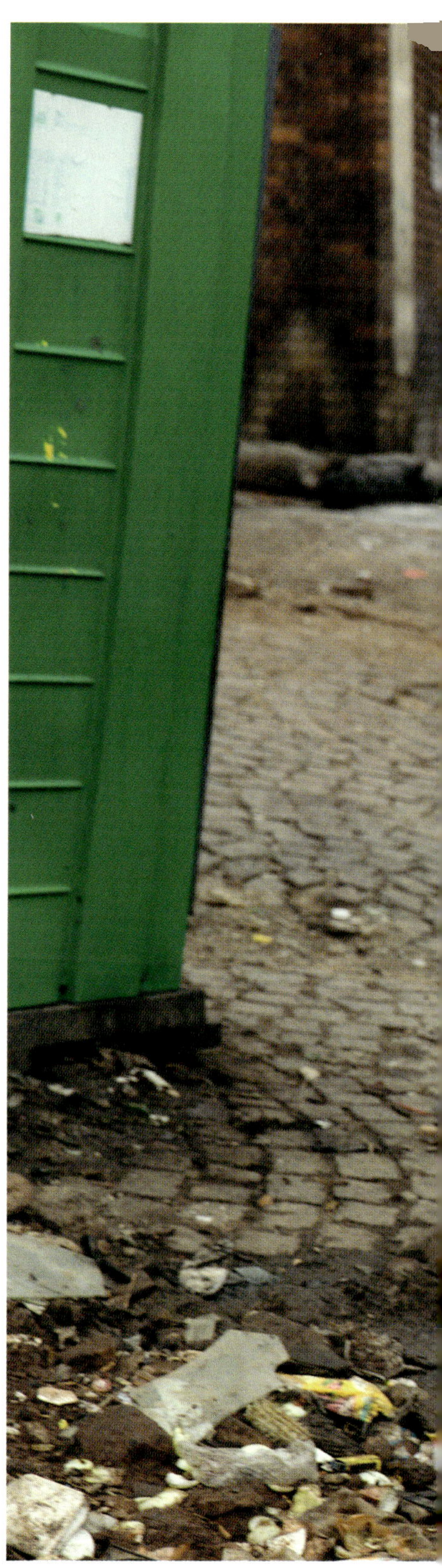

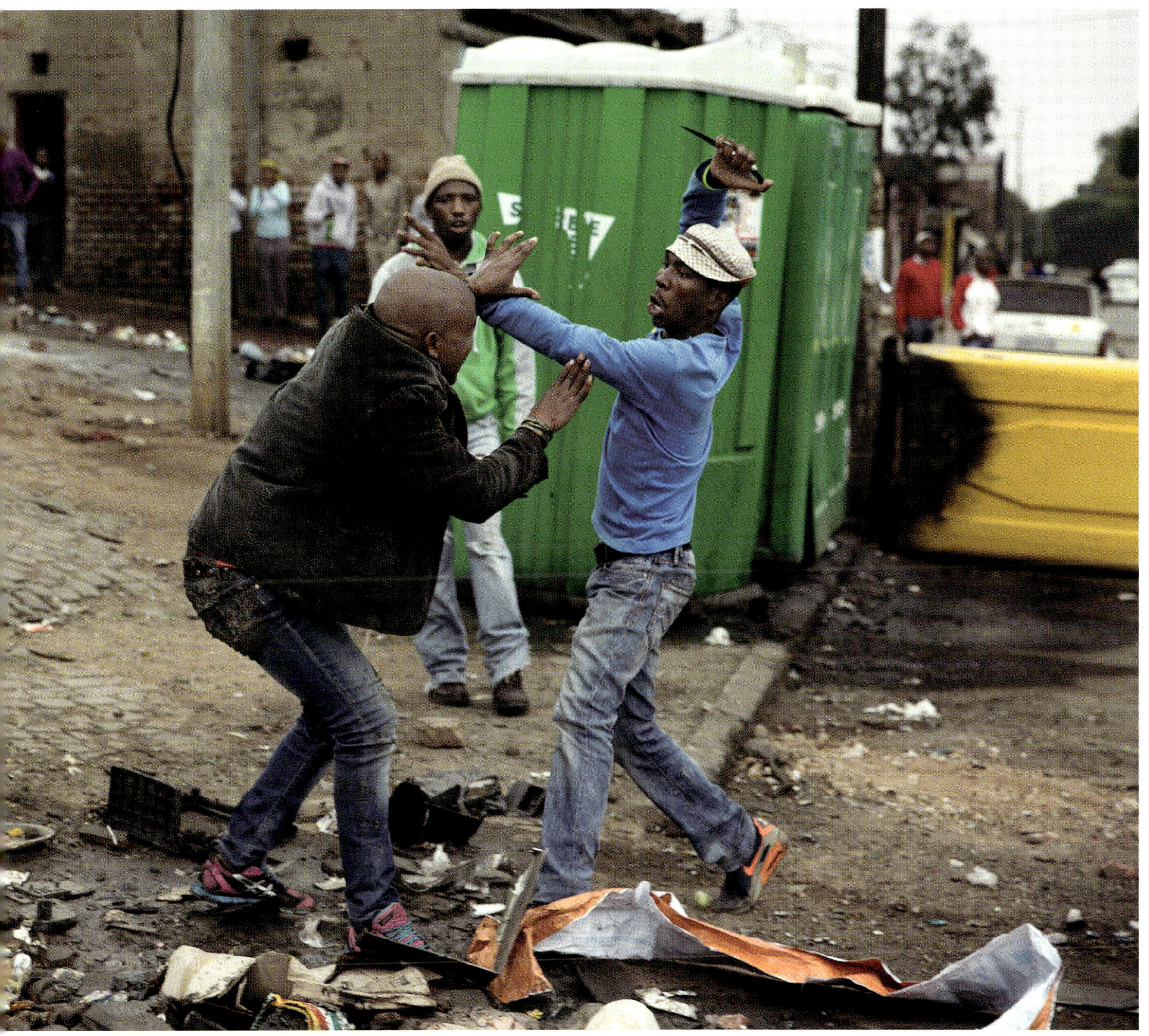

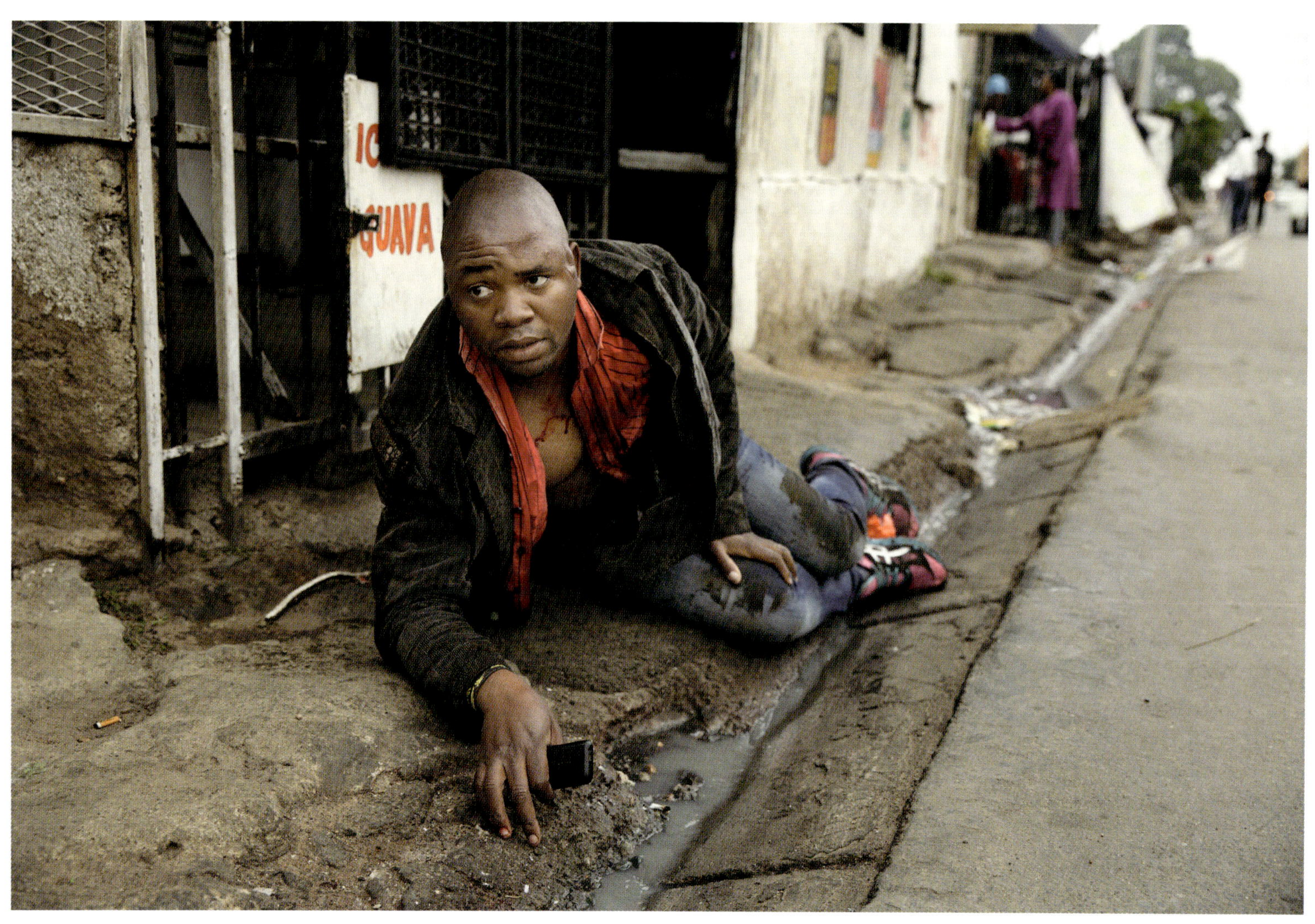

A mortally wounded Emmanuel Sithole looks
in the direction of his attackers. JO

'His name is Emmanuel Sithole'

James Oatway

Alexandra was eerily quiet that morning. It was dull and grey and a strange mist hung over Johannesburg. In the white company VW Polo, Beauregard Tromp and I slowly made our way through the smouldering barricades on London Road. There had been looting during the night. I saw a man with a golf club and some youngsters with sticks disappearing into the shacks. People stepped gingerly through the rubble, making their way to work. Women in fluffy dressing gowns and slippers with their heads covered stood around chatting quietly.

We stopped at a small tuck shop. The zinc roof had been peeled off and the front wall smashed. I took a few photographs before moving down the road to another looted shop. Most of the goods had been taken. The floor was a mess with spilt soft drinks and other junk. A middle-aged man was inspecting the scene. He told me the shop was run by a Bangladeshi man who had fled during the night. I took some more pictures. In the street, I photographed some children who were picking up loose sweets scattered among the debris near an overturned blue plastic toilet.

Then I heard screams and looked up and saw men running zigzag in my direction. A man was being chased. He fell to the ground and the first attacker began to hit him with a big spanner. I ran towards them, taking photographs. Others were shouting and the attacker briefly moved away. That's when number two came running in. I noticed he had a knife in his hand. Through the viewfinder of my camera I saw him raise his arm high above his head and stab at the man.

The men scuffled and both ended up on the ground. Then the first attacker reappeared, swinging his spanner. I kept getting closer, photographing all the time. We were only metres apart. More men appeared. There was lots of shouting. Then they became aware of my presence and began to withdraw. They came very close; Mthinta Bhengu, with knife in hand, glared at me. For a moment I thought it was my turn. I was very scared. I hid behind my camera, almost wincing in anticipation of the imminent assault. But they kept walking ... straight past me. I thought it was over and began to breathe again, but at that moment another man came sprinting in and landed a flying kick on the victim, who was sitting stunned on the ground. I noticed a large kitchen knife in his hand. Another man intervened – he wore a black leather jacket – and the attacker jogged off to join his comrades.

The victim sat there staring at me. I shouted at him to get the hell out of there, but he just looked at me as though he didn't understand what I was saying. I was afraid the attackers would return. They were half-walking, half-jogging down the street. There were many people in the street. Many witnesses.

'Let's go! Let's go!' I shouted, looking between him and the attackers. Finally he got up and started to walk away. 'Are you OK?' I asked. No response. He looked back in the direction of the attackers. 'What's your name?' He struggled to say something but I couldn't work it out. He kept looking over his shoulder. He seemed angry. He disappeared up the road. Then someone called me. 'The man has fallen down!' I ran up the road and found him lying in the gutter clutching his chest. He kept looking down the road as if expecting the attackers to return.

I spoke to the man. 'Don't worry, you're going to be OK. Just relax. You're going to be fine.' Tromp arrived with the car and we tried to get the man in. He kept making a sound like 'heeeyeeee, heeeyeeee'. He was extremely heavy. My cameras kept getting in the way, so I threw them into the front of the car. I remember him smelling strongly of beer. Later we found out that the attackers had poured it over him in the prelude to what I witnessed. I remember his big, strong hands. His thumbnail clipped too short.

A woman told us that there was a clinic just up the road. It was only a few hundred metres away. I stormed in calling for help. We struggled to get the man into a wheelchair. He was so heavy.

'There is no doctor here. You must take him to Edenvale Hospital,' a nurse said. They took his shirt off and stuck a dressing on his chest wound. We battled to put him into the car again.

The journey to Edenvale was excruciating. There were slow vehicles, taxis turning and narrow, bendy roads that made overtaking impossible. The man was struggling and kicking around in the back of the car. I turned in my seat and tried to calm him. I kept telling him: 'Don't worry. Just relax.'

He looked at me now and again – surprise on his face. He calmed down a bit. I kept talking to him – now he was slipping in and out of consciousness. I still didn't think that he had sustained fatal wounds. I had seen people with worse wounds survive. Then his chest wound started to bleed through the dressing.

We finally reached the dull grey edifice of Edenvale Hospital. I ran in, shouting frantically for attention. The staff walked over casually, looked into the car and said 'No, this one's dead. You must call the police.' As if on cue, the man's eyes flickered and his body began to convulse. They brought a gurney and rushed him inside. I peeked through a gap in the emergency room curtain and saw them performing CPR.

A nurse came out and called me over. I went into the theatre and saw the man lying on his back. The nurses and the doctor stood looking at me. 'Is he dead?' I asked. 'I'm sorry. We tried, but the knife had gone straight into his heart. Anyway, his pupils were fixed when he came in.' The nurses went through some numbers on his phone and one made a call from the phone. After hanging up she said: 'His name is Emmanuel Sithole.'

We are the barbarians

Justice Malala

There is nothing more to say. What you will read in this column is what I wrote in 2008, and in subsequent outbreaks of xenophobic violence in this country: about the mealy-mouthed responses of our leaders, the culpability of people such as King Goodwill Zwelithini, who speak without thinking. There is nothing more to say. It has all been said.

We are the barbarians.

So I write this for one man.

When my people stalked Emmanuel Sithole like an animal down Second Avenue, in Alexandra township, on a Saturday in April 2015, when my people beat him brutally with a wrench and stabbed him to death, only one man entreated the killers to stop.

I write this column for that one good man, described by the brave journalists of the *Sunday Times* as 'a man in a leather jacket'.

In the horrific picture by James Oatway on the front page of the *Sunday Times* on 20 April, the killer of Sithole has his right arm raised. In his hand is the knife about to come down into Sithole's chest and through to his heart.

It is not the cruel, focused face of the killer that gnaws at my heart. It is not the blade raised high and about to hurtle down to destroy, to kill.

It is the 11 other people in the picture that so disturbs me. People who stand in the cold and watch. They did not do anything. They watched, at least one with hands to his mouth, watching.

They were not the only witnesses: others watched, said nothing, and did nothing as Sithole crawled away and was taken to hospital by Oatway and his colleagues. Only the man in the leather jacket raised a voice to save Sithole.

The crowd that watched is us. Those witnesses live in Alexandra. They know the killers. They live among them. They love among them. They also know that those killers can kill them too. Afraid and brutalised, they say nothing and do nothing as a man is killed in front of them.

These Alex people are a metaphor for our leaders: we know that the latest round of attacks was in part sparked by Zulu King Goodwill Zwelithini's incendiary 'foreigner go home' remarks.

Speaking at a KwaZulu-Natal 'moral regeneration event' in March 2015, Zwelithini accused government of failing to protect locals from the 'influx of foreign nationals'.

'We are requesting those who come from

outside to please go back to their countries,' Zwelithini said. 'The fact that there were countries that played a role in the country's struggle for liberation should not be used as an excuse to create a situation where foreigners are allowed to inconvenience locals.

'I know you were in their countries during the struggle for liberation. But the fact of the matter is you did not set up businesses in their countries,' he said.

But neither President Jacob Zuma nor Police Minister Nathi Nhleko has the courage to ask him to take to a public platform quickly and apologise. They are afraid that they will marginalise the KwaZulu-Natal constituency of the ANC without having any evidence that what is being said about Zwelithini is actually true.

Zuma and Nhleko are scared to test the waters. If they did they would see that our people's humanity is deeper than allegiance to a monarch. Zuma and Nhleko have lost their courage, just as those people who stood around when Sithole was murdered have.

The Alex people lost their courage because they know that the killers of Sithole, even if arrested, may be back in the community soon and then anyone who tried to help Sithole will be in danger.

Of the dozens of xenophobic murders between 2008 and 2015, the *Sunday Times* reported that there had been only one conviction by the time of Sithole's murder. The system – the police, the prosecuting authorities, the courts – have failed those people who stood around when Sithole died.

They know these institutions couldn't help Sithole and will not help anyone who helped Sithole. What those people saw in Alexandra township on Saturday is commonplace. Violence is endemic in that poor, sad, devastated and neglected community. The only difference between the death of Sithole and that of many others in Alex every day is that this happened in front of a brave and humane press photographer who did his job and took Sithole to hospital.

That man in the leather jacket, the man who said 'Stop!', is the other brief, flickering light of humanity. The killers were armed and he was not. The killers probably know him and where he lives. The witnesses know him and his family. Yet, he had the courage to call out to those killers and tell them to stop. He had the courage to keep telling them to stop as they carried out their terrible deed. The man in the leather jacket is my hero.

Courage, anywhere, is one man or woman with a voice. We have seen little courage in South Africa lately. Zuma and his cabinet have flip-flopped and have failed to confront the issue head-on. Organised business has been quiet, except for a few brave voices.

The only voice that has been anything equivalent to that of the man in the leather jacket has been that of civil society.

Our leaders are failing to act with courage and humanity. They are failing to be the man in the leather jacket.

This column was first published in *The Times* newspaper.
The man in the leather jacket was later identified, but remains anonymous here, as he faces threats from those who think he should not have intervened.

Justice Malala is an author (*We Have Now Begun Our Descent*), television host and newspaper columnist.

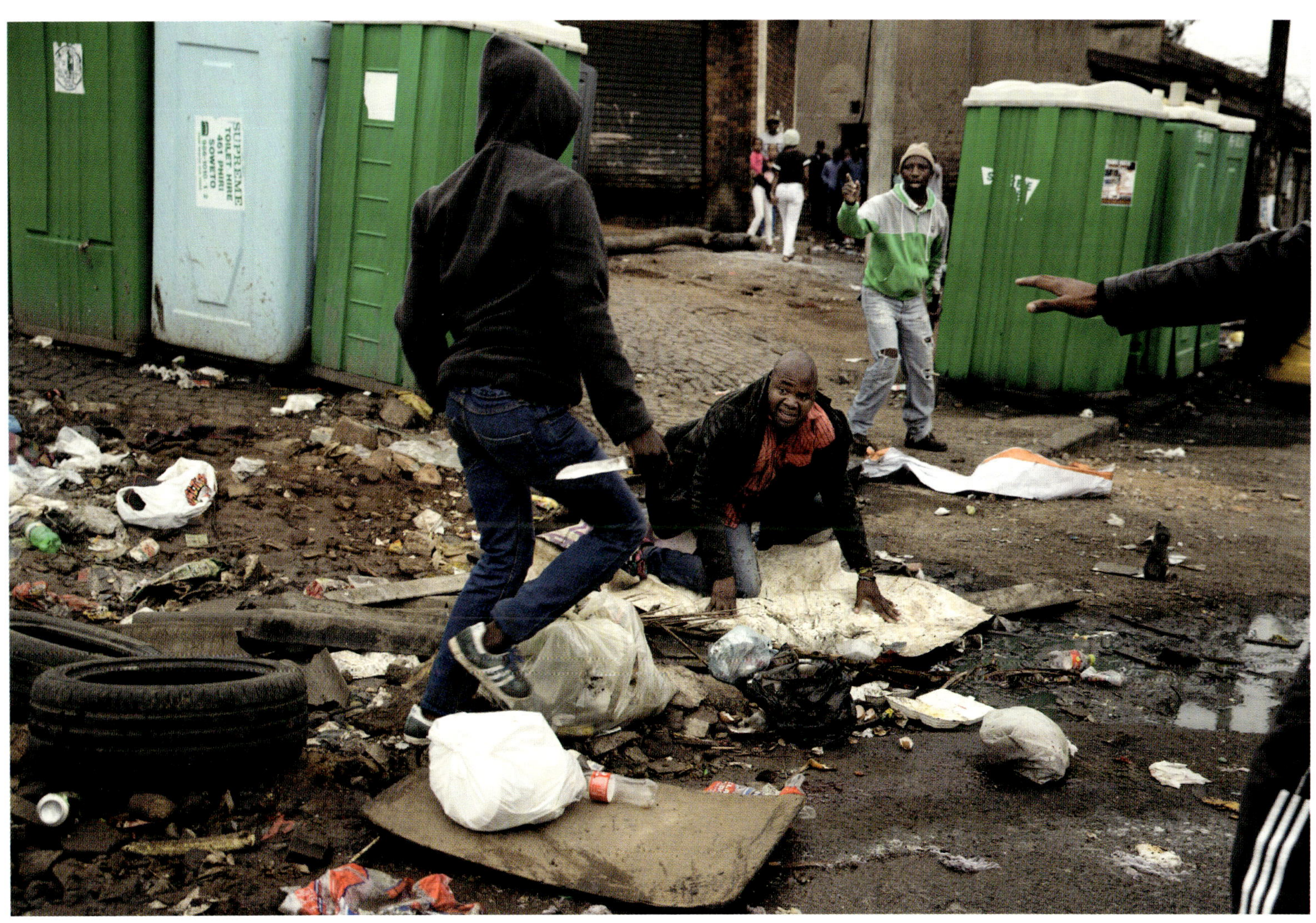

A youth approaches Sithole but is stopped by 'a man in a leather jacket' whose arm appears at the right of the image. JO

South African men's hostels are a hotbed for much of the anger against migrants. With thousands of residents forced into cramped and squalid conditions, and mine closures leading to increased unemployment, inhabitants feel the government has abandoned them. After the slaying of Emmanuel Sithole in April 2015, a police special task team launched a high profile raid on Wolhuter Men's Hostel (widely referred to as Jeppe Hostel) in Johannesburg. The media were tipped off before this heavy show of force that left hostel residents angry that their dignity had been violated in the way they were treated during the raid.

Hostel residents gather before a demonstration. Many of these men are themselves migrants from other areas in South Africa who have come to the City of Gold in search of work. AS

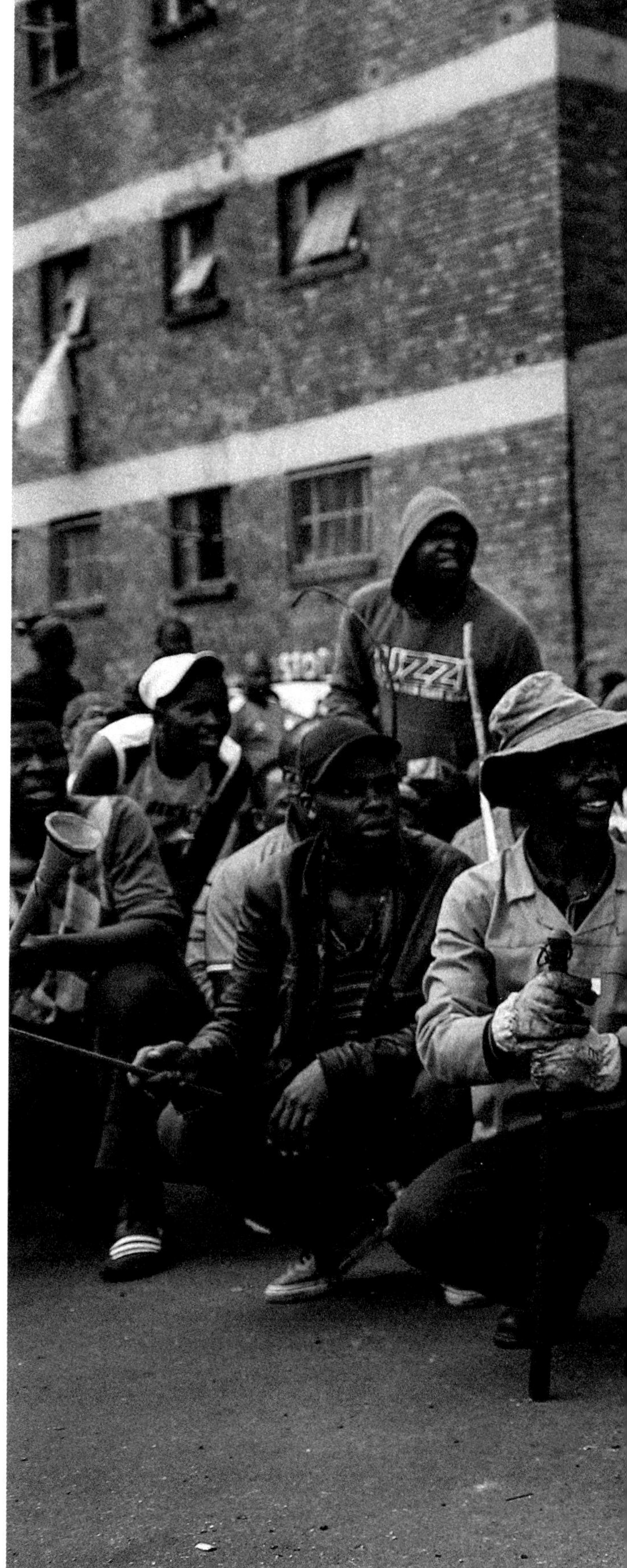

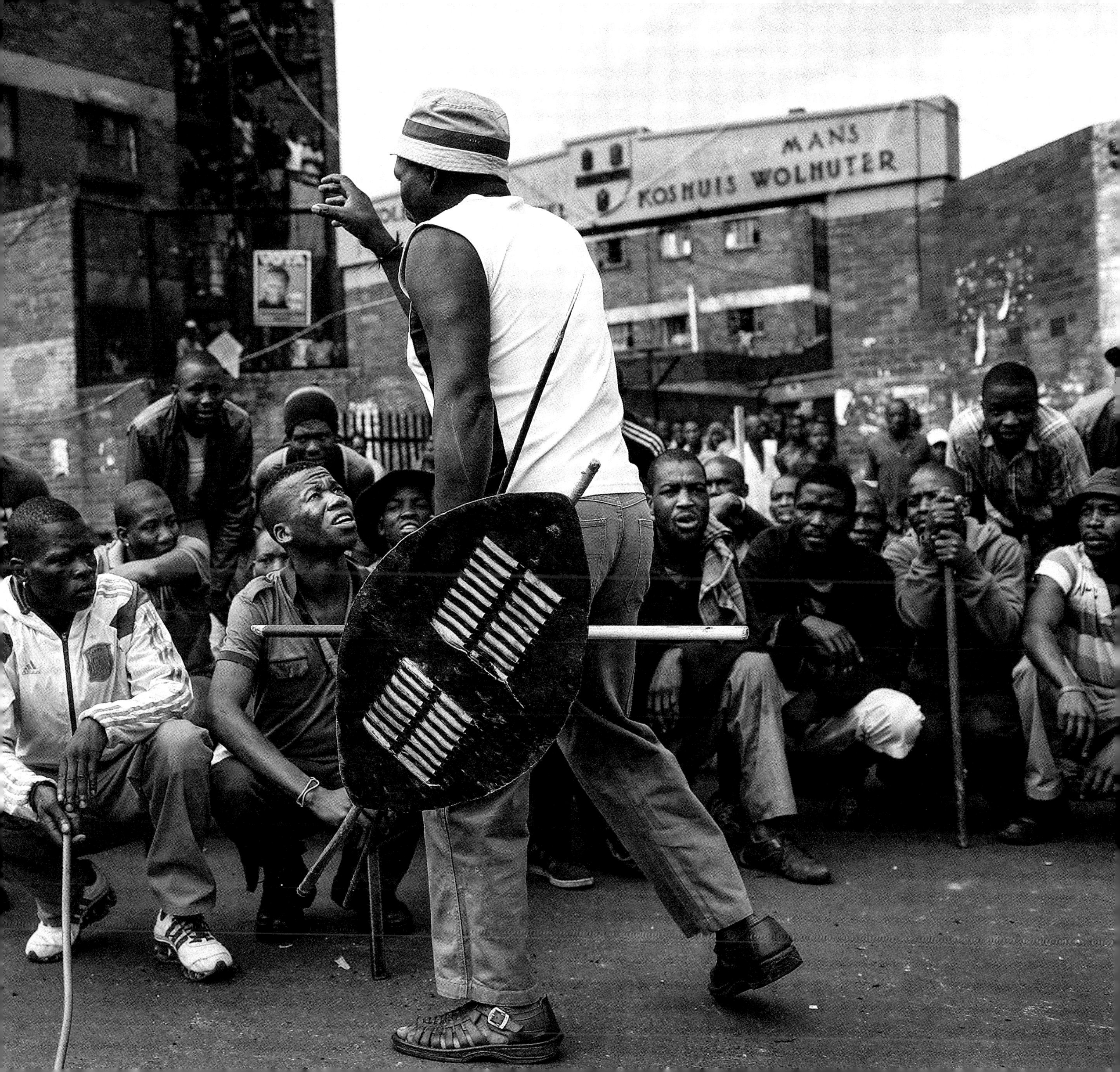

MANS
KOSHUIS WOLHUTER

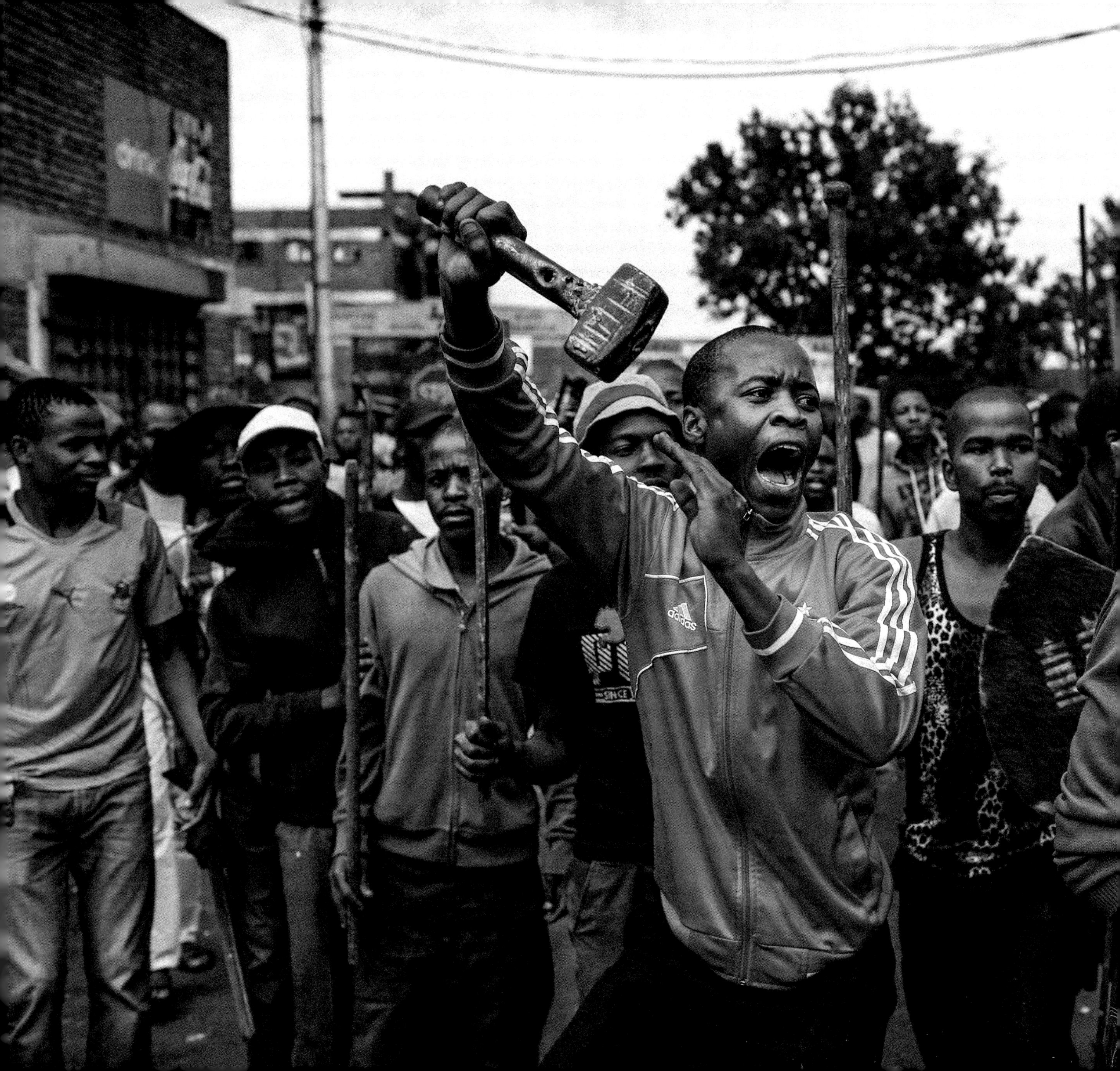

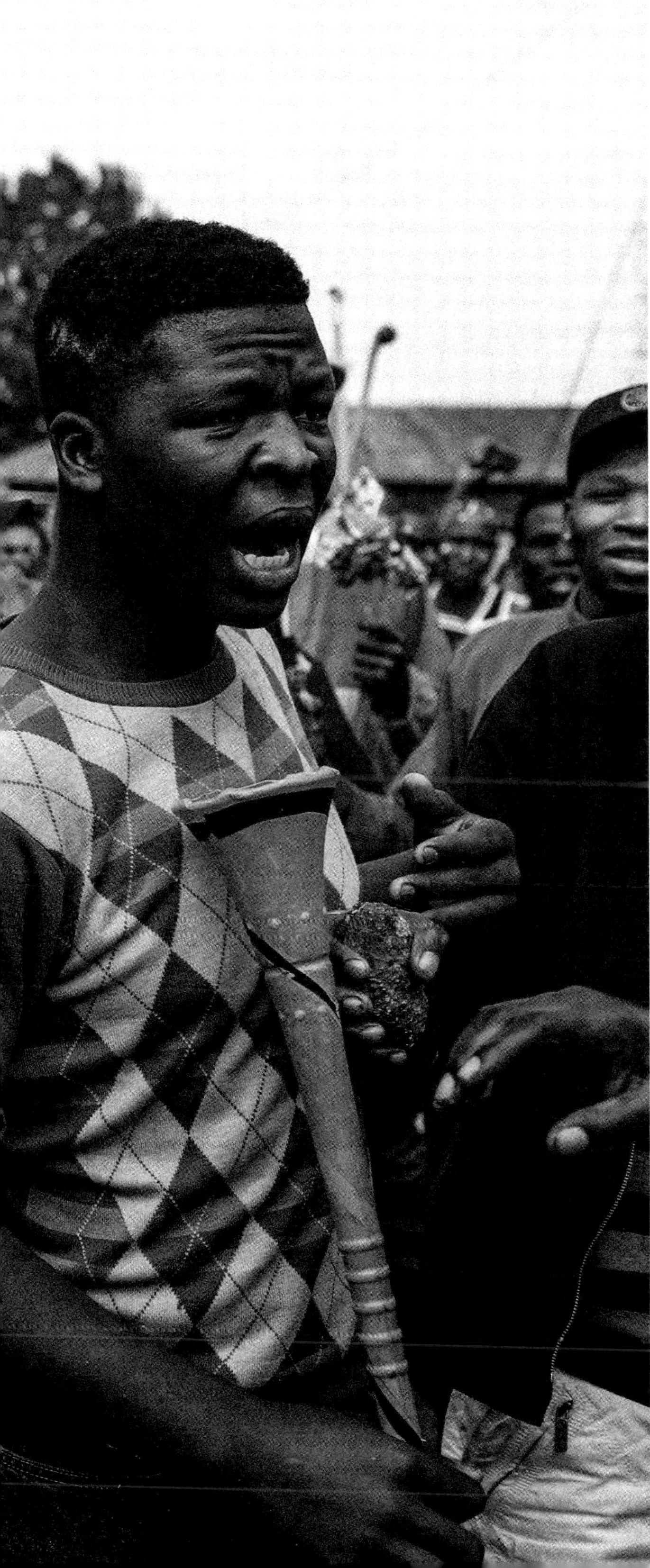

Armed with weapons ranging from a rock to a masonry hammer, hostel dwellers – large numbers of them unemployed – vocalise their anger at migrants who they believe are taking food off their tables. AS

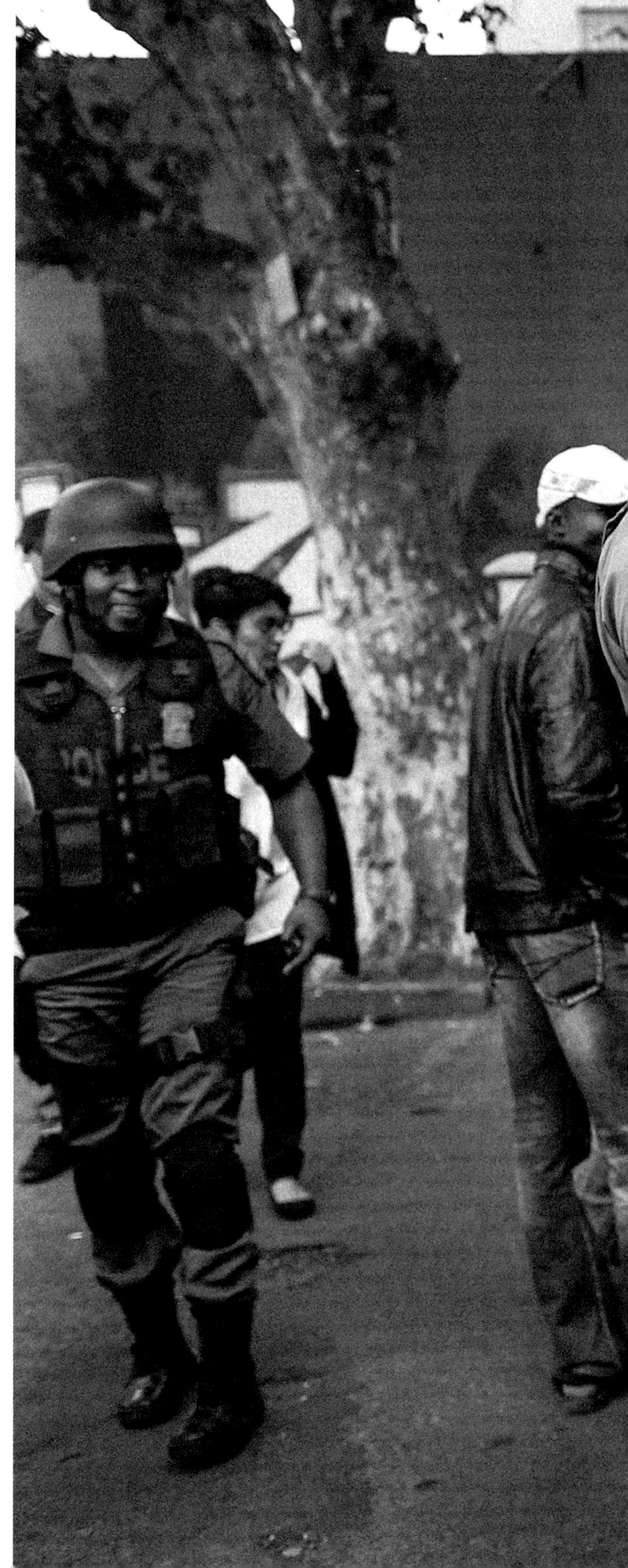

SAPS members try to discourage a group of migrant men, infuriated at the looting and attacks, from fighting back against a militant crowd of marchers. AS

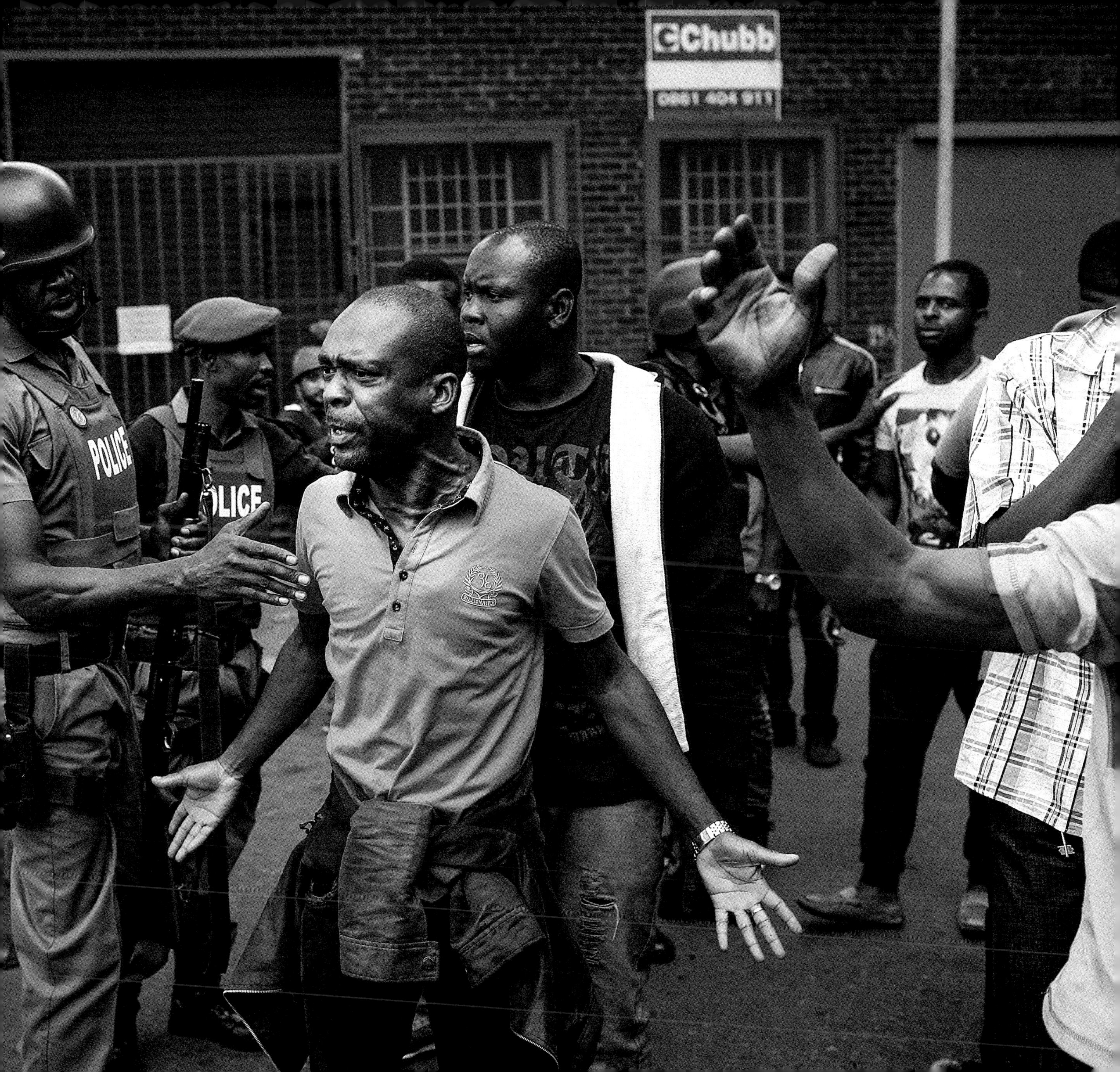
Chubb
0861 404 911
POLICE
POLICE

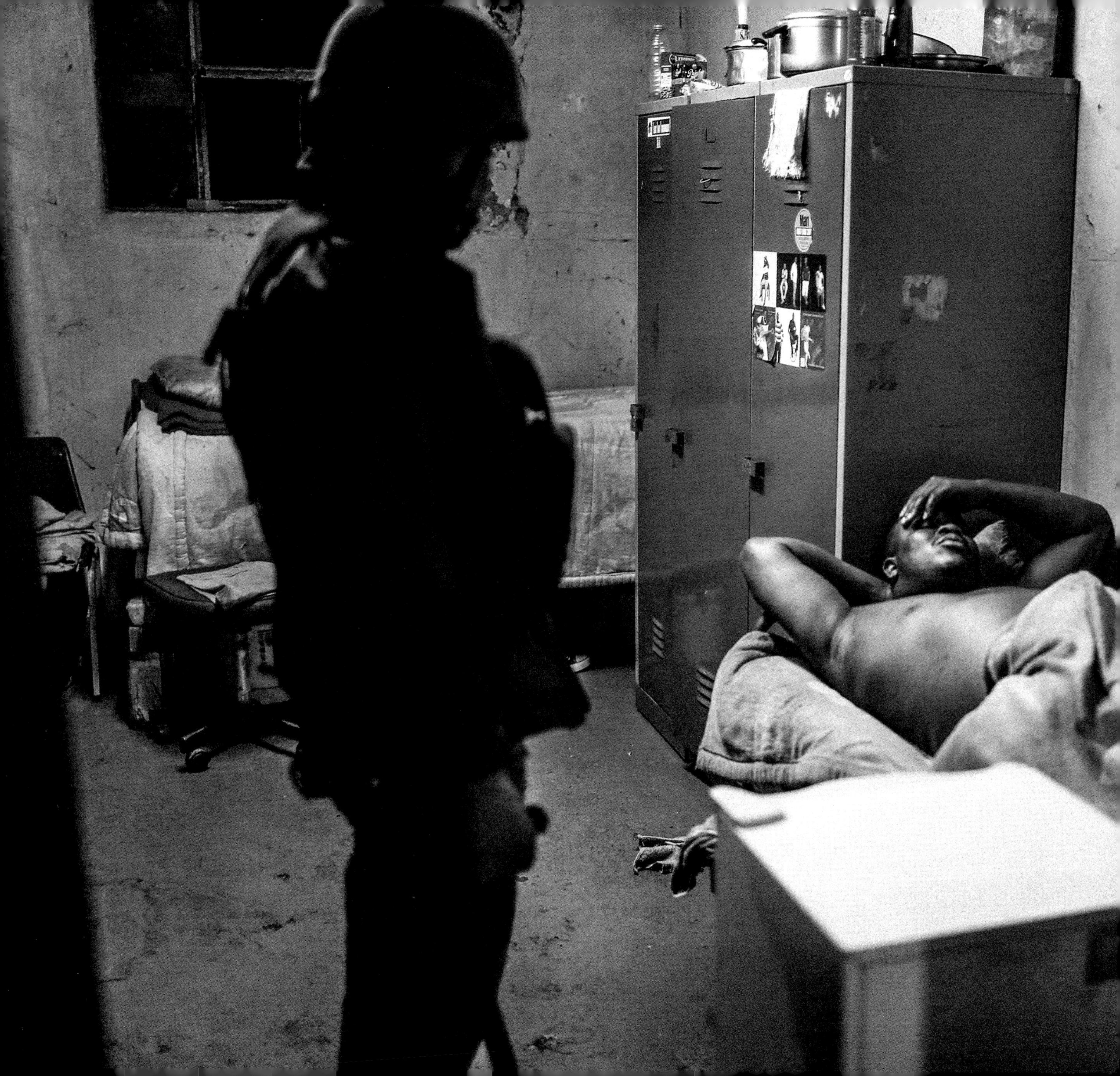

A policeman rouses a resident during a night raid on Jeppe
Hostel, where men live in barracks-like conditions. AS

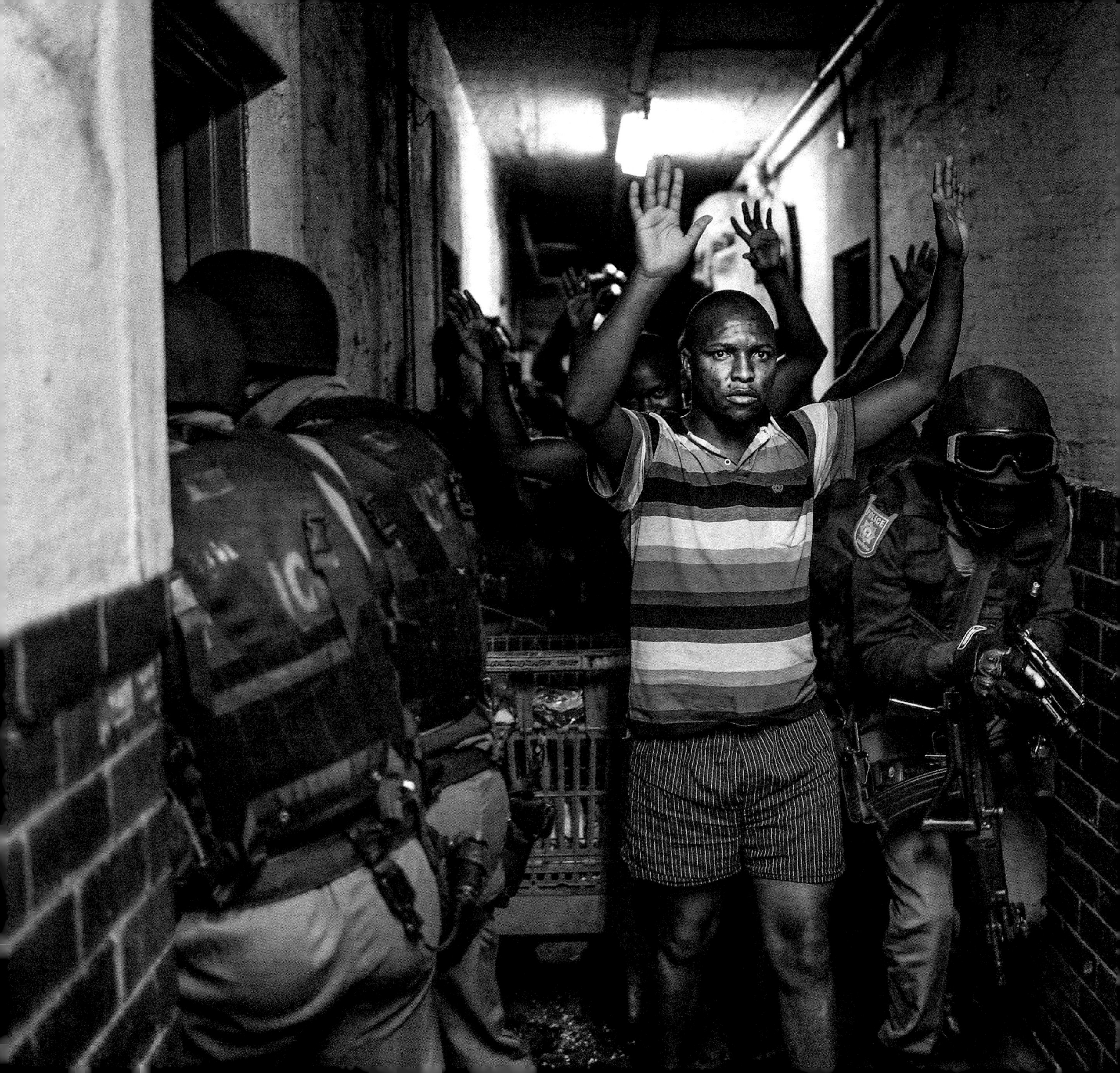

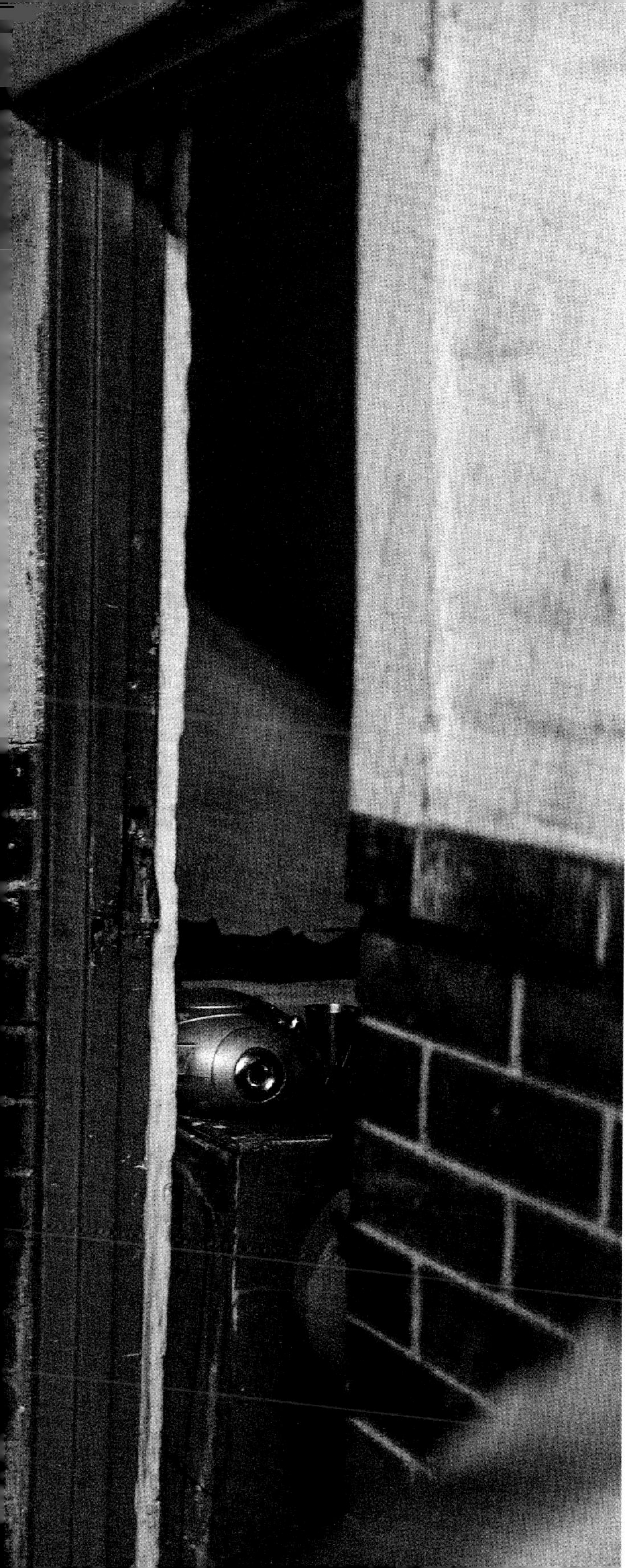

Men are forced from their rooms as police search for
weapons and those suspected of being perpetrators
of xenophobic violence. AS

Made to lie in an undignified manner in the corridors,
many hostel dwellers felt humiliated and angered
by this aspect of the police action. AS

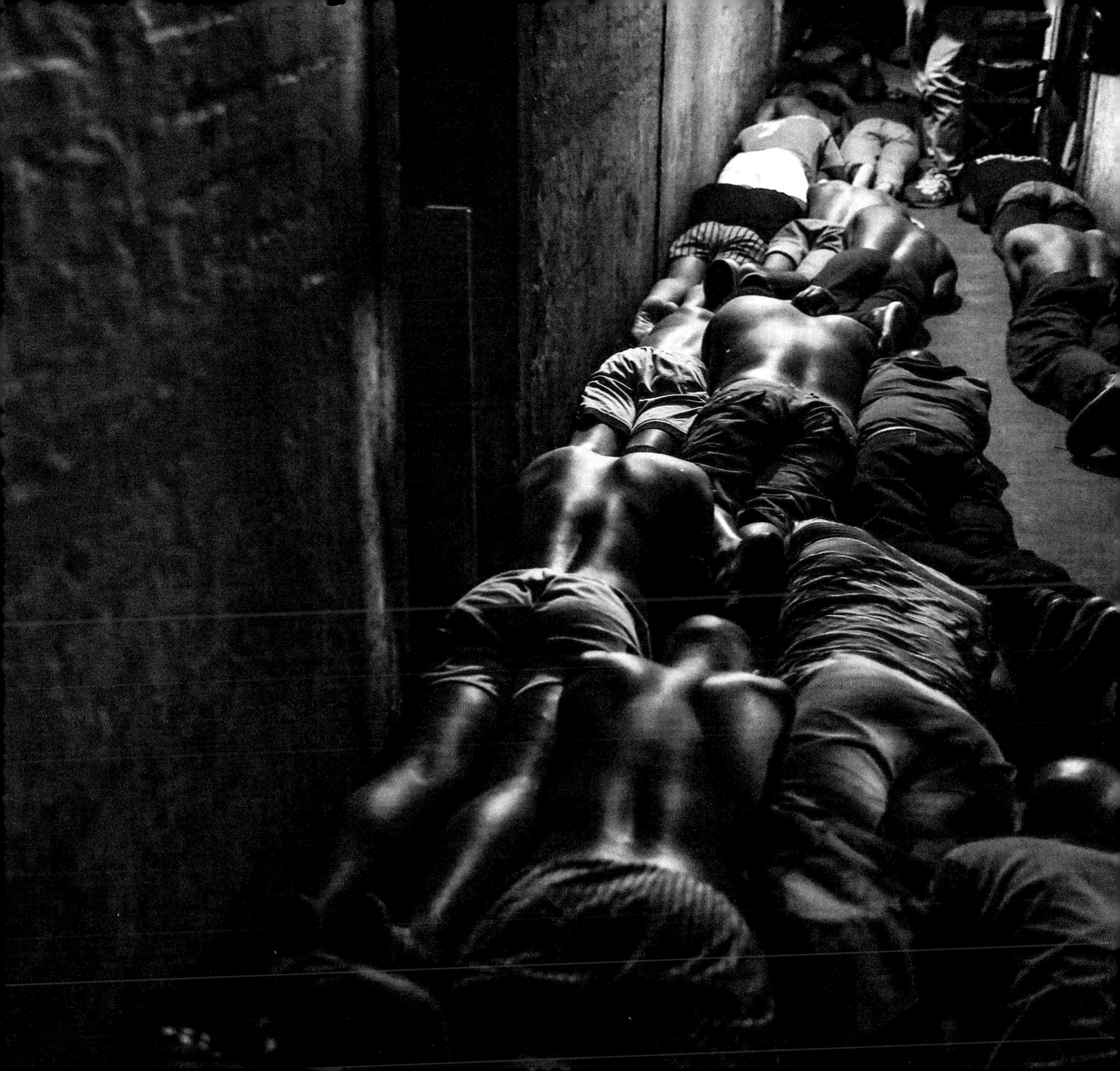

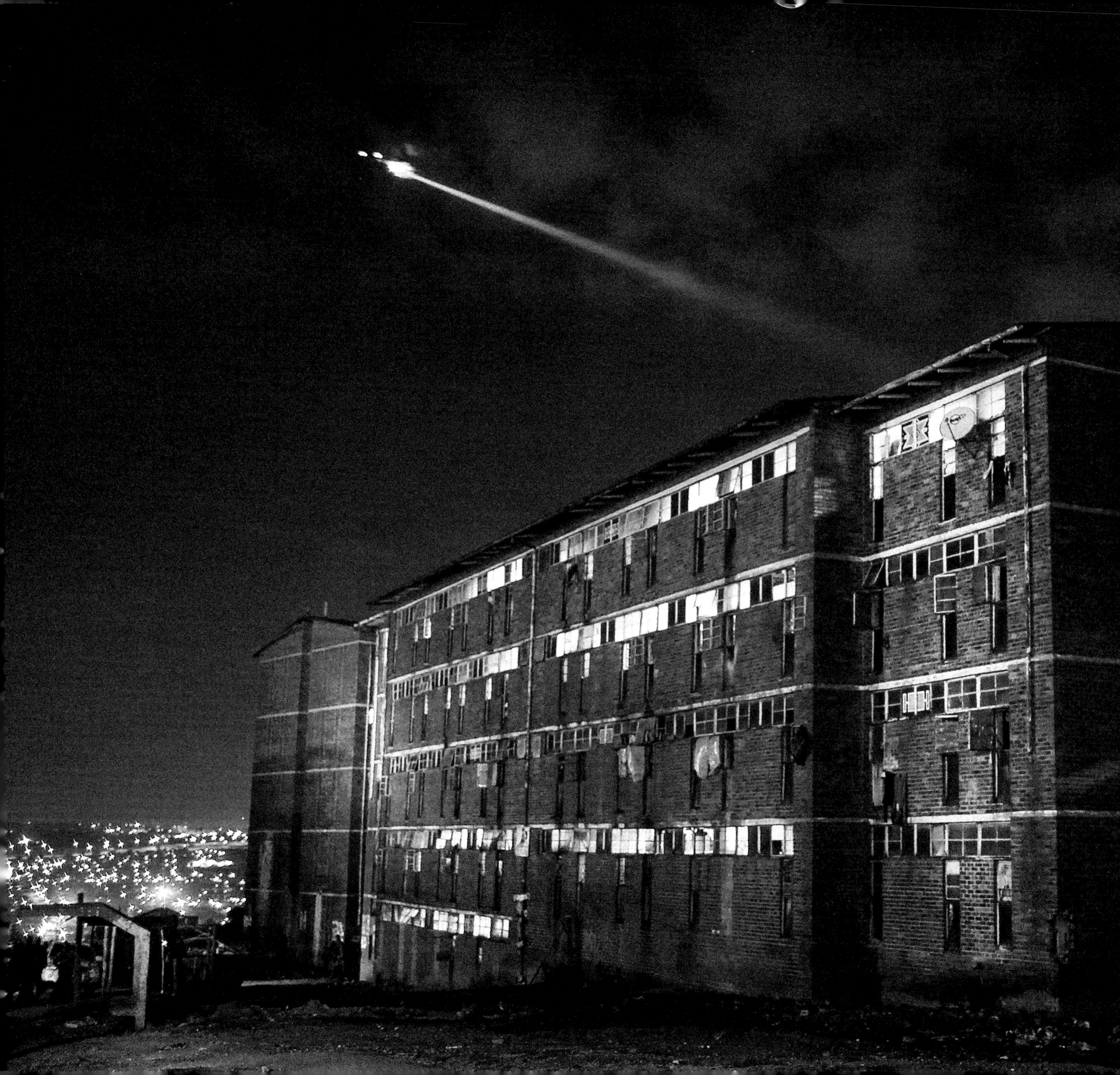

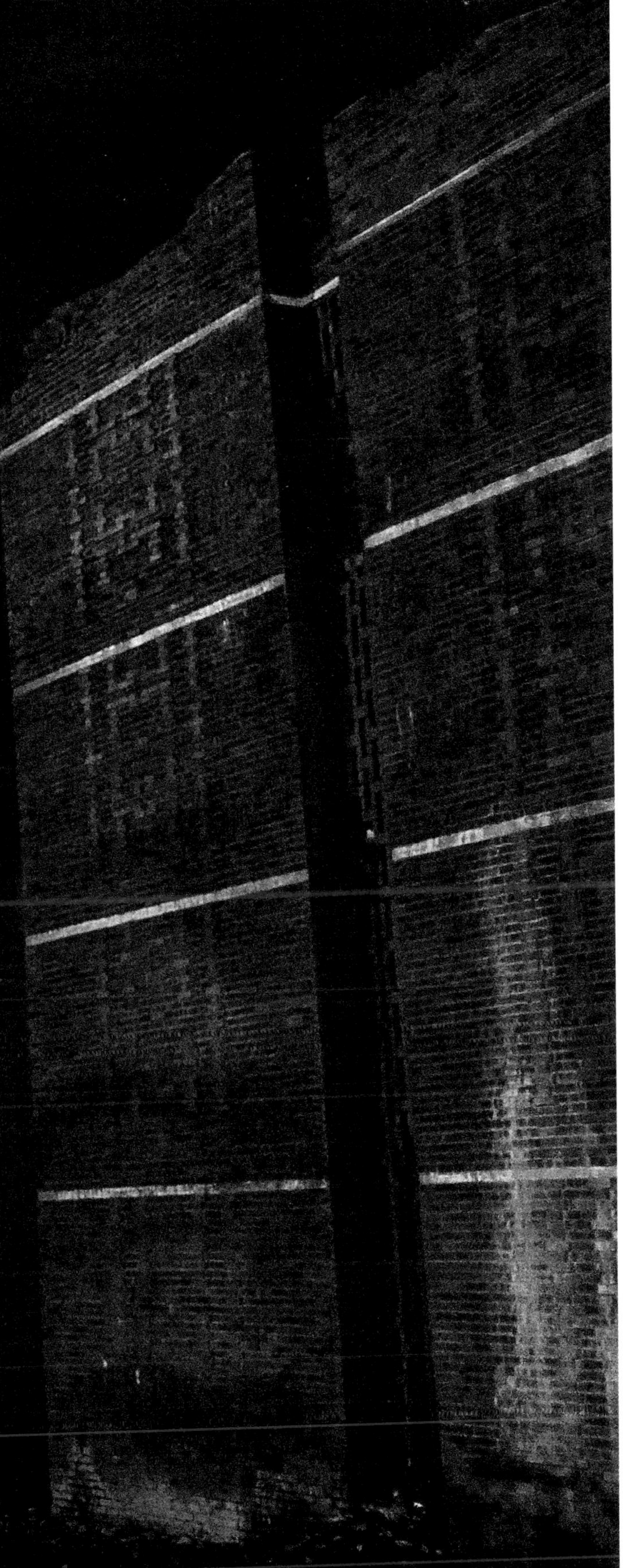

A police helicopter hovers above Madala Men's Hostel in Alexandra during a late night raid to search for weapons used in recent attacks. AS

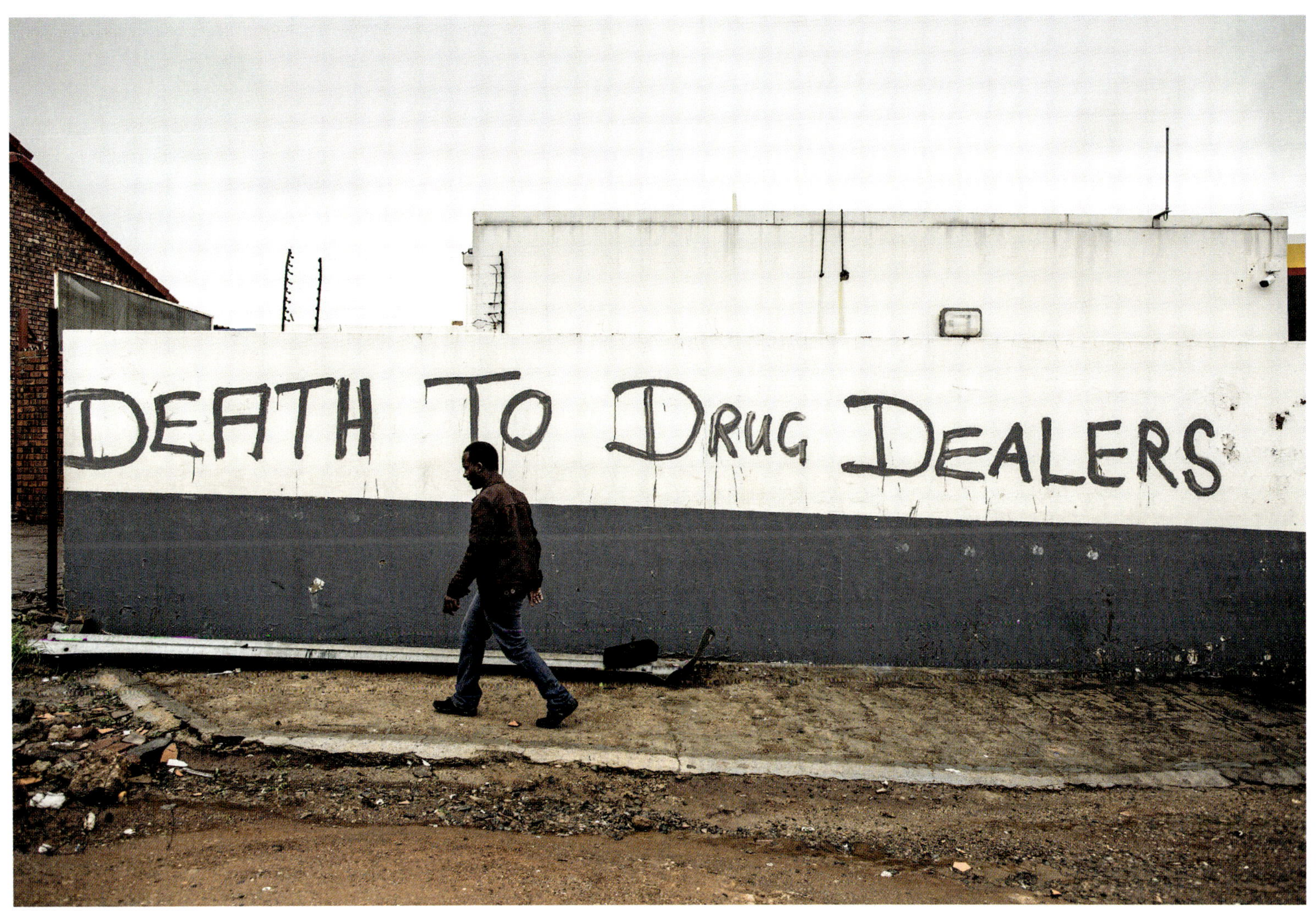

DEATH TO DRUG DEALERS

A community protest against 'criminals and drug-dealers' in Pretoria West in February 2017 turned into a series of random attacks on migrants during which this church minister was injured. JO

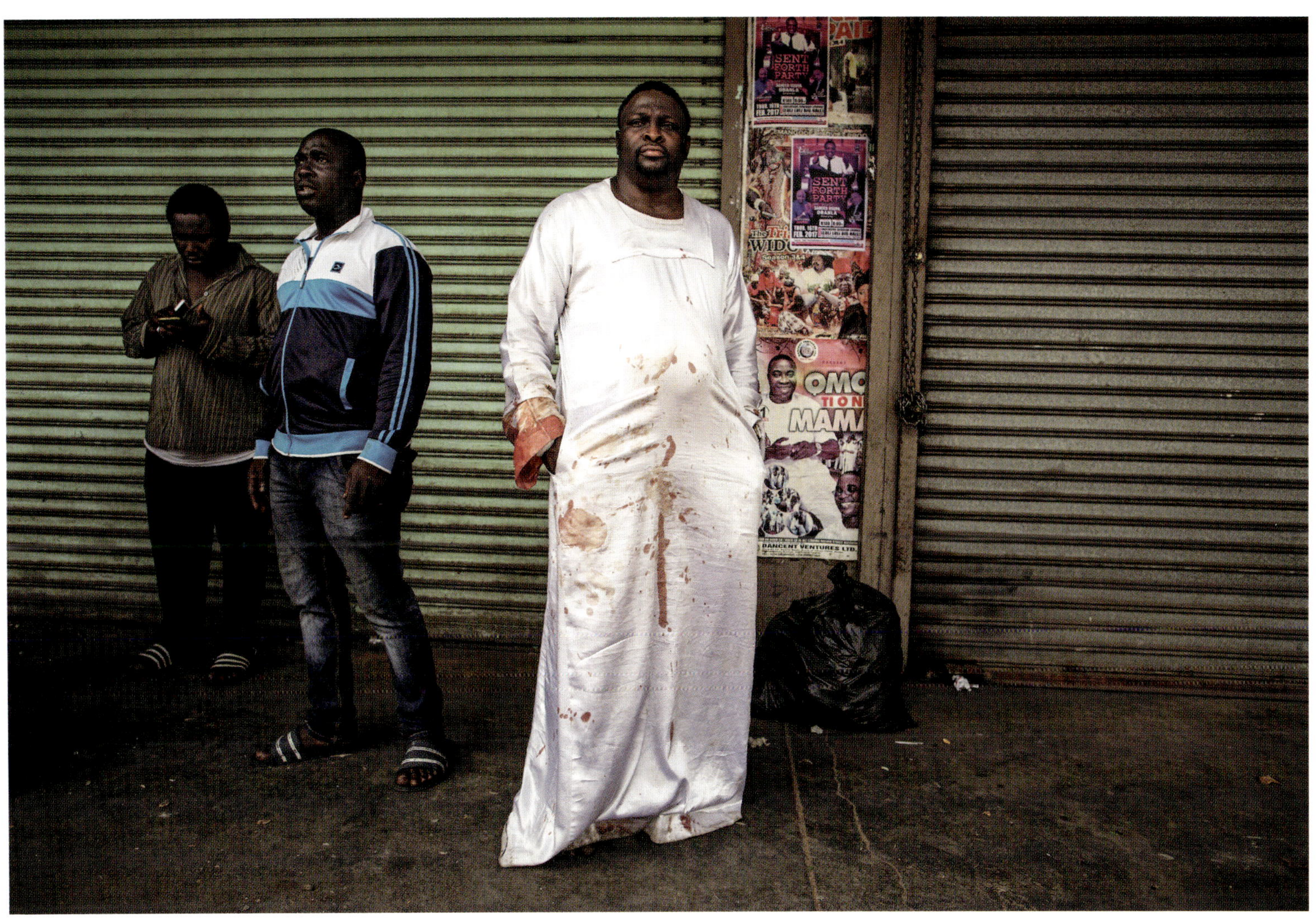

SENT
FORTH
PARTY
WIDOW
OMO
TION
MAMA
DANCENT VENTURES LTD.

Shopowner Sipho Sibiya alongside his premises in
Atteridgeville at a time when xenophobic rhetoric
was rife, and tensions were running high. JO

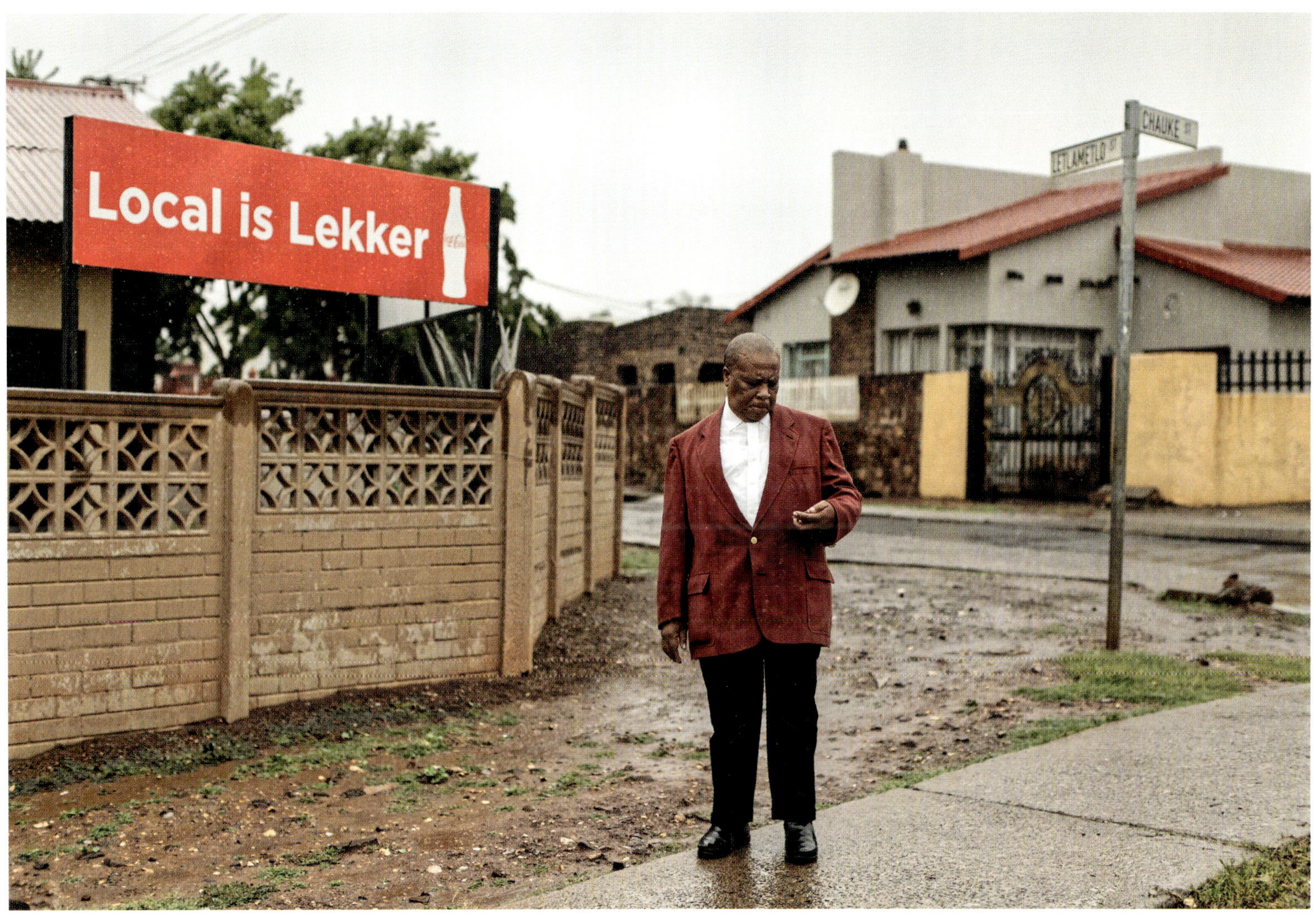

93

A man peers through the gate of a building in Pretoria at
angry locals who are demanding entry. They accused those
inside the premises of having weapons. AS

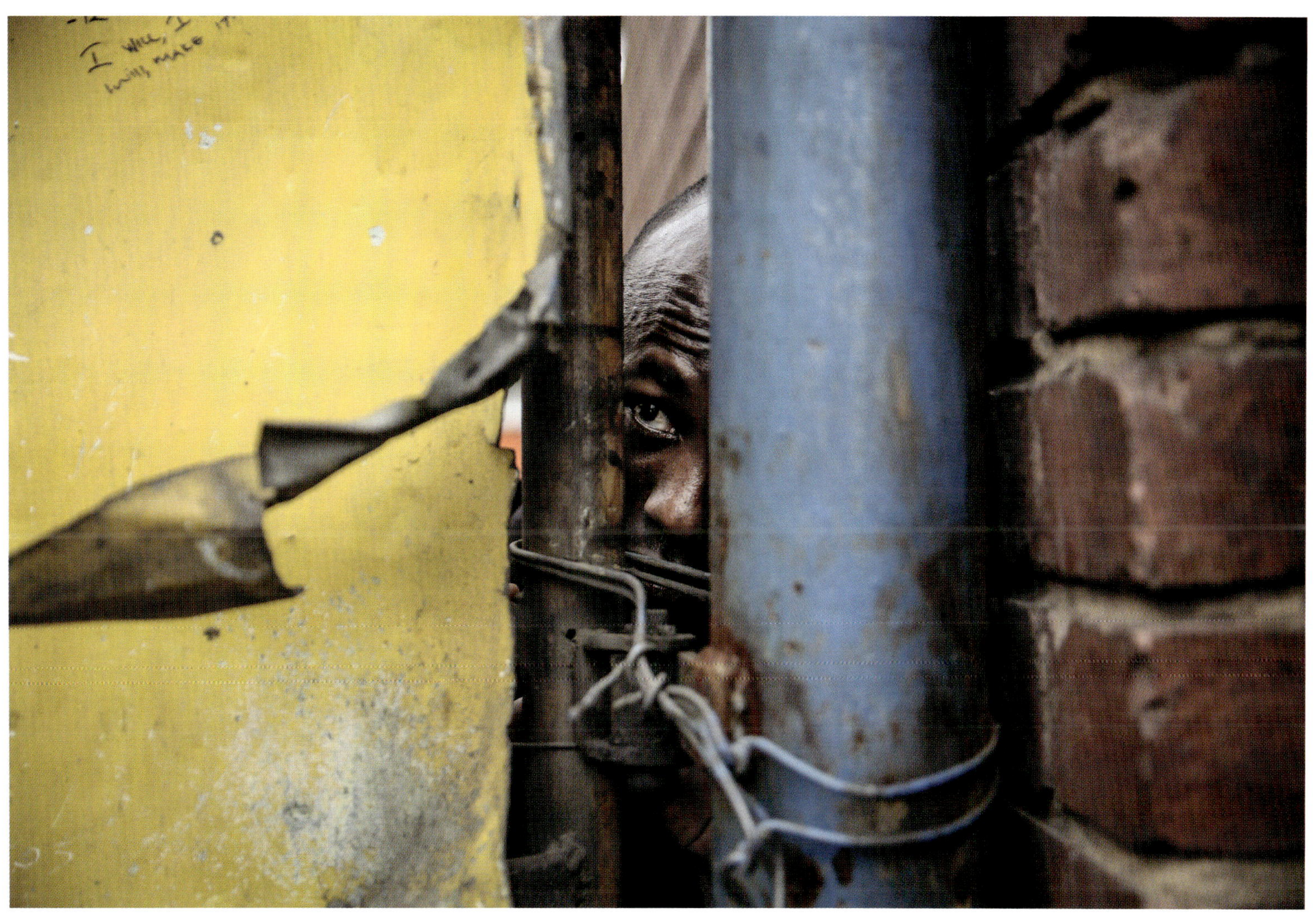
I WILL, I
WILL MAKE IT

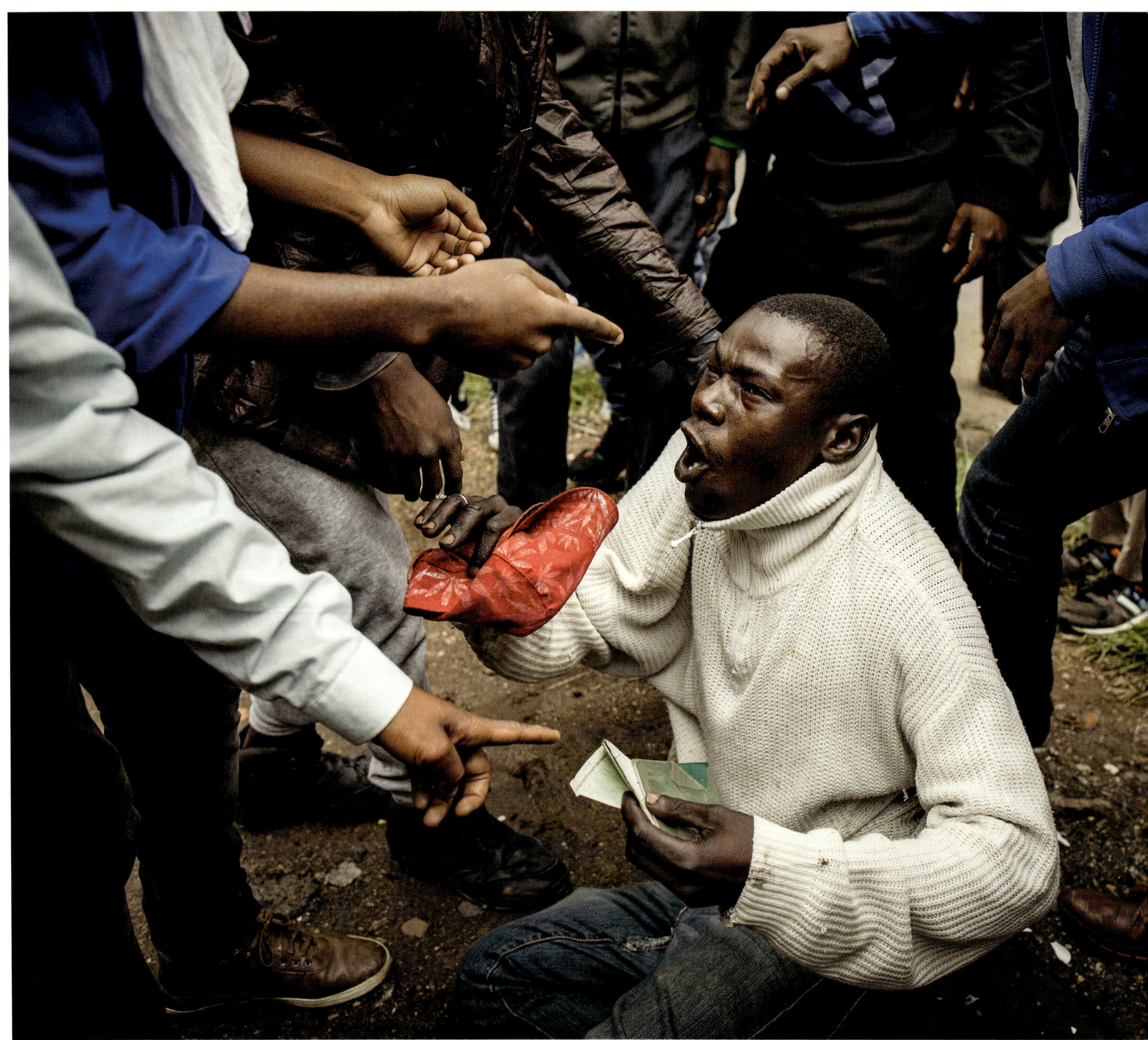

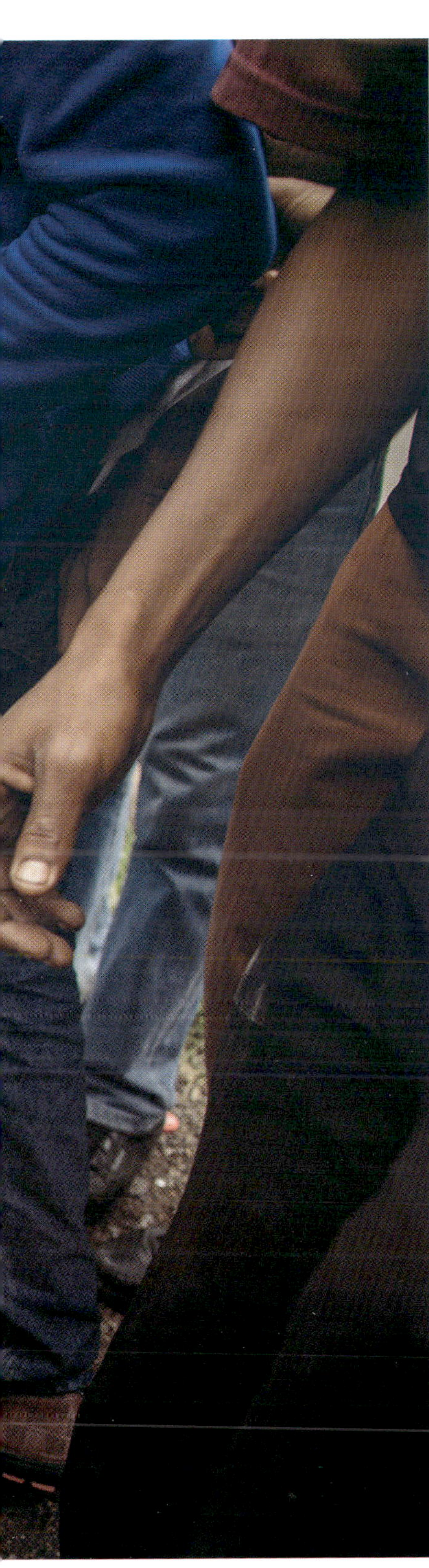

A heavily outnumbered man is saved by producing his South African 'book of life' after being attacked during an 'anti-crime' march that turned into an 'anti-migrant' hunt. JO

In 2008 Central Methodist Church in
Johannesburg became a sanctuary
to thousands of refugees who were
displaced initially by political violence
in Zimbabwe, and then by xenophobic
violence in South Africa. But by 2015,
after a criminal element had infiltrated
the refuge and it had fallen into a state
of disrepair, the church was forced
to evict the inhabitants.

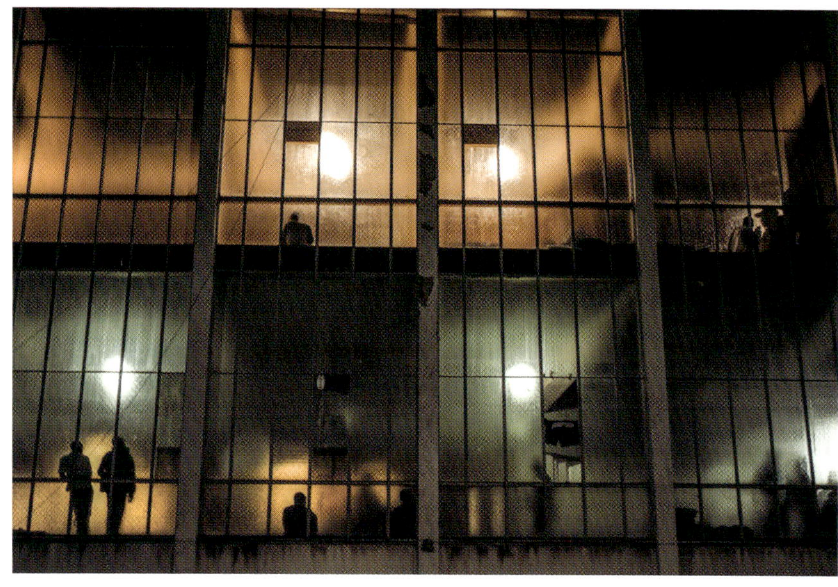

Central Methodist became a beacon of hope for
the destitute and homeless in Gauteng. JO

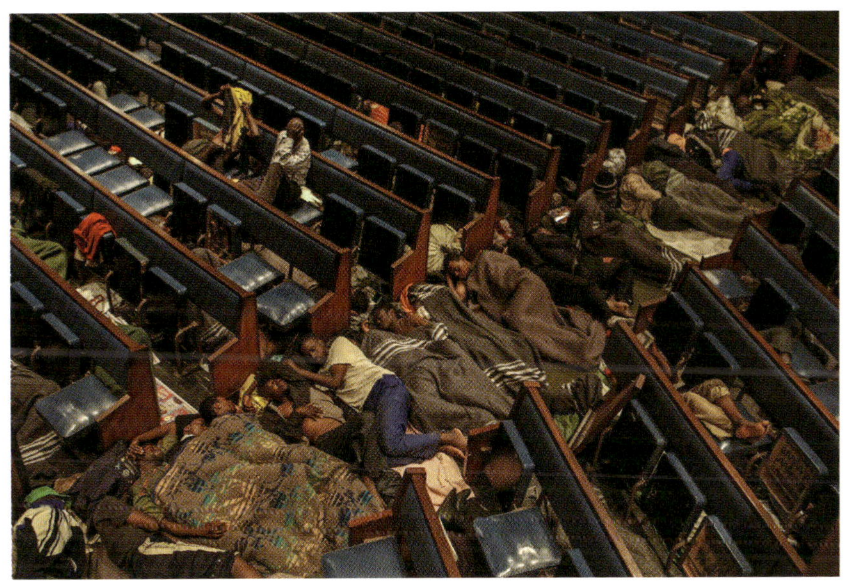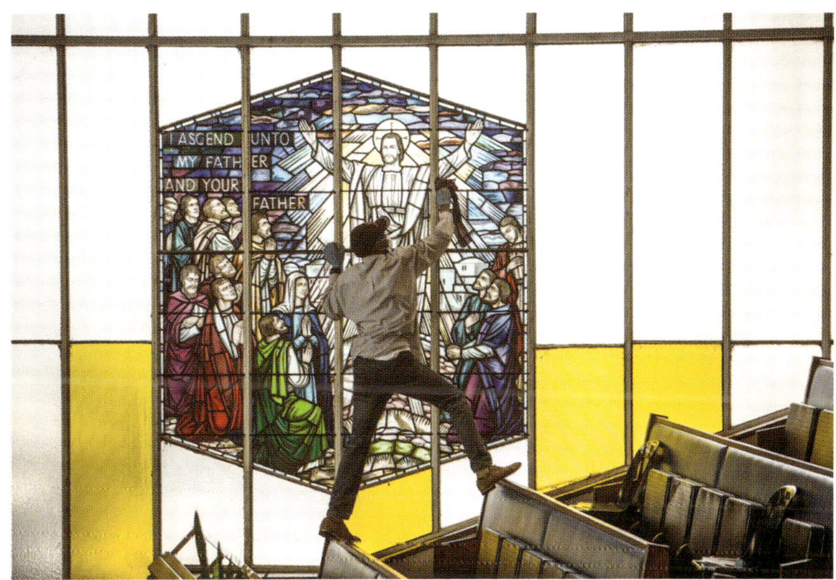

As years passed, overcrowding in the church became a health risk, and alcohol and drug abuse and allegations of crime eventually forced its leaders to close the doors. JO

After the refugees vacated the premises at the end of 2015, repair work began on what had effectively become a slum building. Congregant Paulin Chikomb, above, who was part of the clean-up team, later became a wellness counsellor for traumatised migrants in the city. JO

Adnaan Yassin Abdullahi fled Ethiopia following army clampdowns and
arrived in South Africa in 2008 as xenophobic violence swept the country.
He now runs a restaurant in Johannesburg. JO

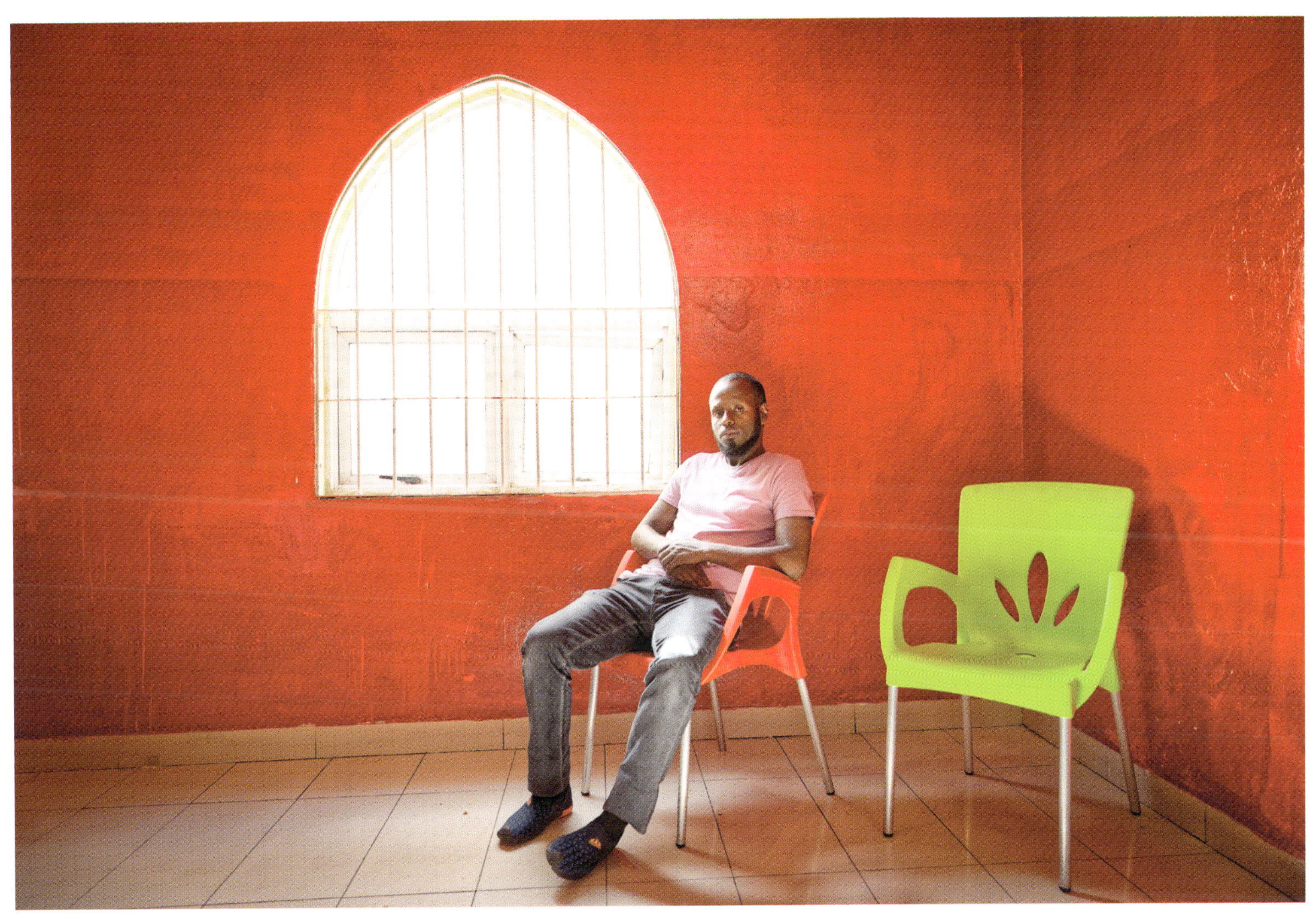

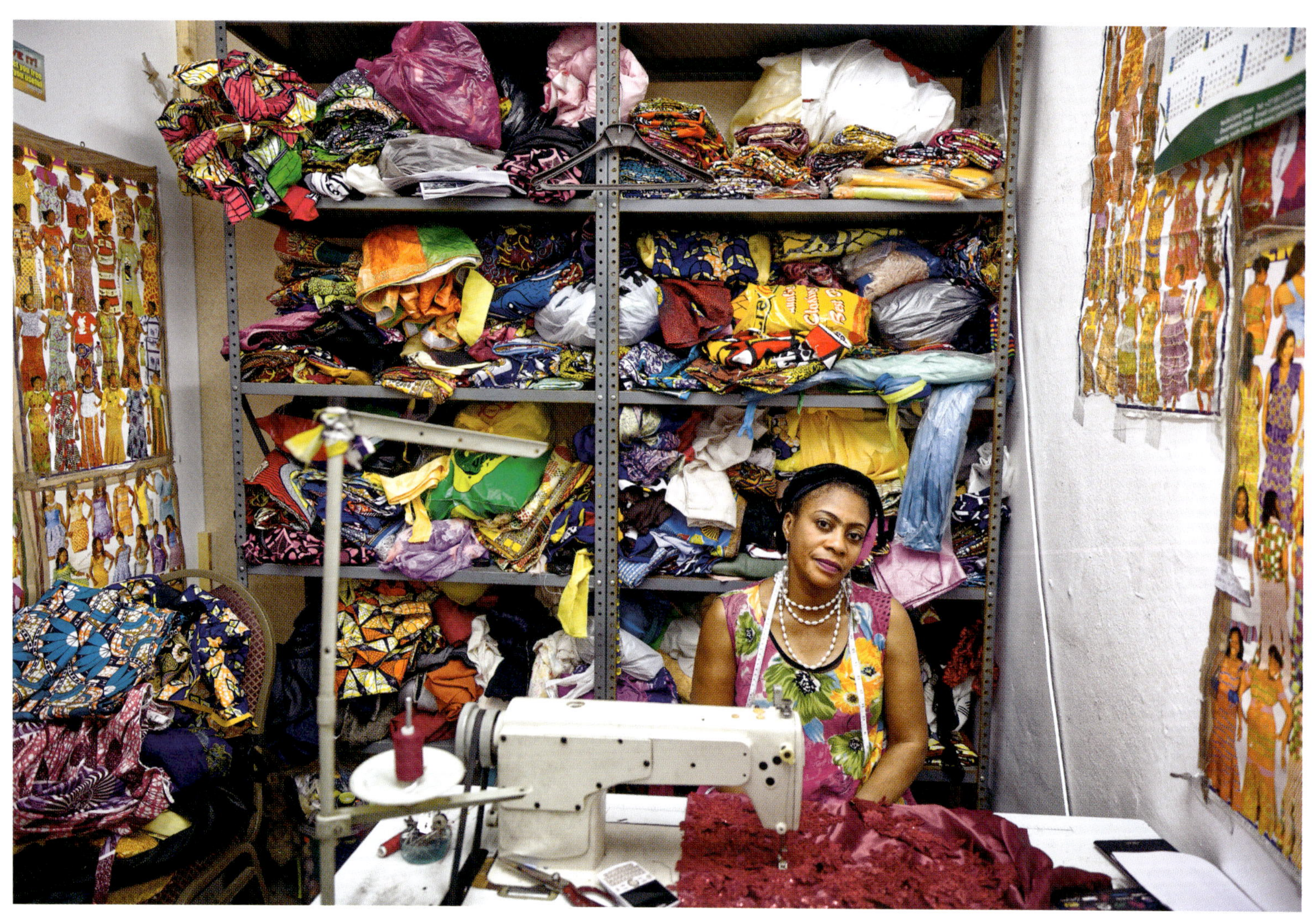

Chantal Nsunda was born in Angola, but later lived in the Democratic Republic of the Congo. In 1997 she moved to South Africa where she now runs a small but successful dress-making business. JO

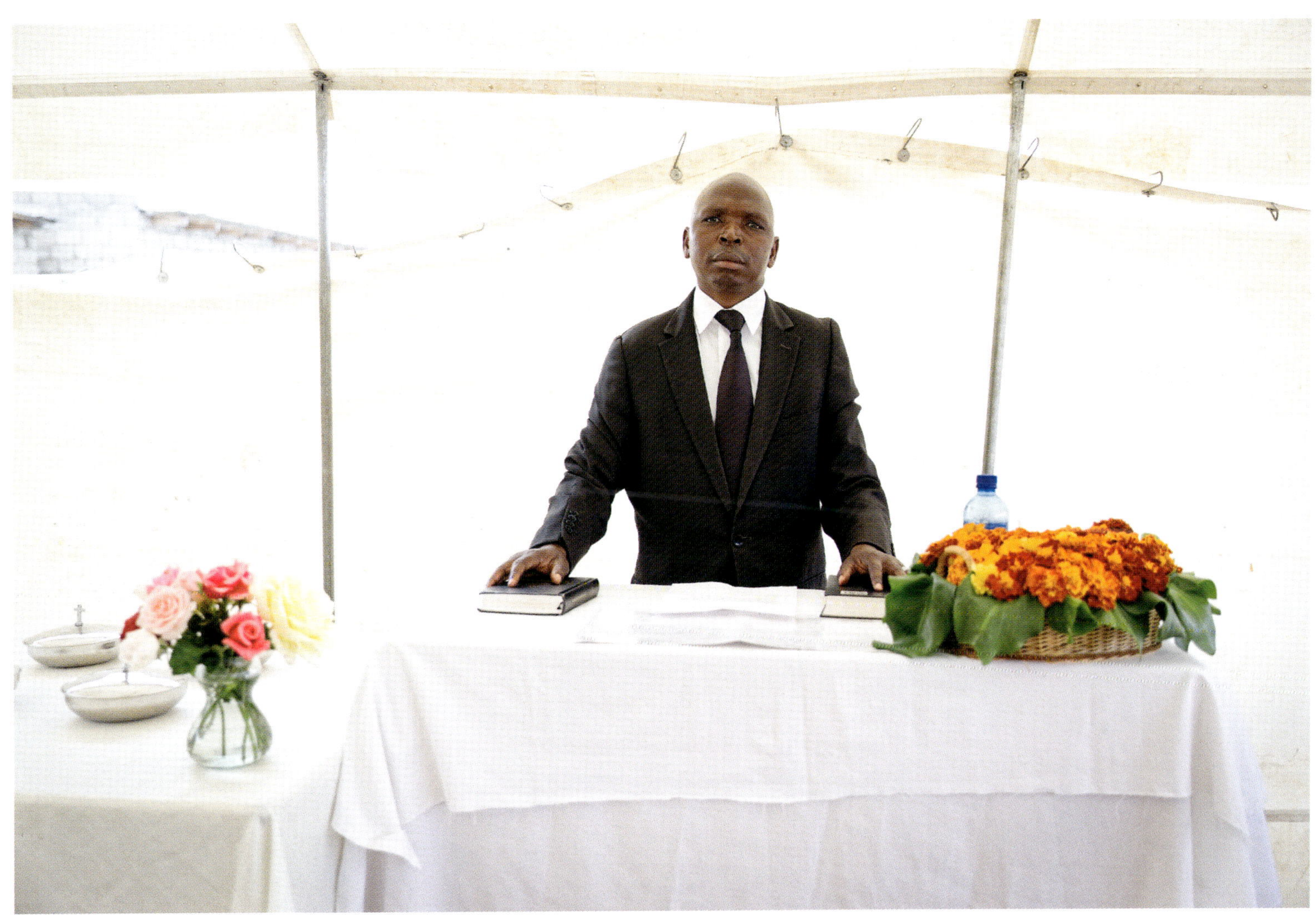

New Apostolic Church minister Rashid Shaba leads a congregation in a tented church in Gauteng. He was a schoolteacher in Malawi, but now works as a gardener and sends most of his money back to his children up north. JO

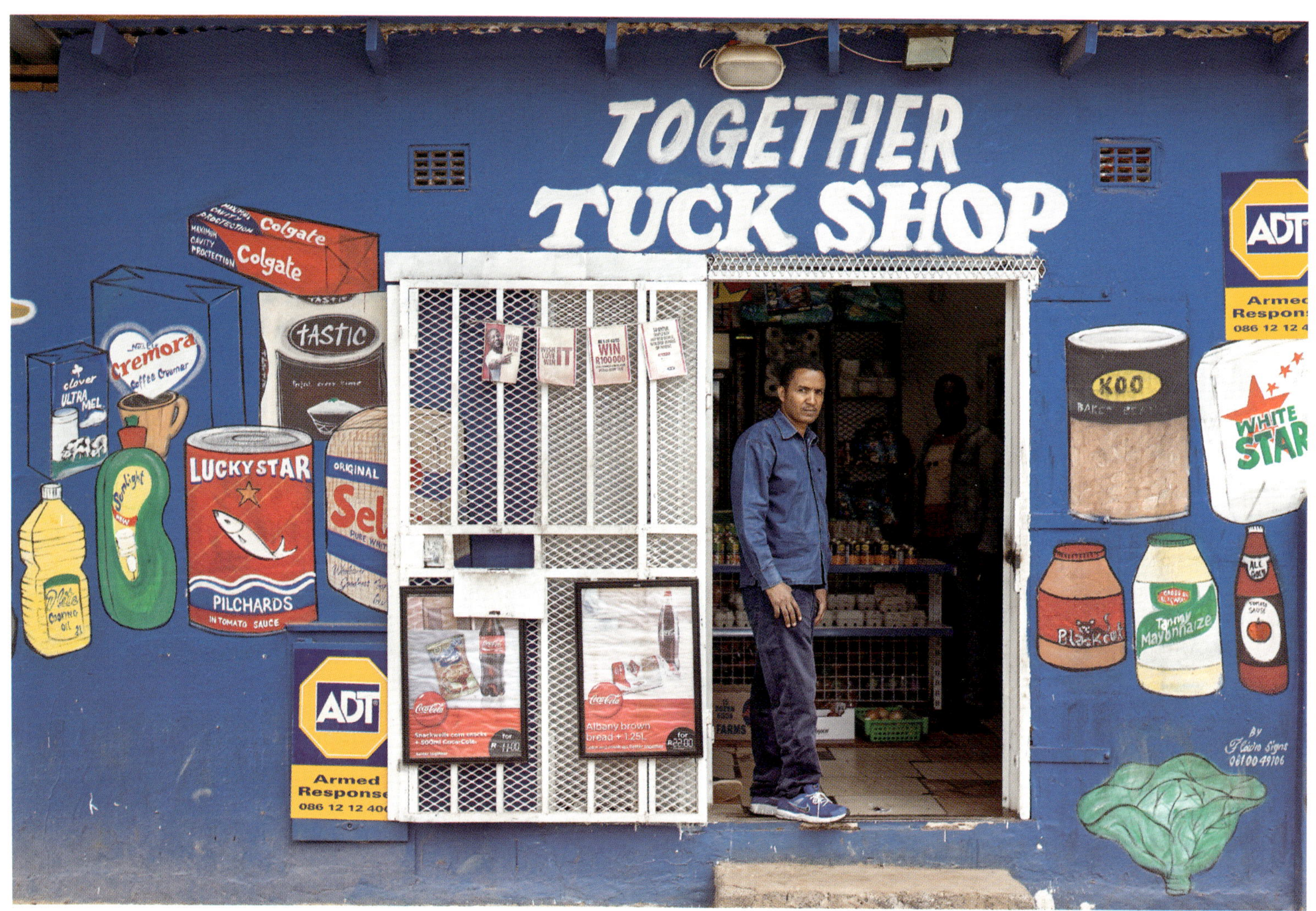

Since Ethiopian-born Getachew Sugebo arrived in South Africa in 2004, he has been a victim of xenophobic violence, and his shop has been broken into 'many times'. JO

Our neighbours lost

Koketso Moeti

2020. As many celebrated the start of a
new year and new decade, draconian new
restrictions on refugees came into effect
under South African law.

Among other things, the regulations – which
are part of an amendment to the law – restrict
refugees' ability to visit their home countries;
to take part in political action; and to interact
with their home governments' institutions or
representatives.

The government's justification for this
amendment is 'national security' – a threat
that it has not clearly defined.

This alarming development is just one
of many examples of how 'law and order'
is increasingly being invoked to drive a
xenophobic agenda. Such new policies are
simply the latest manifestation of xenophobic
attitudes that have existed for some time, but
which are becoming more prevalent among
politicians and government officials.

As an example, in 2019 Police Minister
Bheki Cele claimed that foreign nationals
posed a criminal threat. This came after
months of xenophobic electioneering ahead
of the general election during which some
candidates and parties blamed migrants for
a variety of state failures.

In August 2019, a spate of violent attacks
broke out in the Johannesburg inner city and
surrounding areas. It began with a confrontation
between traders, who government officials
claimed were 'foreign nationals', and police,
following raids that were carried out in the
Johannesburg inner city to crack down on
'counterfeit goods'. This confrontation was
labelled as an attack on police officers and
therefore 'an attack on our state and its
sovereignty'. Before long, mobs of people
attacked immigrant shopowners, and looted
or set fire to their shops.

The suggestion in all these actions is that
in order to protect 'us' South Africans, law and
order needs to be restored by criminalising
'them'. This is the mobilisation of xenophobic
violence by building widespread support to
criminalise and dehumanise migrants.

And I have seen this shift first-hand. People
I regularly meet at the bus stop on my way to
work generally supported the attacks. Whereas
our discussions before were usually about
the cost of living, the state of governance
and, yes, even sometimes about our negative

perceptions of the police, suddenly there was high praise for police 'taking action on crime' and dealing with 'those illegal people', 'those criminals'.

One woman in particular — someone who could easily be my mother, grandmother, sister, cousin or friend — went on and on about how 'nice it is to see the police doing their jobs' and how they should 'just get rid of or kill these criminals'. Whether or not what she shared were views she has always had I will never know.

But what was striking was how she used the language of law and order, the same language used by political elites and those — including some media — who uncritically parrot those views.

And this isn't unusual. Xenophobic language is increasingly becoming normalised.

So, it comes as no surprise to notice that migrants, who for years I have met at the same bus stop, no longer catch that morning bus. For a short while during the violence, a young woman who lives in my street would be escorted by her father. They would stand at a distance from us, only coming closer when the bus arrived. Since then, she – along with many others – have disappeared.

This is not to suggest that South Africa does not have a crime problem; it does, among the many other crises plaguing the country. But law and order must not be invoked at the suggestion that people are criminals because they are 'foreign nationals'; nor heavy-handed treatment and denial of essential services based on nationality.

Political elites, some who are government officials, have consistently preyed on existing prejudice and warranted concerns and anxieties of the people. Human beings have been described as 'illegals', which not only effectively criminalises a person's mere existence, but also invokes imagery of hordes of 'criminals' set to do harm.

Former Johannesburg mayor Herman Mashaba has even gone as far as suggesting that 'foreign nationals' are not only criminals, but are also 'disease-ridden'.

This cannot be separated from the recurring xenophobic violence experienced in South Africa, which is only the most visible manifestation of prejudice. As horrific as these incidents are, it's a continuation of the daily discrimination and dehumanisation faced by migrants

It's important to recognise how these are linked. As pointed out by David Livingstone Smith, author of the book *Less Than Human*, among many other things, dehumanisation is a way of subverting inhibitions that prevent us from violently harming people – as we see them as less than human.

This is an extremely difficult time for migrants and other marginalised people, not just in South Africa but all around the world.

The virulent xenophobia of US President Donald Trump, UK Prime Minister Boris Johnson and Brazil's Jair Bolsonaro is well known. In Hungary, draconian laws targeting migrants have been put in place. In India, xenophobic incidents have been on the rise since the election of Narendra Modi as prime minister in 2014.

Elites across regions are increasingly attempting to cast migration as a danger to everyone – deflecting from the real crises, which are poverty, rising inequality, an unprecedented environmental crisis and a general sense of instability.

There are no easy solutions to this problem, both the recurring violence and the ways in which it is enabled.

This also applies to politicians and government officials who spew hateful views, and to those of us who perpetuate them in our daily interactions. Interventions that are rooted in evidence and understanding of the key drivers of violence are critical. Most importantly, though, we all must engage in a long-overdue reckoning with the country's extensive history and present practice of using exclusion as well as law and order as ammunition when mobilising for violence.

This needs to be urgently addressed, otherwise we will continue to be needlessly divided – while natural resources and poor black people, irrespective of our nationalities, continue to be exploited by elites.

Koketso Moeti has a long background in civic activism and in 2019 was made Atlantic Fellow for Racial Equity. She is also an inaugural Obama Foundation Fellow and an Aspen Institute New Voices Senior Fellow. She serves on the Civic Tech Innovation Network and is Deputy Chairperson of the SOS Coalition. Koketso's writing has been published by *City Press*, *Al Jazeera*, *The Guardian*, *Africa is a Country*, *Salon* and the *Mail & Guardian*, among others.

2019

As 2018 drew to a close, xenophobic monitoring platform Xenowatch[1] recorded 529 violent incidents in South Africa since 1994. These attacks had resulted in 309 deaths, tens of thousands displaced and thousands of businesses looted. In March 2019, Silindile Mlilo and Jean Pierre Misago released an overview of this violence[2] that concluded with the warning that while Gauteng, Western Cape and KwaZulu-Natal remained the most affected provinces, xenophobic violence was increasingly spreading across all the country's nine provinces. Without effective preventive measures, the review report cautioned, these areas were likely to experience repeated brutality. And so they did. In August that year, Johannesburg's inner city was wracked with anti-migrant attacks, and by late September the total number of incidents had risen to 598[3] … and this number is set to escalate steadily as the days, months and years pass without the root causes of this destructiveness being addressed.

1   Xenowatch is an open source platform aimed at monitoring xenophobic violence in South Africa, created by the African Centre for Migration & Society (ACMS) at the University of the Witwatersrand.

2   Xenophobic Violence in South Africa: 1994–2018. An Overview by Silindile Mlilo and Jean Pierre Misago for Xenowatch. This overview is based on a detailed report (Characteristics and Causal Factors of Xenophobic Violence across South Africa 1994–2018) prepared by Alexandra Hiropoulos for ACMS.

3   While Xenowatch provides information of these incidents, many more are suspected to have occurred since 1994. Such an undercount is not uncommon with crime statistics related to vulnerable communities such as migrants.

On 7 August 2019, the streets of Johannesburg's inner city erupted. Police had earlier launched a raid on migrant traders to confiscate counterfeit goods. But vendors took up resistance and pelted their vehicles with rocks, forcing them to withdraw. Six days later, police returned to 'reassert the authority of the state'. Hundreds of traders were arrested, this time without striking back. Then, emboldened by the police action, a wave of looters, some armed with sjamboks and crude weapons, swept in. Chanting xenophobic songs, they rampaged through the area, smashing stalls, shops and vehicles in a lawless spree that police were only able to subdue by using riot control ammunition.

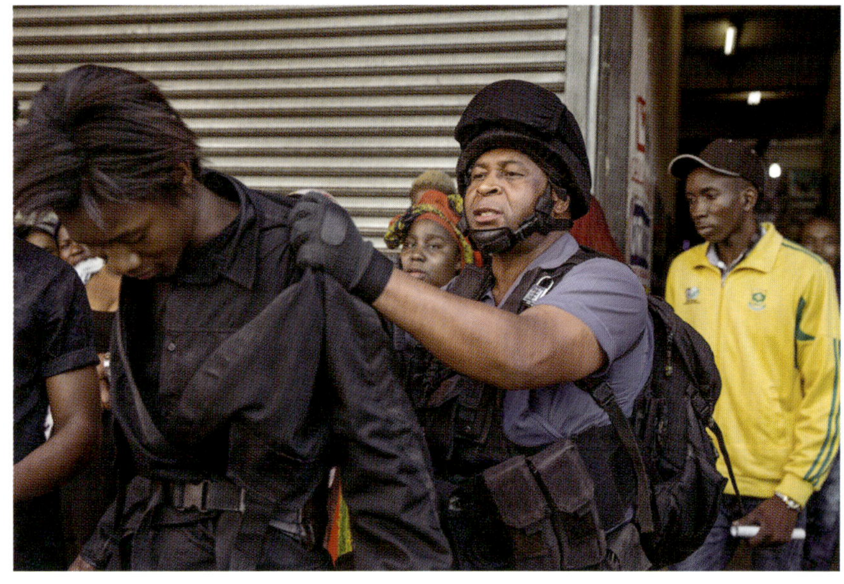

A policeman removes a person from a beauty parlour in the Fashion District quarter of the city during the second round of police action. 'Undocumented migrants' were also targeted in the raid. JO

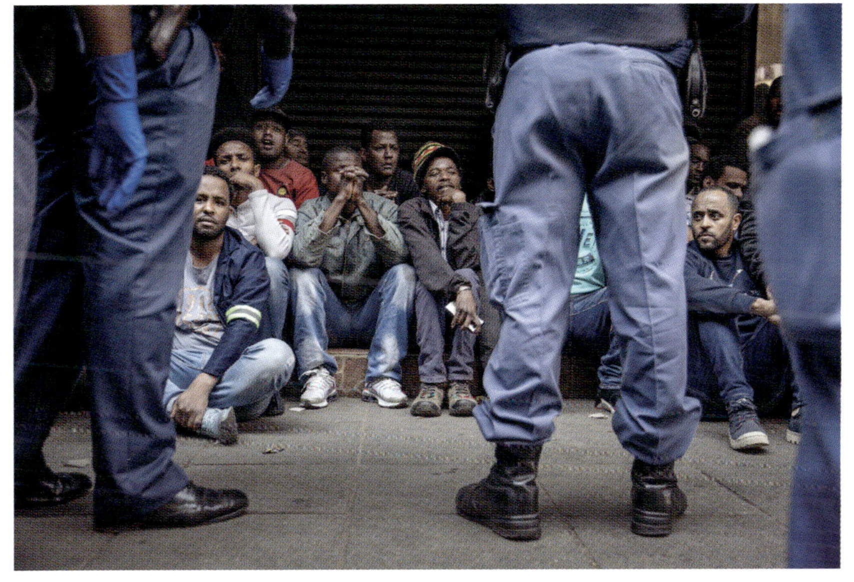

Hawkers and traders are lined up before being taken into custody.
Five police officers were later caught allegedly attempting to
resell confiscated goods back to the traders. JO

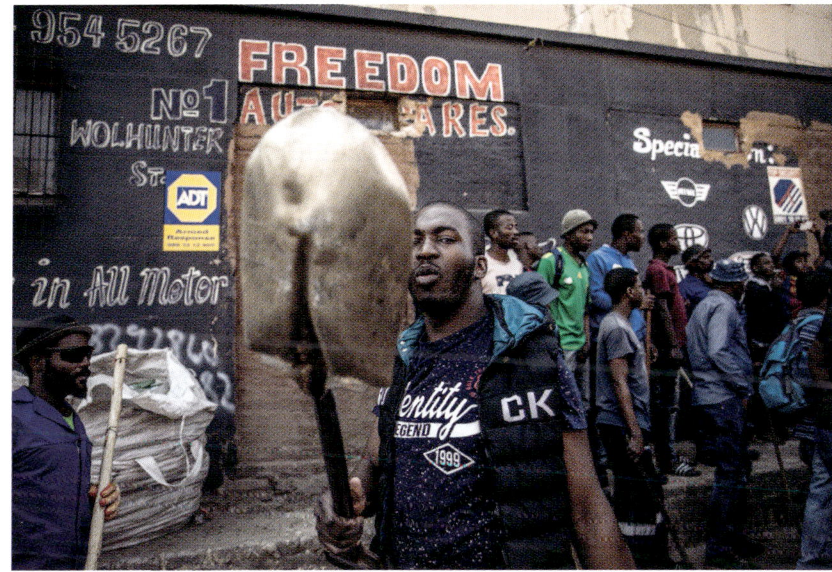

A crowd of local hostel dwellers descends on the area before
trashing shops and stalls and looting goods. Many South Africans
believe migrants are robbing them of job opportunities. AS

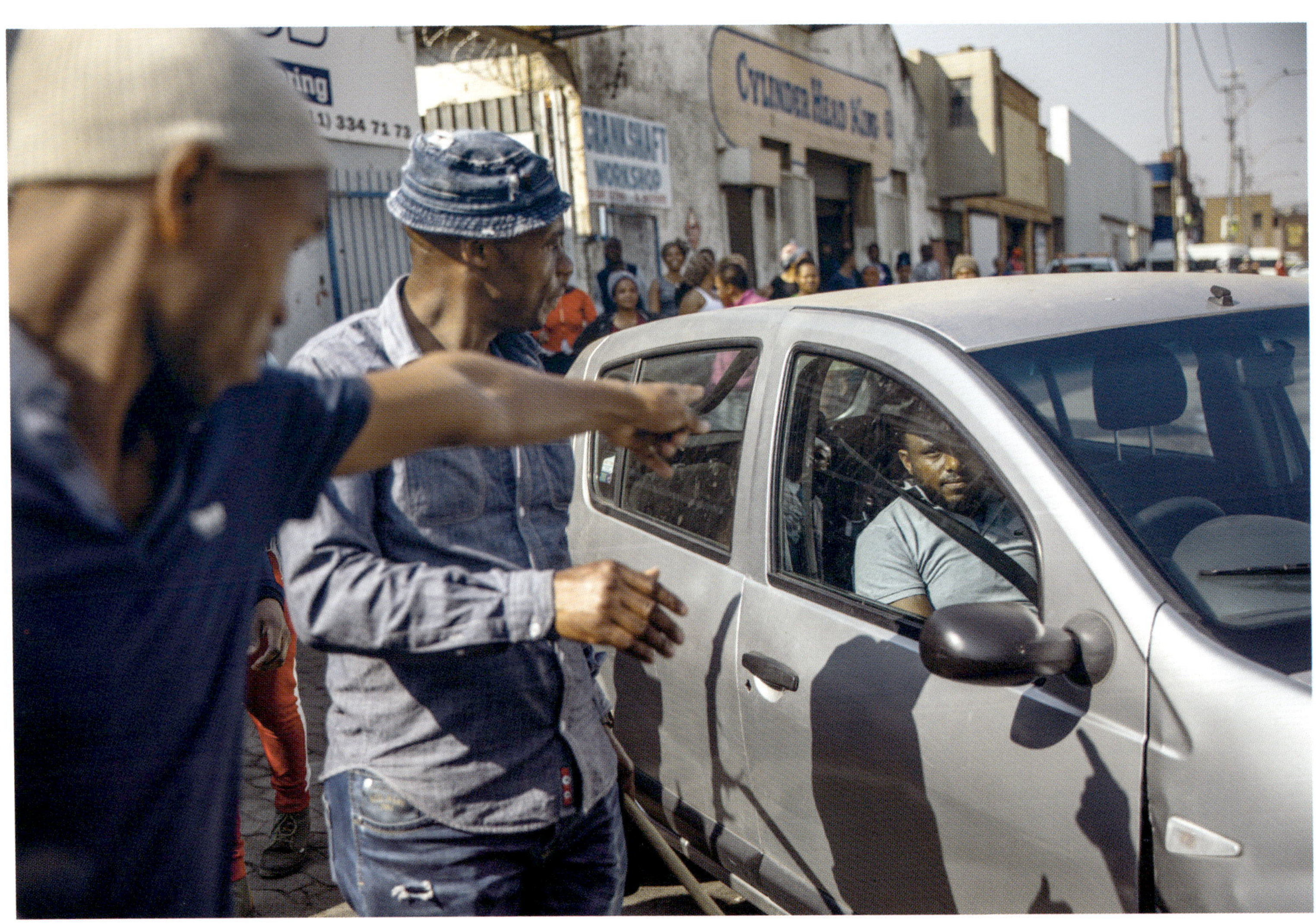

Locals threaten a driver who they suspect is a
migrant before a member of their group intervened
and the motorist was allowed to leave. AS

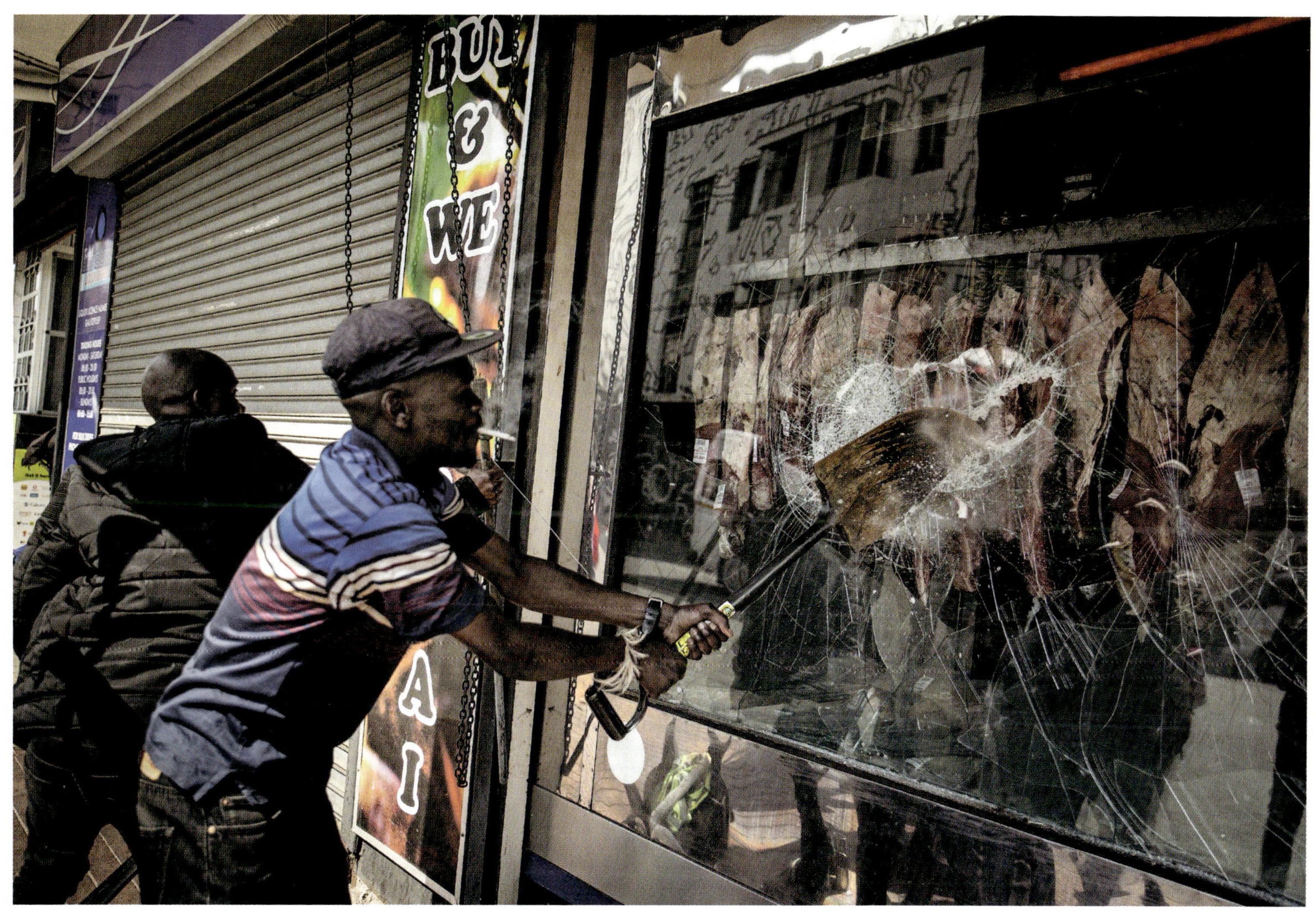

As angry bands of smash-and-grabbers run amok through
the inner-city streets, a man lays waste to a butchery
window before the meat was looted. JO

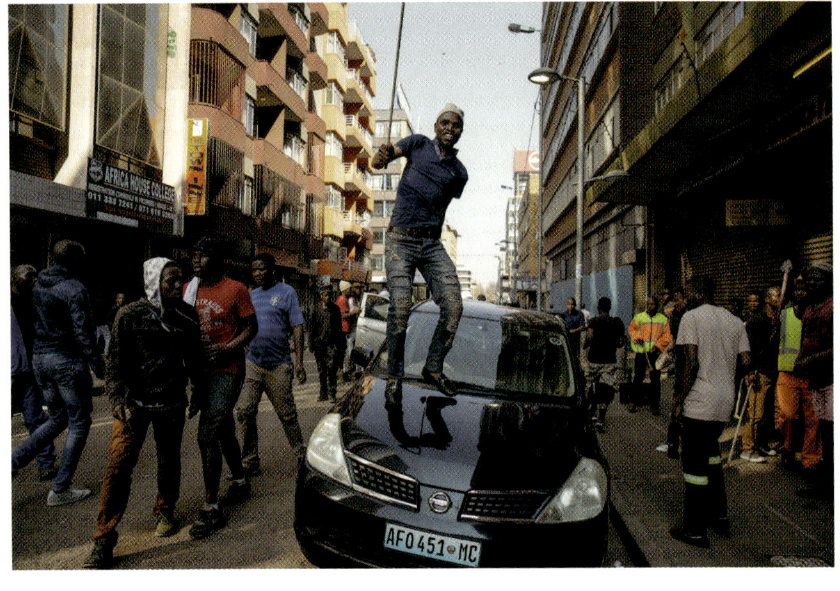

As the marchers sing in isiZulu 'We'll get our hands on them. Why has the government failed us', one man makes his anti-migrant stance clear by leaping onto a vehicle with cross-border plates. JO

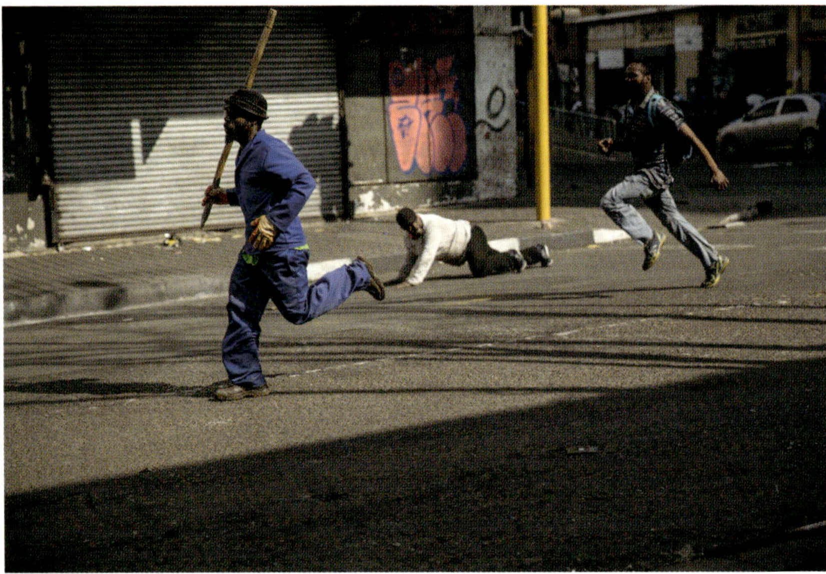

Rioters flee as police open fire with rubber bullets and stun grenades to bring a stop to the plundering of migrant and local businesses. AS

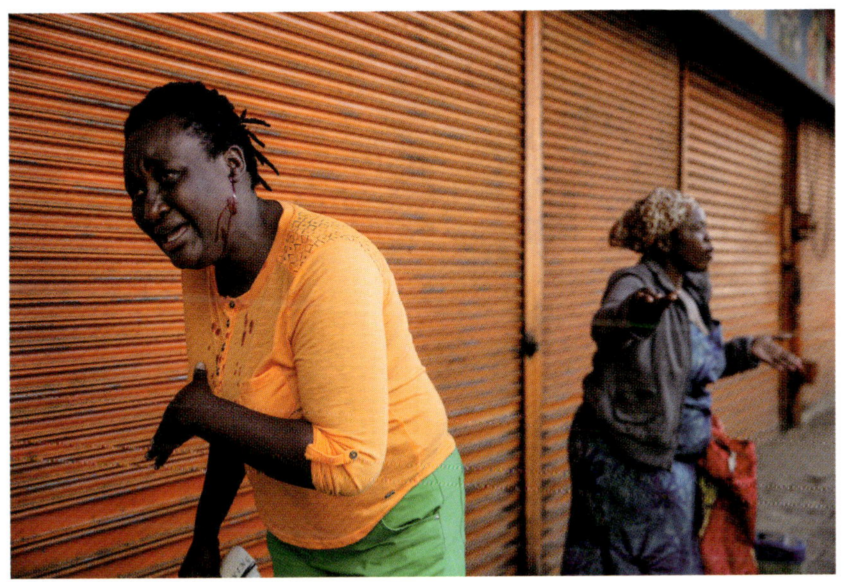

A hawker cries after being hit on the ear by a rubber bullet
fired by officers who targeted her and other vendors. JO

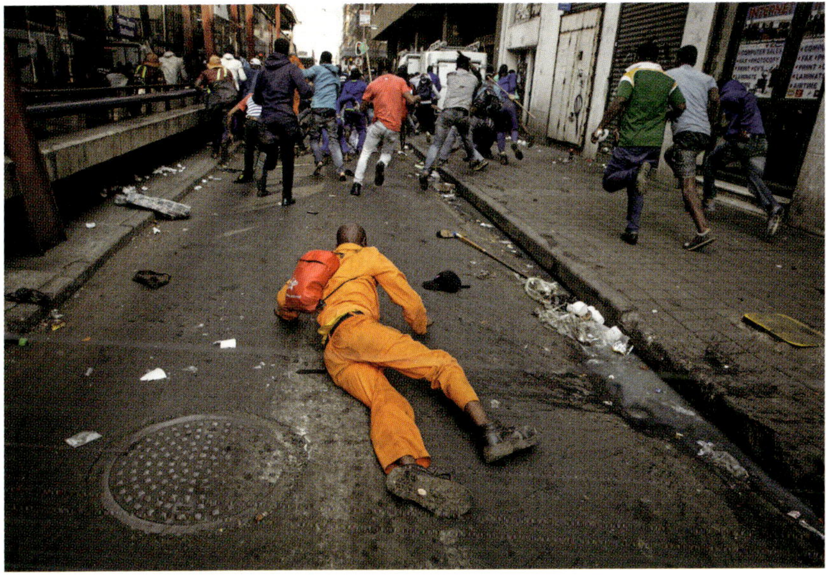

A crowd beats a hasty retreat, leaving a fellow disrupter to his
fate, as police discharge teargas and rubber rounds. JO

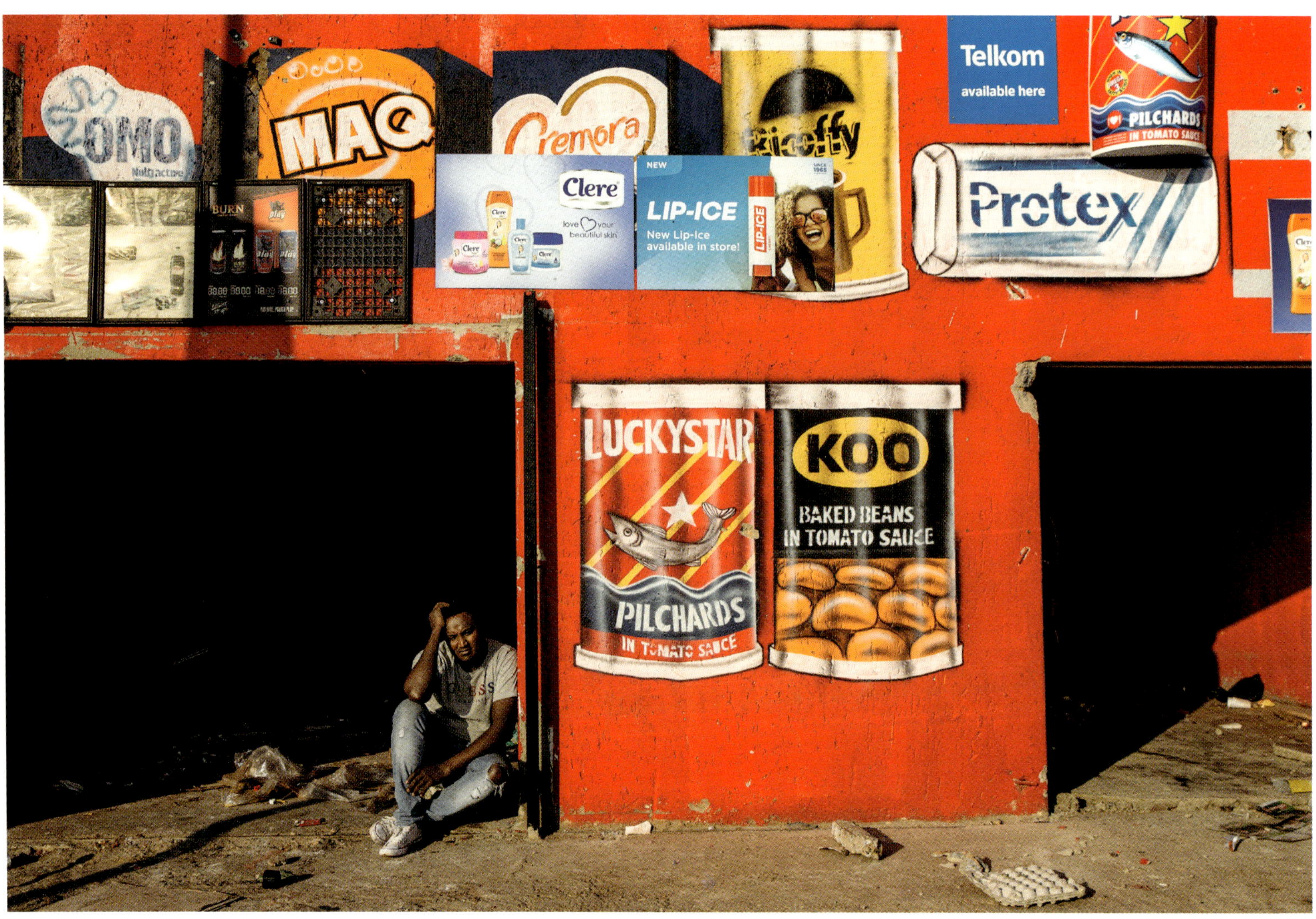

A trader sits in his shop that has been looted overnight in Zola, Soweto. These types of businesses are not only the lifeline of many migrants in the country, but also benefit South Africans who depend on their proximity and affordability. JO

Every one of us must be
deeply concerned

Dr Jean Pierre Misago

Anti-migrant sentiments and practices are on
the rise in both the developed and developing
world,[1] and in South Africa, studies consistently
document strong negative sentiments and
hostility towards foreigners among the public
and government officials.[2]

Xenophobic attitudes cut across all social
strata[3] – it is not just a problem of the poor, the
black or the angry, unemployed youth. Pervasive
strong anti-immigrant sentiments are informed
by misplaced perceptions of immigrants as a
threat to national security and to citizens' lives
and livelihoods.[4]

Xenophobia is a hate crime the logic of
which goes beyond the often accompanying
and misleading criminal opportunism. The
real motive of the violence, as unambiguously
expressed by the perpetrators themselves, is to
drive foreign populations out of communities.[5]

But the consequences of this violence reach
far beyond the targeted migrant groups. They
have profound negative socio-economic,
political and security implications for us all.

In this country, xenophobic violence is
often characterised by the looting, destroying,
torching and vandalising of foreign-owned
livelihood assets, particularly spaza shops or
community-based small businesses. These
businesses are not only the lifeline of many
immigrants in the country but are also beneficial
to ordinary community members in poor
informal settlements and townships due
to their proximity and affordability.

Ordinary community members suffer a
double loss when these assets are destroyed.
First, this means they will have to pay more
for basic necessities in distant and more
expensive shopping malls. Second, they
also lose livelihood assets in the process
as destroyed property (homes and business
places) belongs to South African citizens.
Foreign nationals are just tenants, and the
rentals they pay are a critical income to many
South Africans in those communities.

In addition to the loss of lives (in the majority
of cases, South African citizens are also killed
during the violence), this loss of livelihood
assets makes South African citizens forgotten
victims of xenophobic violence.

Rather than being for the socio-economic
wellbeing of the community as it is always
claimed, research indicates xenophobic
violence is primarily 'politics by other means':

local instigators or 'violence entrepreneurs' organise the attacks for their political and economic interests,[6] and every victory creates further incentives for exclusion. And it is not just foreign nationals who are excluded. Indeed, examples are many where local players regularly exclude other South Africans through claims about opportunities for 'locals'.[7] This outsider exclusion fragments the economy and limits the benefits of trade and domestic mobility.

Anti-outsider violence is also affecting the country's economy beyond the community level. The 'truck driver war' in 2019 is a good example. While intended to drive all foreign drivers out of the trucking industry, the violence targeted both foreign and South African drivers, truck owners and the truck industry itself. This is a dangerous development that should worry even some of us who do not usually pay attention. It does not seem unreasonable that similar attacks can be organised against other (or our own) industries such as tourism and hospitality, education, civil society, etc, where it is perceived that outsiders are stealing jobs from locals.

This violence has a negative impact on the country's economy as a whole, as it threatens the much-needed foreign investment, food security and job creation.[8] On the continent, South African-owned businesses have suffered because of xenophobic violence here at home. Indeed retaliatory attacks or boycotts were organised against South African-owned businesses such as MTN, Multichoice and Shoprite, and South African-owned shopping malls in a number of African countries including Nigeria, DRC, Zambia, Malawi and Mozambique.[9]

Xenophobic violence is a serious threat to regional economic integration from which our country benefits.

It also presents serious domestic political and security concerns. It fuels, and is in turn fuelled, by political populism as political leaders and public officials increasingly blame immigrants for systemic failures to deliver basic services.[10] Political populism and the resulting impulse to exclude threatens constitutional democracy and is likely to reinforce existing – and draw new – boundaries and divides at every level across the country.

So we see that xenophobic violence is not just about removing foreigners from communities. It is more generally about the dangerous politics of localism and entitlement, and rationing access to rights and opportunities. It is about individuals and groups deciding that the Constitution is not their guide. It is about deciding that the courts and police are not the place for resolving disputes. It is about groups or individuals deciding who has rights and who does not, who lives and who dies.[11] This undermines the rule of law and puts everyone at risk since, after all, we are all outsiders, one way or another.

This is even more worrying when the state seems complicit in processes that undermine the rule of law. Xenophobic attacks are often carried out in the presence and full view of the police (the state),[12] which implies the state's support or at least tacit endorsement. Further, interventions to address xenophobic violence in the country have failed largely because of the state's denialism, lack of political will and impunity, all of which encourage perpetrators to strike whenever it suits their interests.[13] A state that is complicit in undermining the rule of law is a danger to itself, its legitimacy and its citizenry. As Landau notes, this is 'fundamentally a story of a ruling party unable and afraid to truly take on the responsibility of governing a deeply divided, angry country'.[14]

Due to growing socio-economic hardships and increasing political populism, xenophobic or outsider exclusion in South Africa is likely to continue and intensify. This is a grave concern for all country residents, foreigners and citizens. Xenophobic exclusion threatens the country's socio-economic prosperity, democracy and nation building, as well as the rule of law. As such, it puts everyone at risk.

If for nothing else, self-preservation should be an incentive for everyone to work together to address the country's virulent xenophobia, or at least mitigate the effects of its various manifestations.

1   Crush, J. and Ramachandran, S. (2009). Xenophobia, International Migration and Human Development. United Nations Development Programme Human Development hdr.undp.org/en/reports/global/hdr2009/.../HDRP_2009_47.pdf.
2   Dodson, B. (2010). Locating xenophobia: Debate, discourse, and everyday experience in Cape Town, South Africa. *Africa Today*, 56(3), 2–22.
3   Crush, J. (2008). South Africa: Policy in the face of xenophobia. Migration Information Source, Migration Policy Institute.
4   Crush, South Africa.
5   Misago, J.P. (2017). Politics by other means: The political economy of xenophobic violence in post-apartheid South Africa. *The Black Scholar*, 47(2), 40–53.
6   Misago, Politics by other means.
7   Misago, J.P. and Landau L. (2019). Truck driver 'war' about more than migration. *New Frame*, 28 June 2019.
8   AgriSA (2019). Xenophobic violence destroys the economy. https://www.iol.co.za/business-report/economy/xenophobic-violence-destroys-the-economy-agrisa-31862641.
9   Misser, F. (2019). South Africa: Causes and consequences of the xenophobic attacks. https://www.southworld.net/south-africa-causes-and-consequences-of-the-xenophobic-attacks/.
10 Saunderson-Meyer, W. (2019) Xenophobia: Reprehensible but irresistible? *Politicsweb*, 11 January 2019. https://www.politicsweb.co.za/opinion/xenophobia-reprehensible-but-irresistible.
11 Misago and Landau, Truck driver 'war'.
12 Bornman, J. (2019) The people who sparked the xenophobic violence. *New Frame*, 11 September 2019.
13 Misago, J.P. (2019). Is the state complicit in xenophobic violence in South Africa? *Daily Maverick*, 13 August 2019.
14 Landau, L. (2019). What's behind the deadly violence in South Africa? https://www.nytimes.com/2019/09/16/opinion/south-africa-xenophobia-attacks.html.

Dr Jean Pierre Misago is a Senior Researcher with the African Centre for Migration & Society at the University of the Witwatersrand in Johannesburg, South Africa

In August 2019, members of a group calling
itself 'Concerned Residents of Orange Grove
and Alexandra' began evicting tenants they
claimed were migrants living in houses
'hijacked' from the Johannesburg Property
Company. They cited frustration that migrants
were given free houses while locals were on the
waiting list, but some tenants had sub-lease
agreements with private owners. At the time,
security analysts attributed the increase in
such vigilante groups in part to the xenophobic
rhetoric of senior politicians.

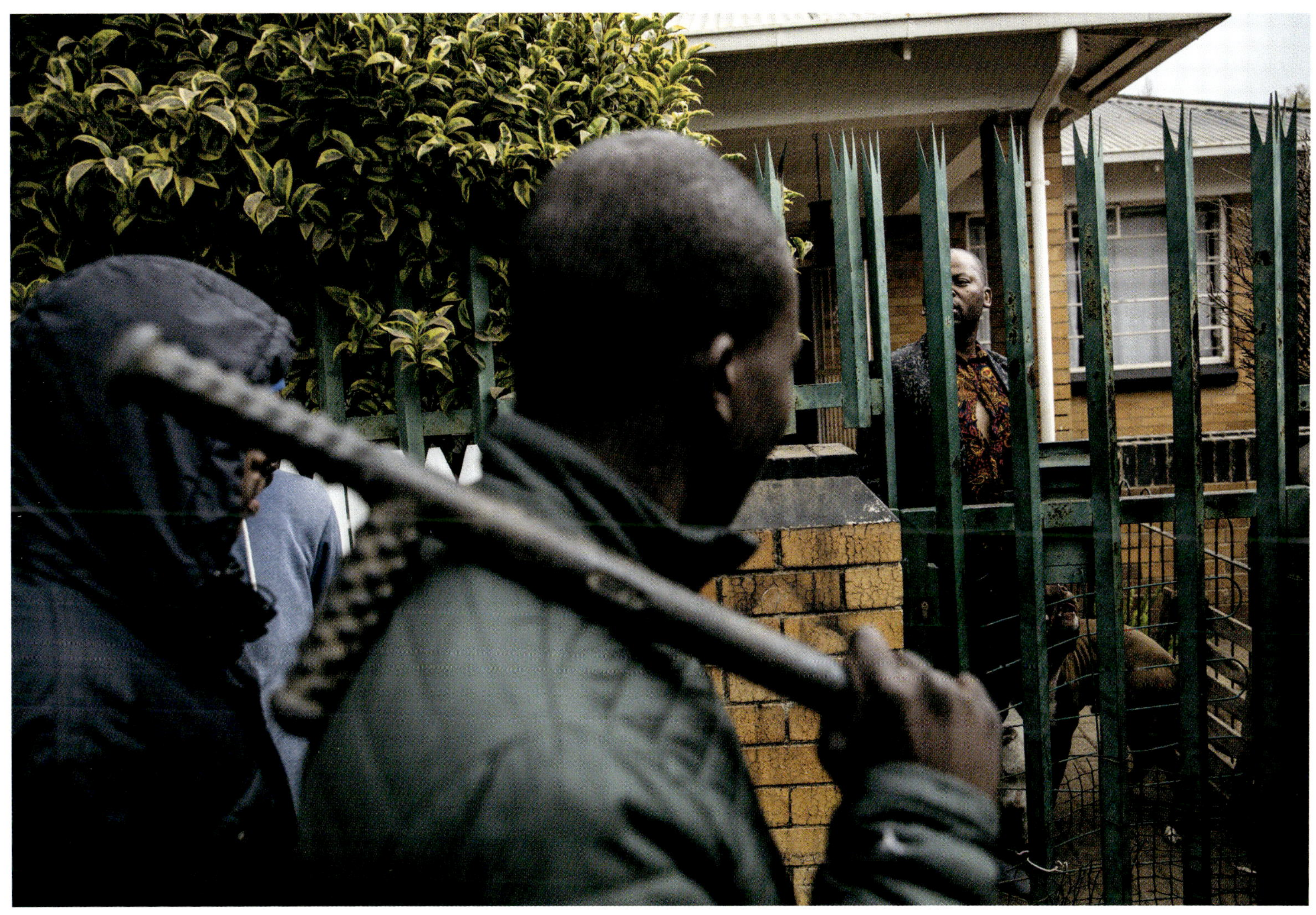

Vigilantes demand entry to a house in Orange Grove. The occupant, who claimed to be South African, was forced to open the gate and was turned out onto the pavement with all his possessions. AS

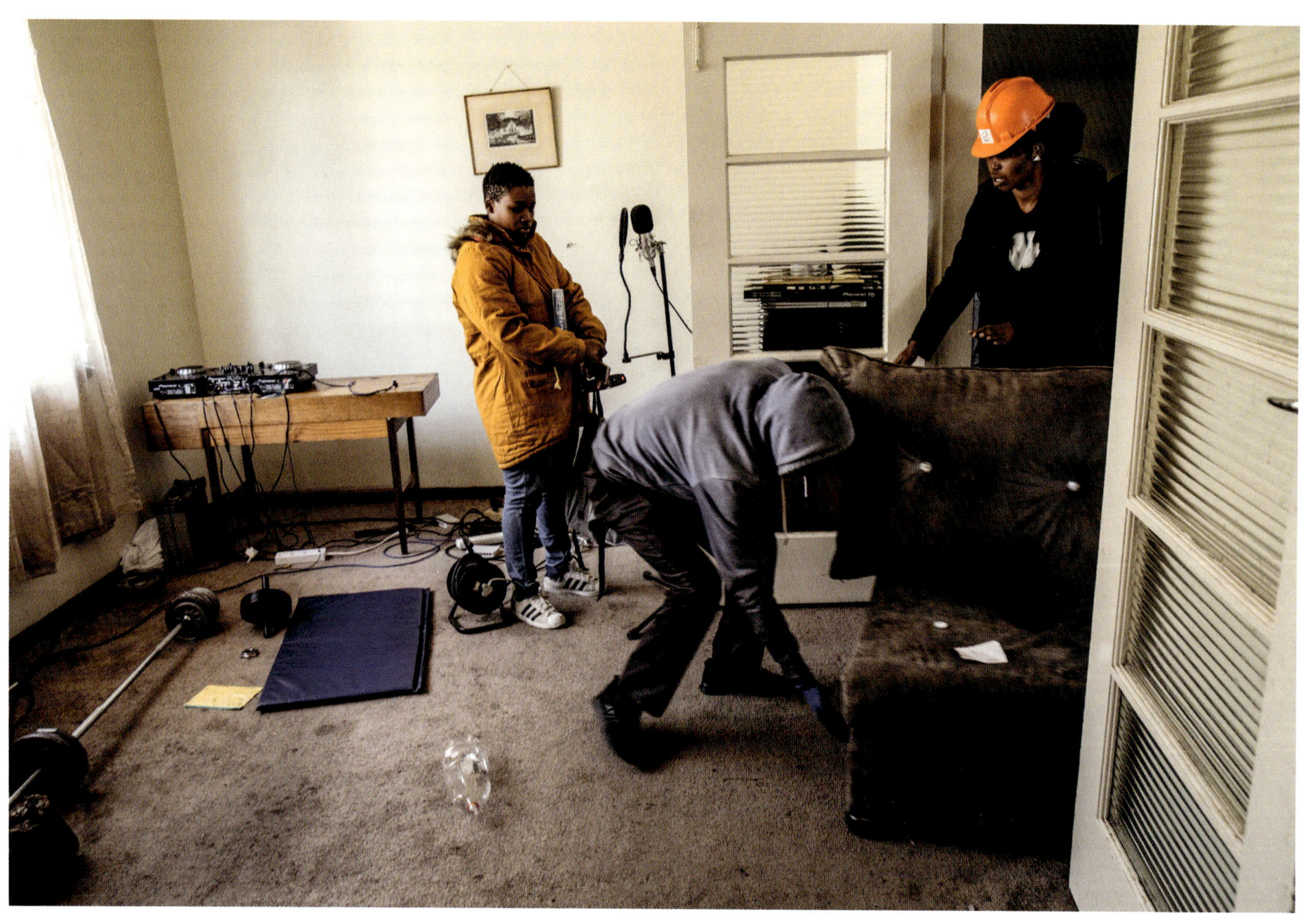

A tenant watches helplessly as her belongings are removed from the house she and her family have been living in. They were accused of being cross-border migrants, and therefore illegal occupants. AS

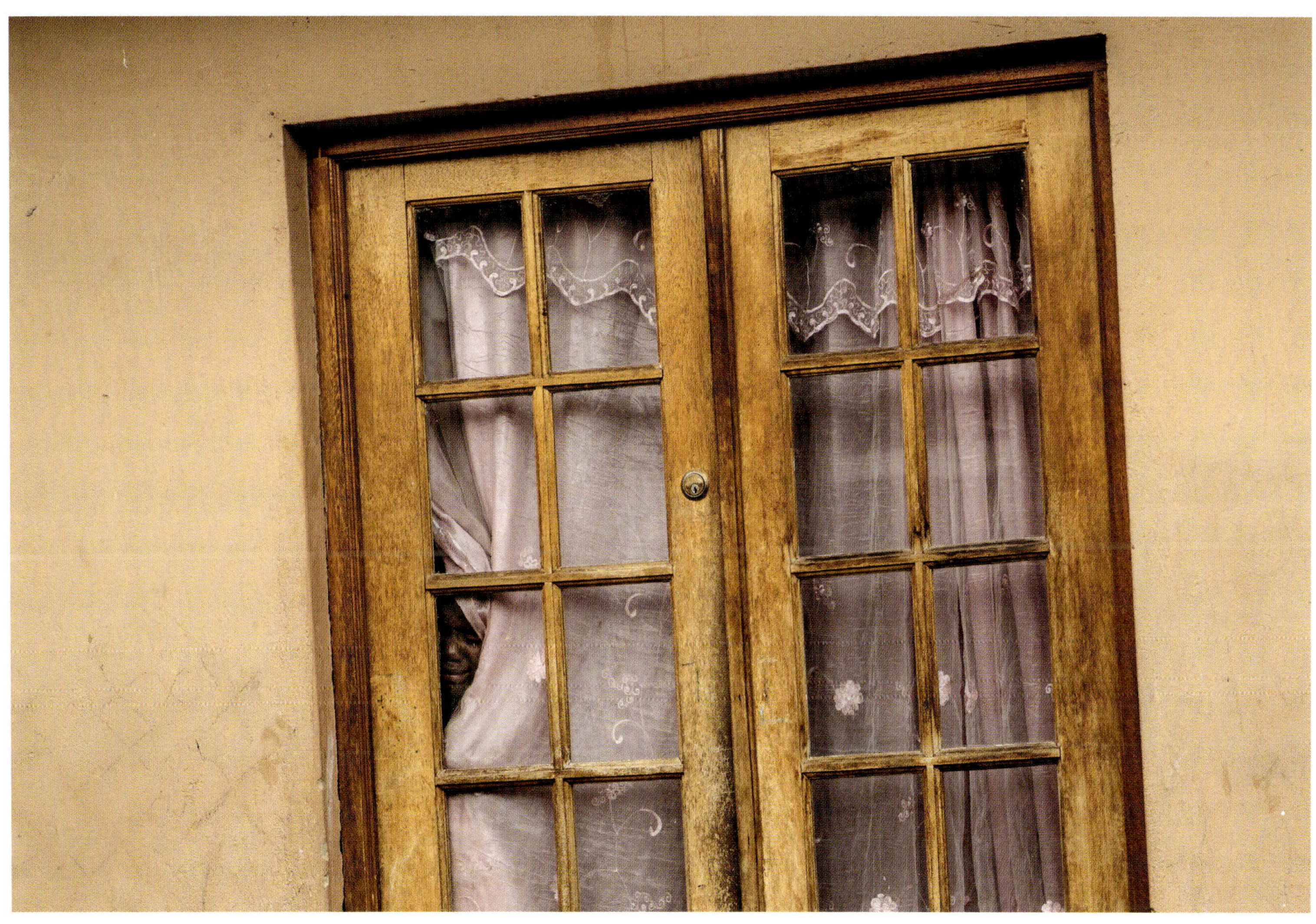

A 12-year-old girl peers through a window of a cottage on the property where a group of men had come to evict the occupants of the main house. AS

For five days in early September 2019, Johannesburg streets were once again scenes of chaos. At least a dozen people were killed, many injured and displaced, and hundreds arrested as shops were raided and premises and vehicles set alight by enraged crowds. Ironically, some of the small businesses attacked were locally owned. Of the 12 people reportedly killed, the government said ten were South African, arguing that 'criminality rather than xenophobia' was responsible for the situation. But a Human Rights Watch report released in 2020[1] found that at least 18 foreigners died in the violence; and in an article at the time for *New Frame*[2] journalist Jan Bornman concluded that 'when looking at the circumstances in which some of the South Africans were killed, it becomes evident that they were killed in direct acts of xenophobic violence.' The riots coincided with a nationwide truck driver strike protesting against the employment of truckers who were not local. Following this spate of violence, South African-owned businesses in other African countries were targeted in revenge attacks.

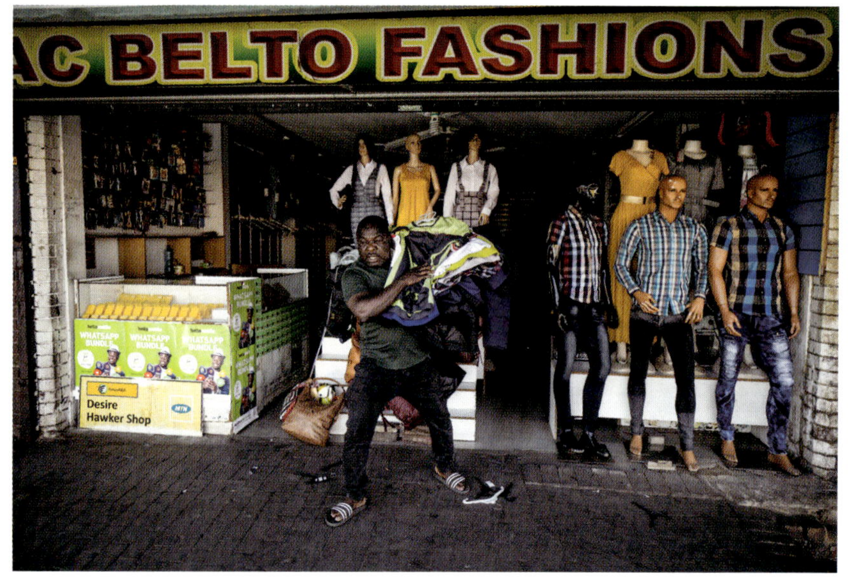

A man scrambles to remove goods from a shop in Germiston on the East Rand before crowds looted the area. AS

1   'They Have Robbed Me of My Life': Xenophobic Violence Against Non-Nationals in South Africa. www.hrw.org/news/2020/09/17/south-africa-widespread-xenophobic-violence
2   www.newframe.com/xenophobia-denialists-should-be-held-culpable/

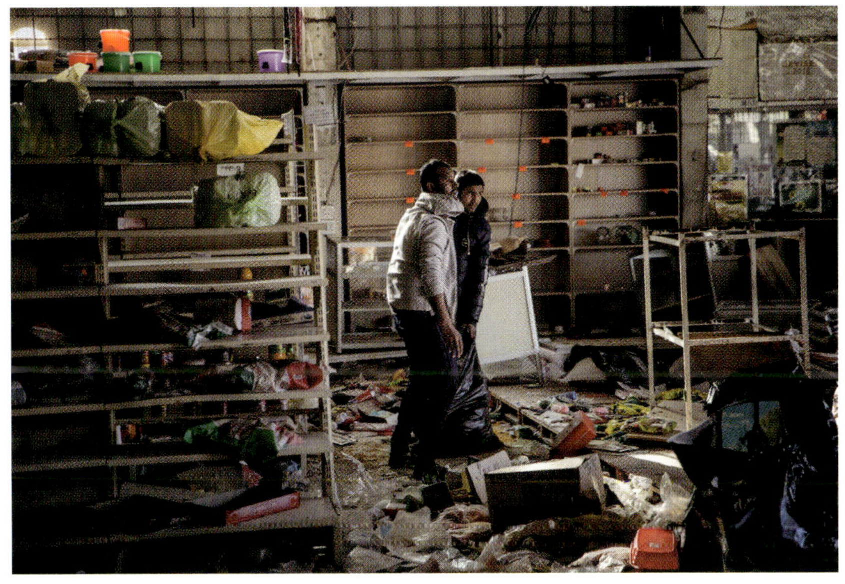

Traders survey the damage to their Malvern shop
after a night of looting and arson. AS

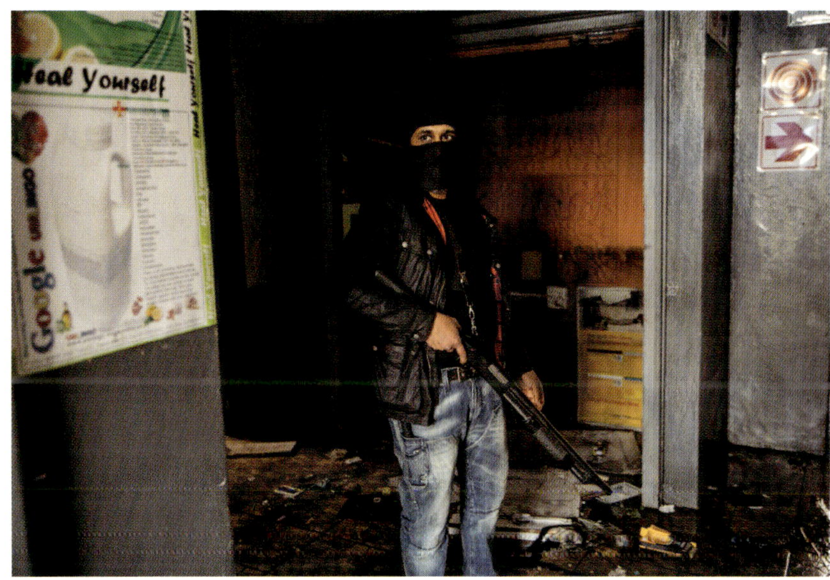

A community member at the entrance to a ransacked arcade in Jeppestown.
Every shop in the nearby Jozi Mall was looted during the unrest. AS

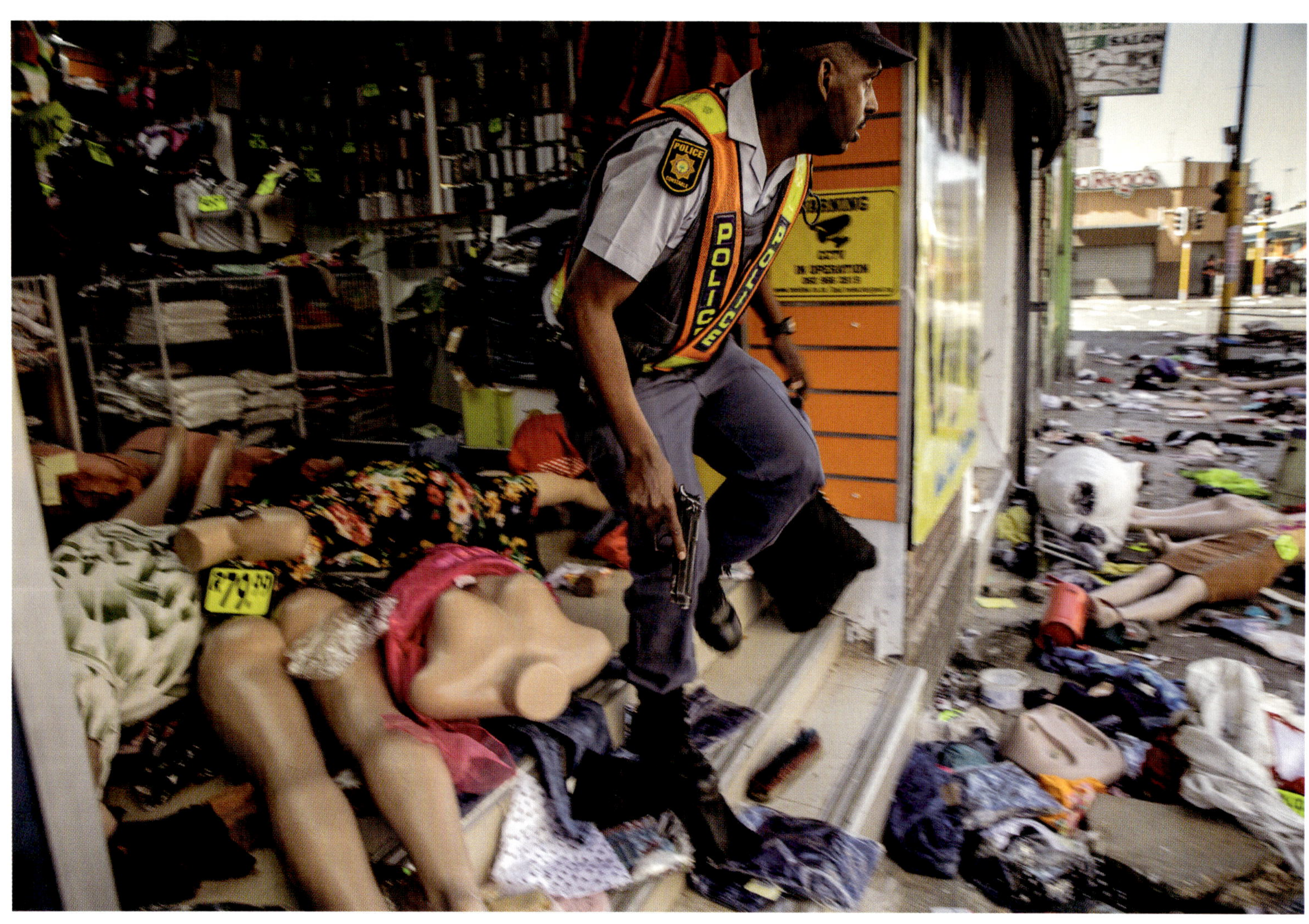

Police react to the rioting in which as many as 50 businesses owned by Africans
from the rest of the continent were reportedly destroyed or damaged. AS

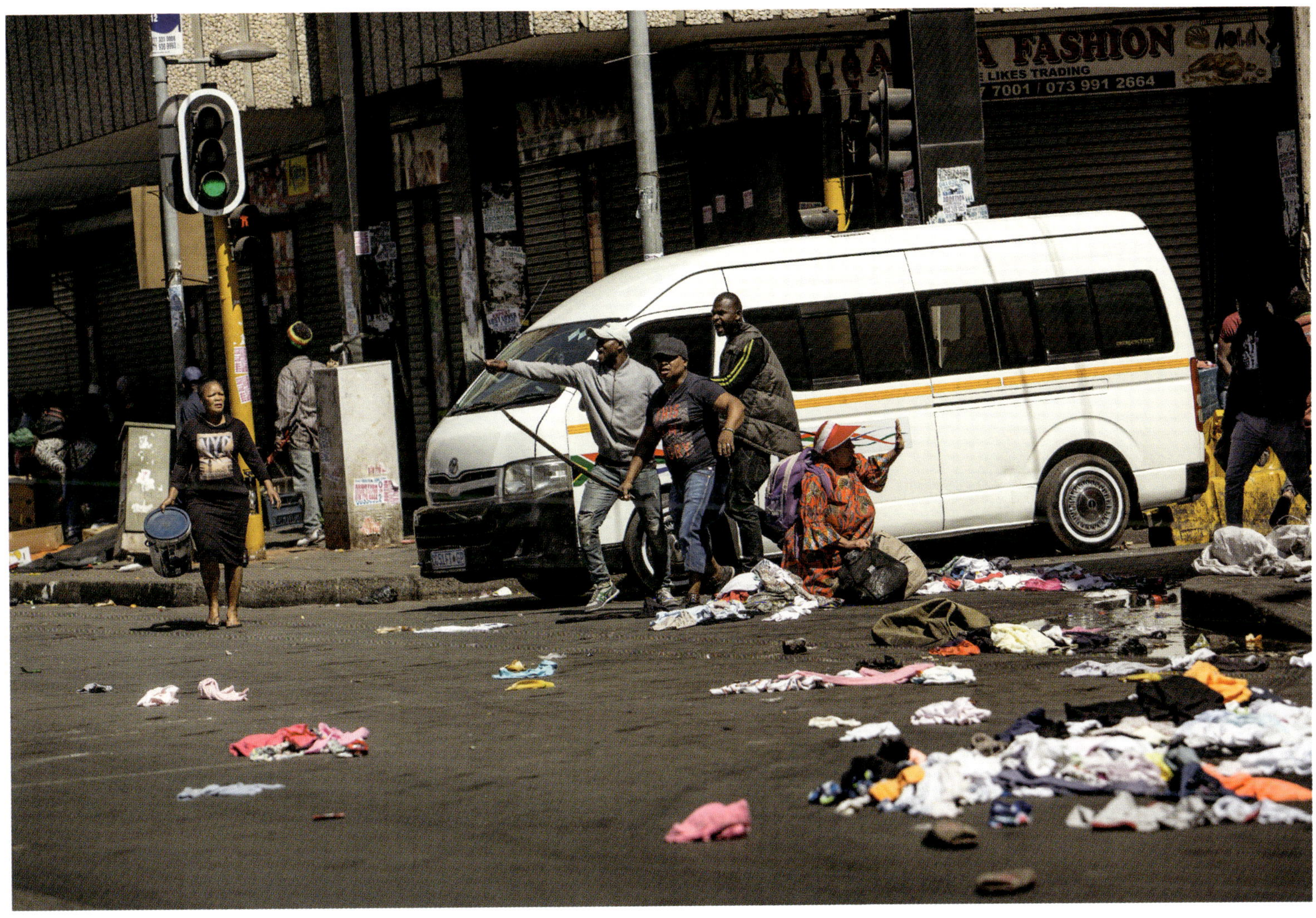

A group of men arm themselves and prepare to fight off looters
running rampant through the Johannesburg CBD. AS

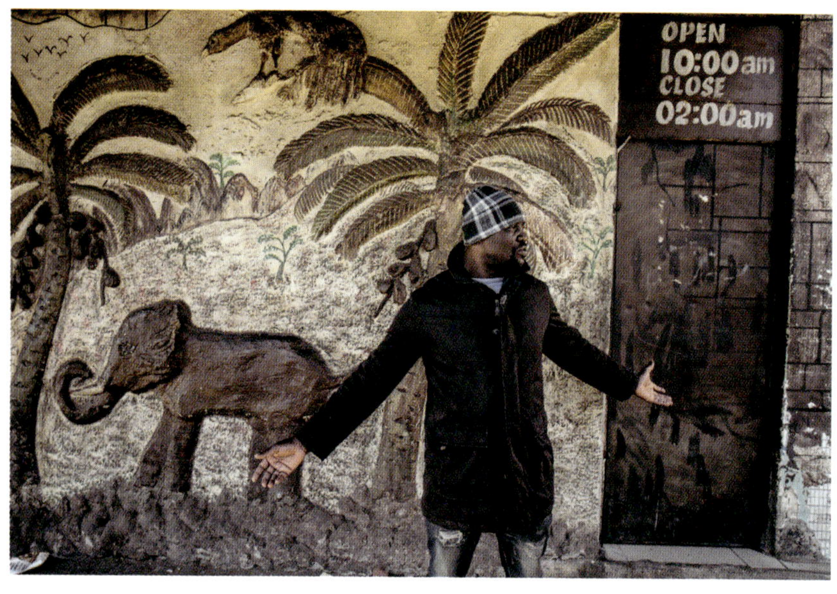

A man stands outside a looted bar in Malvern after a night of heavy destruction in the area. Similar violence broke out in surrounding areas of Johannesburg City, Germiston, Thokoza, Katlehong, Alberton and Alexandra, as well as in Durban and Pretoria. AS

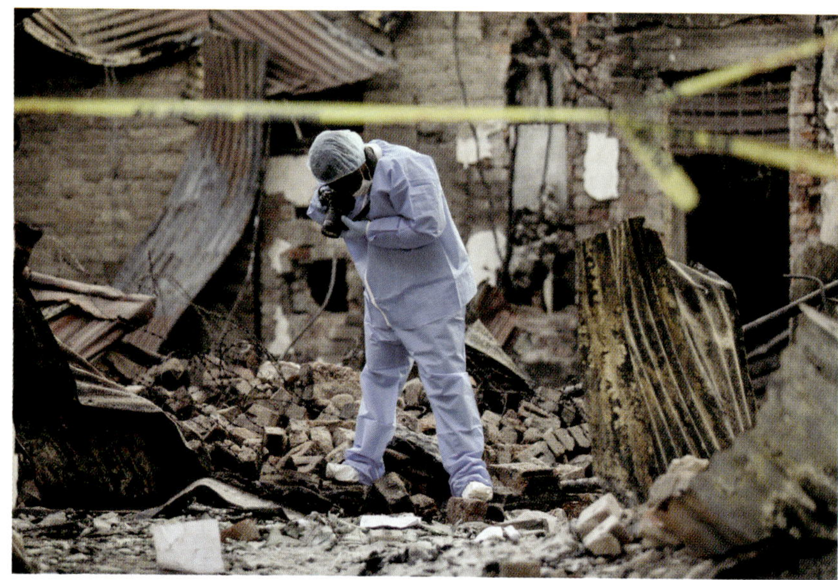

Two bodies, burnt beyond recognition, were discovered inside gutted shops in Alexandra in the aftermath of a looting spree near the Pan Africa Shopping Centre. AS

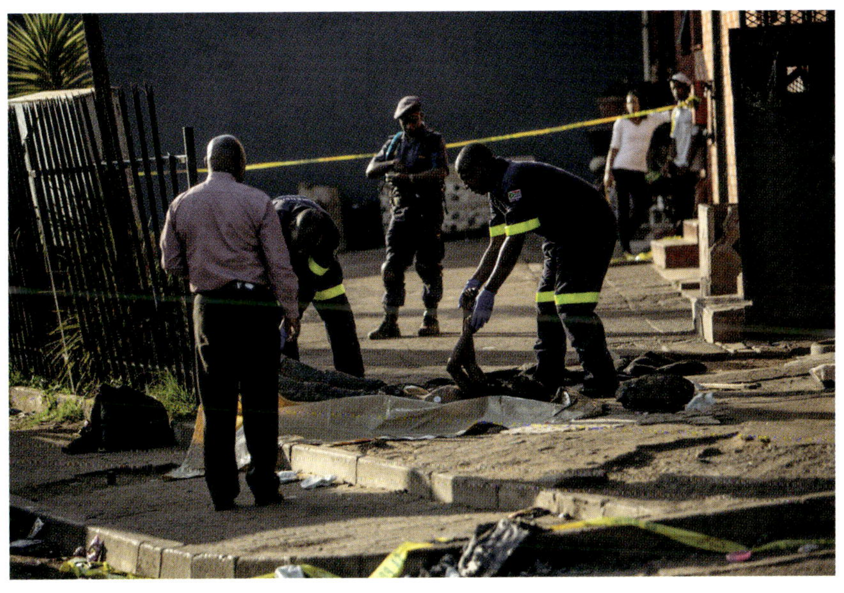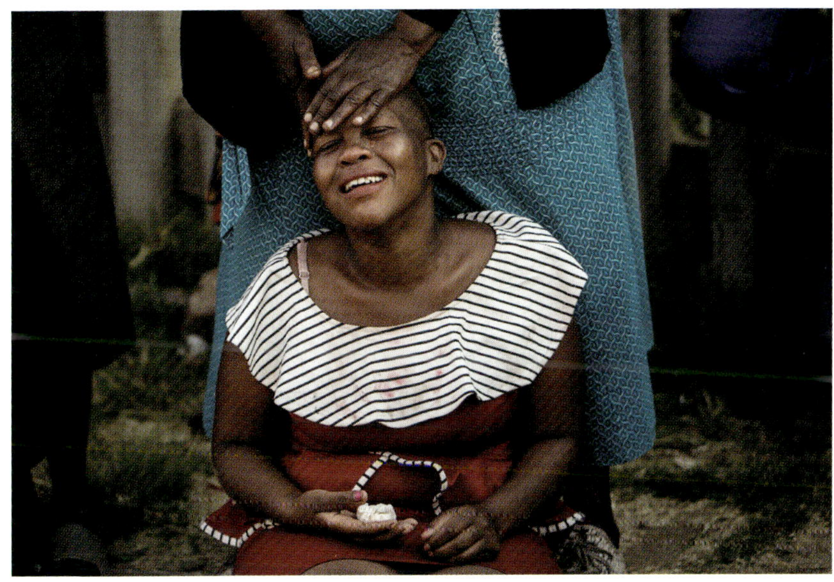

Members of the Forensic Pathology Services prepare to remove the body of Isaac Sebaku, 24, who was shot in the face while allegedly ransacking a spaza shop in Coronationville. Sebaku's sister, Tsholofelo, arrives on the scene later in the day while his family strongly deny he was involved in the looting, claiming he was an innocent bystander. AS

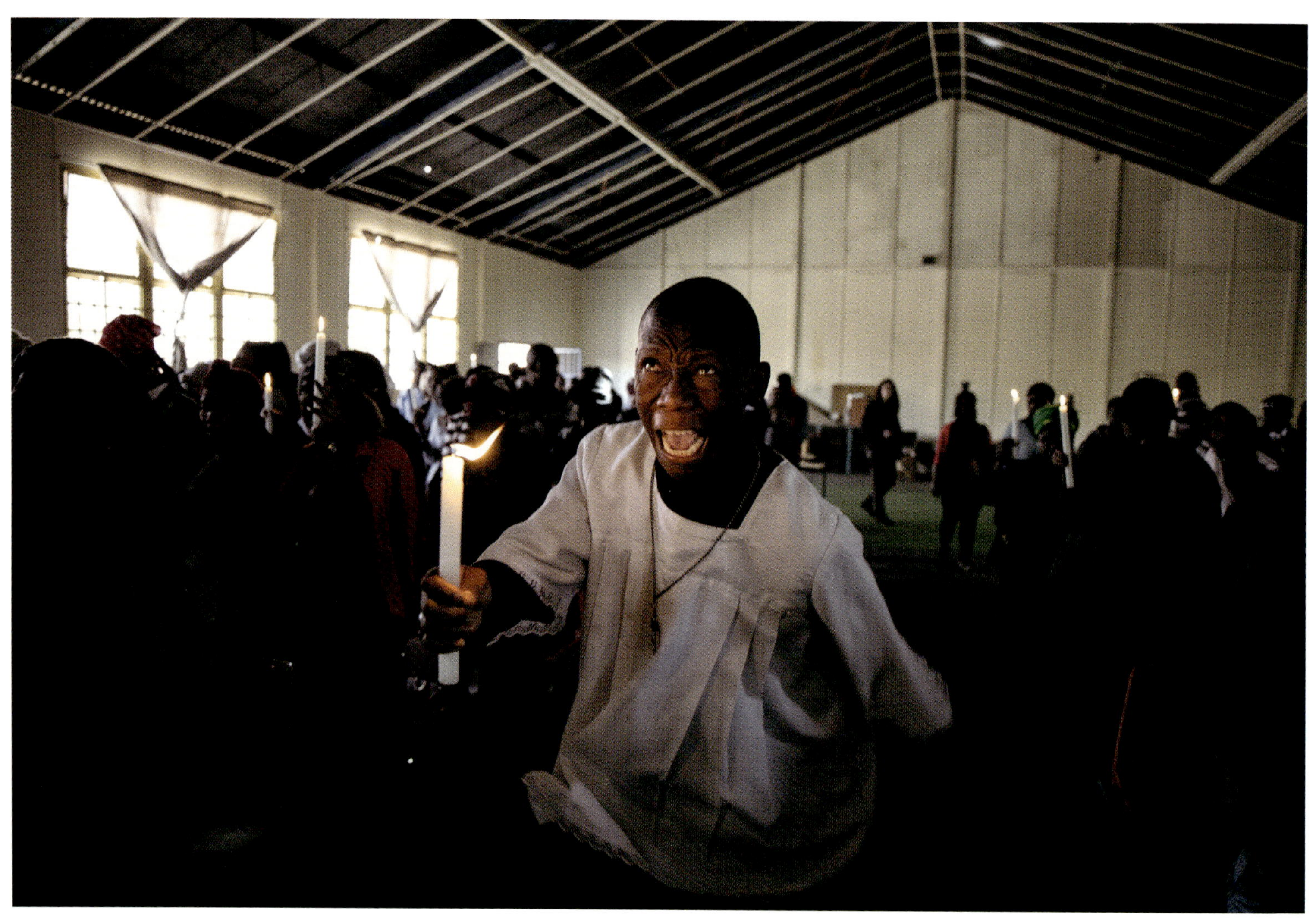

Reverand Omphemetse Dimo leads a memorial service in Coronationville on Johannesburg's West Rand for Isaac Sebaku who was killed during xenophobic unrest. A second South African, Karabo Ditire, was also killed in the area, allegedly by a stray bullet fired by a shopowner trying to protect his premises from looters. Ditire's family claim he had been washing his young daughter's clothing outside his shack when he was struck. AS

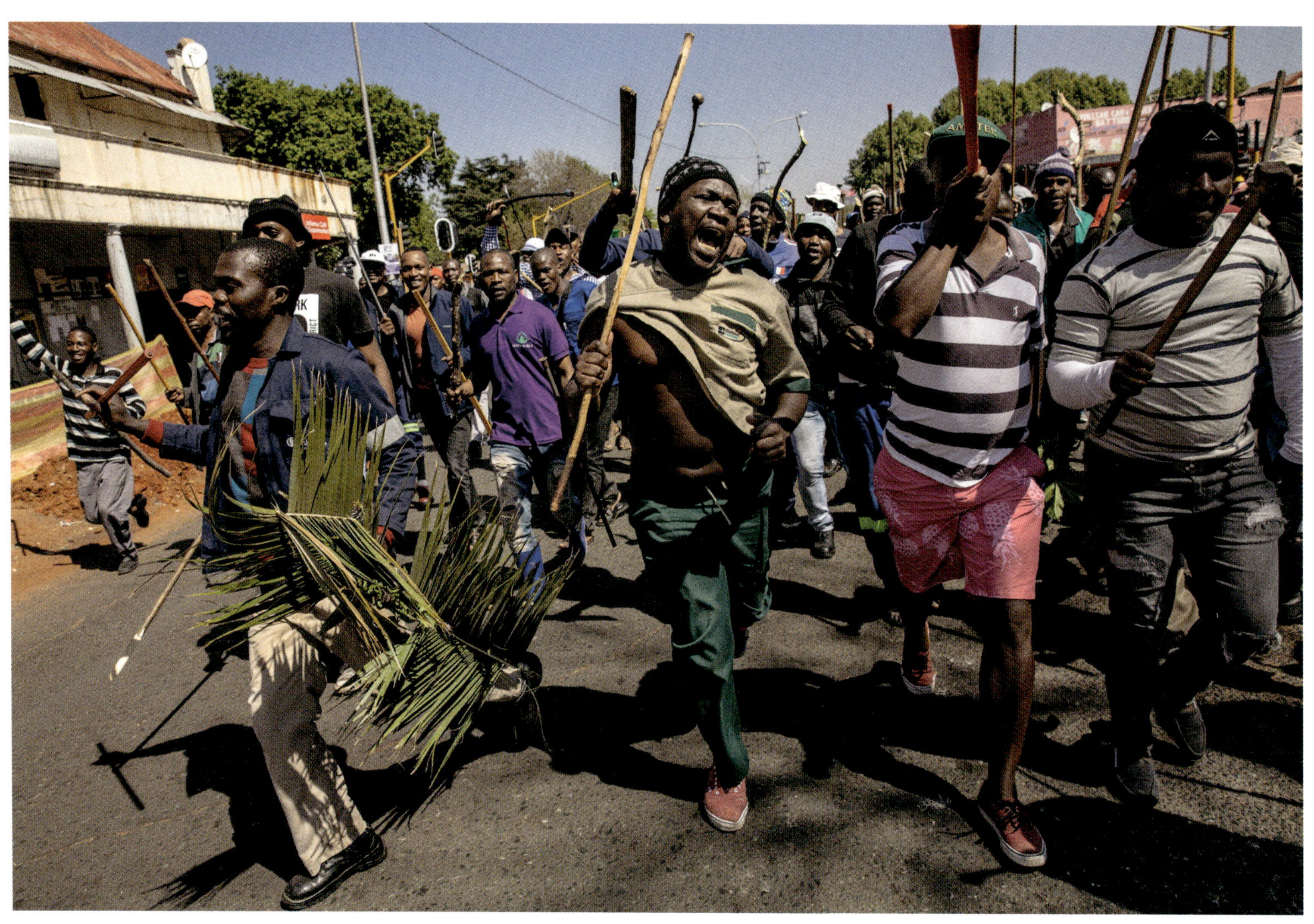

Hostel dwellers singing 'Foreigners must go, they must go back'
surge towards Murray Park in Malvern where IFP leader Mangosuthu
Buthelezi called for an end to xenophobic attacks. AS

Inside the anger

Jan Bornman

Sitting on a step near a rubbish bin inside the KwaMai-Mai Hostel and Traditional Market in Johannesburg, Zweli Ndaba admits he's feeling angry and frustrated, sentiments born out of numerous attempts to meet with Johannesburg Mayor Herman Mashaba, Gauteng Premier David Makhura, the national and provincial police, and other government departments.

For months in 2019, as chairperson of a group calling itself the Sisonke People's Forum, he had wanted to raise concerns about rising crime levels, unemployment, the lack of housing and the proliferation of drugs in communities. But after his pleas fell on deaf ears, Ndaba reached out to hostel dwellers and the All Truck Drivers Foundation (ATDF) to organise a national shutdown.

He claims the action was never meant to be xenophobic, but the grossly anti-migrant rhetoric that emerged from the violence in Gauteng in early September 2019 is irrefutable. As xenophobic attacks spread across the city, 12 lives were lost, livelihoods were destroyed, and hundreds of people displaced.

'I think no one is happy about seeing a South African person smoking drugs, sleeping under a bridge, not working,' says Ndaba. 'The people of South Africa, they showed their anger.

'We've been knocking on the doors of the government. We went twice to the office of Premier Makhura and they were just laughing at us. I ... phoned the [Police] Minister Bheki Cele. He wasn't answering ... I invited the police commissioner of Gauteng, Mr [Elias] Mawela, to a public meeting. He never even bothered to reply...'

So Ndaba created and circulated the flyer calling for the shutdown. It reads: 'Sisonke People's Forum ... invite all the residents of this country ... to come together as South Africans with one voice of ENOUGH IS ENOUGH, ON SELLING OF DRUGS, ON PROPERTY THEFT, AND ON OUR WORK TAKEN BY FOREIGN NATIONALS.'

It called for the blocking of access to communities and industrial areas 'until our voices is heard', concluding: 'South Africa for South Africans. This is not xenophobia but the truth.'

The Africa Diaspora Forum apparently handed over this and other flyers containing xenophobic messages to the police, days before violence broke out, but no action was taken.

After a week of violence, Cele scheduled an urgent imbizo with hostel dwellers, but cancelled it, citing other commitments. Instead, Mangosuthu Buthelezi, as the traditional prime minister to Zulu King Goodwill Zwelithini, agreed to meet with hostel dwellers at Murray Park in Malvern. Ndaba was among them.

Many of the men – angered by rising unemployment and inequality, and harbouring feelings of powerlessness arising from government officials ignoring their complaints – have been blamed for the violence and looting that spread across Gauteng.

Residents from the Wolhuter, George Goch, Denver and Cleveland men's hostels came to make their voices heard, hoping Buthelezi would accept their demands. Marching to the park, they sang: '*Awahambe amakwerekwere, awabuyele emuva.* [Foreigners must go, they must go back.]'

Buthelezi called for calm and condemned the violence. 'What we have seen in the past few days is unacceptable,' he said. 'The attacks on foreign nationals and their businesses are purely xenophobic.

'I understand the tensions, the complaints and the anger. I understand that there is validity to the complaints, on both sides. I also understand that wrongs have been committed by both sides. This has not come out of nowhere.'

While he was pleading for peace, the majority of the group, still jeering, got up and left the park, clearly dissatisfied with Buthelezi's stance. They were angry and resentful that Cele had not appeared. But they eventually came back, and when Buthelezi had finished, some of them took to the stage.

'People of South Africa,' said one man, 'there is only one thing that we have come for here today: *Kuzabakho uxolo mhla ugovernment lo usiphetheyo wathatha amaforeyna wawabeka lapho asuka khona* [There will only be peace when the government in charge of us deports all the foreigners back to their countries].'

Another man said: 'Shenge,[1] government must give the day when the foreigners will go to their countries...'

Yet another complained about housing. 'We, people of South Africa, don't have houses. The government has taken houses and given them to foreign nationals. We want to know when are they returning our houses,' he said.

After the meeting, the hostel dwellers marched down Jules Street, smashing windows and throwing rocks. As they got to Jeppestown, the violence escalated. The crowd splintered, heading into various parts of Johannesburg; and by night's end, two people had been killed, a number injured and a mosque petrol-bombed.

Siphiwe Mhlongo, chairperson of the hostel izinduna (headmen) in Gauteng, condemned the destruction and physical harm done, but cautioned against dismissing people's concerns because they had committed violence.

'Their concerns and complaints are that companies are taking advantage of foreign nationals. They are paying them a low salary and also in housing department, there are suspicions that they [foreigners] are buying houses. That's why people are delayed to be getting their houses,' he said.

'And thirdly, is the drugs. There is a belief

that drugs came with them. So that's the main three issues that are of great concern to our people,' Mhlongo said.

'We are condemning this violence. We want it to stop,' he said. '…[but] hostel residents are angry because they don't have answers.'

Mayor Mashaba's office confirmed they had received two separate pieces of correspondence from Ndaba and the Sisonke People's Forum wanting to raise concerns about drugs and employment in the city.

'…Owing to the nature of the issues he sought to discuss, and keeping in mind the need to secure a successful resolution thereof, a decision was taken to refer him to the SAPS and the Department of Home Affairs. Mr Ndaba was duly informed of this decision,' a spokesman said.

Both Commissioner Mawela and Premier Makhuru's offices were not able to confirm whether they had received meeting requests from Ndaba.

Ndaba asks: 'When they [politicians] say we need to live in harmony, what is the harmony they talk about? Because we are seeing a lot of countries just bunching into South Africa, sharing just that piece of the bread that South Africa has.'

1   Clan name for Buthelezi

This is an edited version of the original article first published by *New Frame*:
https://www.newframe.com/the-people-who-sparked-the-xenophobic-violence/

Jan Bornman is a journalist with *New Frame*.

Violence soon spread to Katlehong on the East Rand
where rioters blocked the streets with rocks to prevent
police access before ransacking shops in Sontonga
Mall. On the morning of 5 September, the bodies of
two people were found. One of them was a 35-year-old
father, Isaac Sithole, who had been beaten and burnt
alive in Mandela Section. Another resident said a baby
was also killed when rioters set fire to a shack; and in a
selfless act of remarkable bravery, South African George
'Sung Sung' Kwachana was killed as he tried to shield
a Shangaan-speaking woman from attack. Hundreds
of migrants fled the area, most of them seeking refuge
in shelters provided by the city of Ekurhuleni, which
ironically means 'place of peace' in Xitsonga.

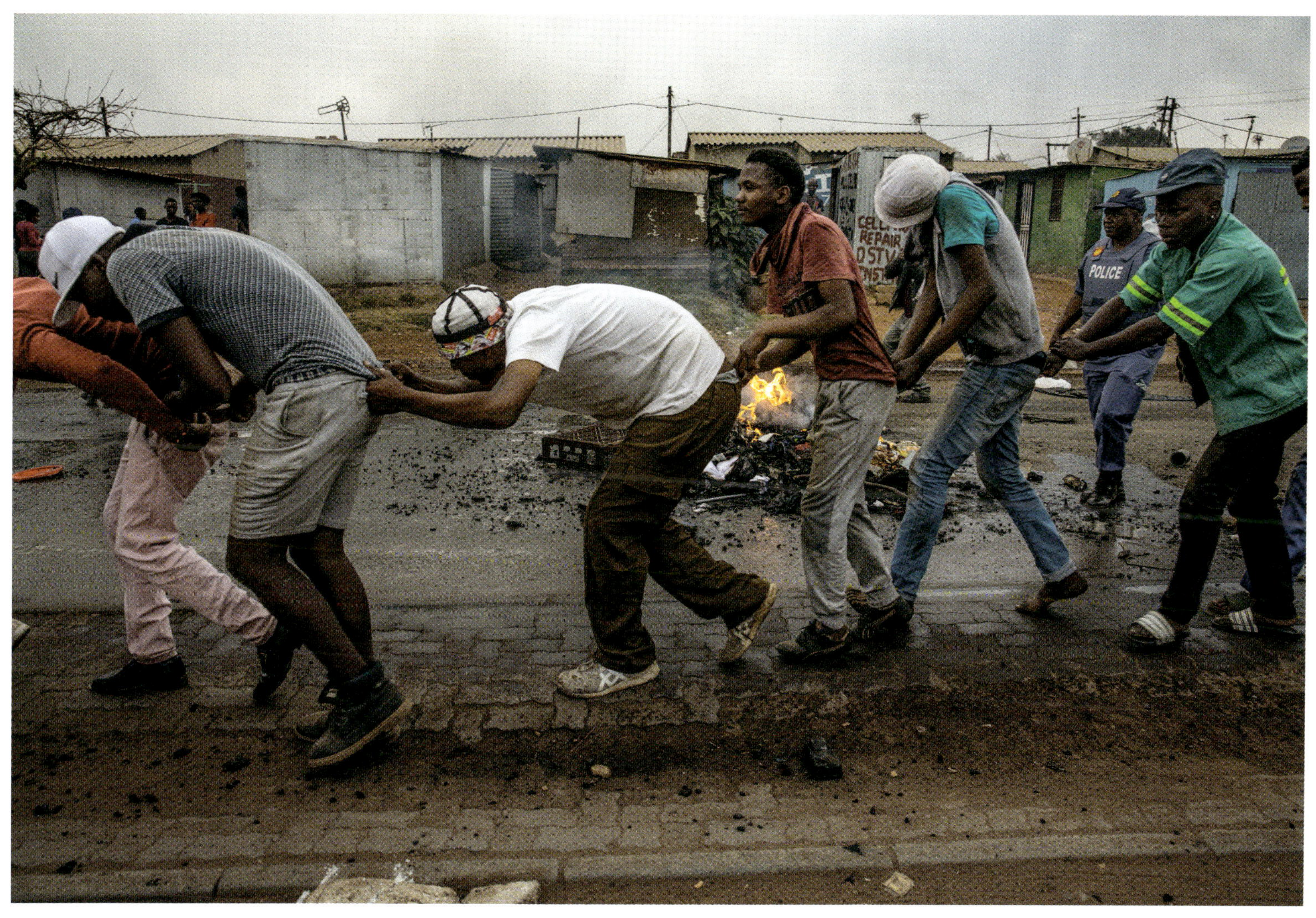

Police arrested 74 people in Katlehong during days of violence
in the township, which is considered one of the most poorly
served areas in Gauteng. AS

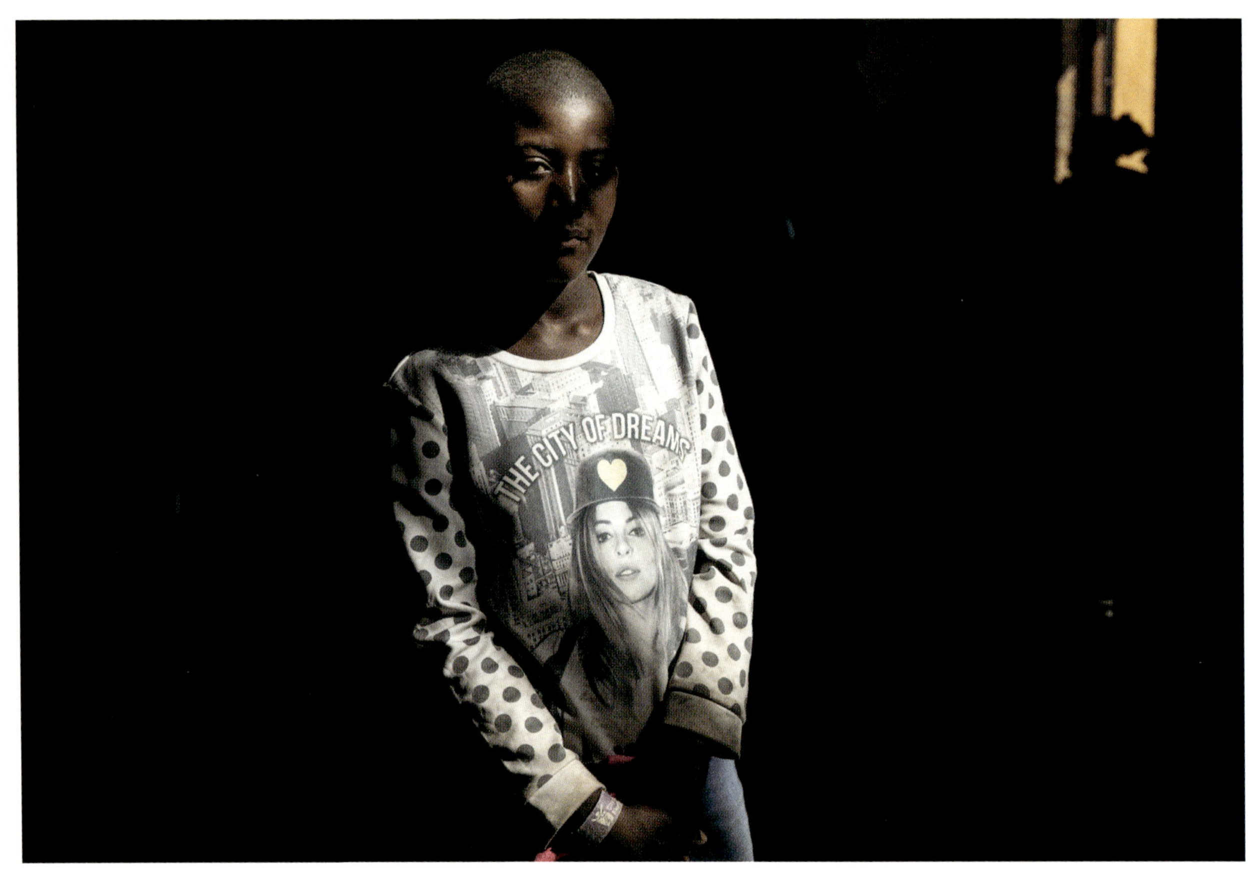

A young girl from Mpumalanga shelters in the D.H. Williams Hall in Katlehong, after she and her mother had been chased from their home because they speak Xitsonga. AS

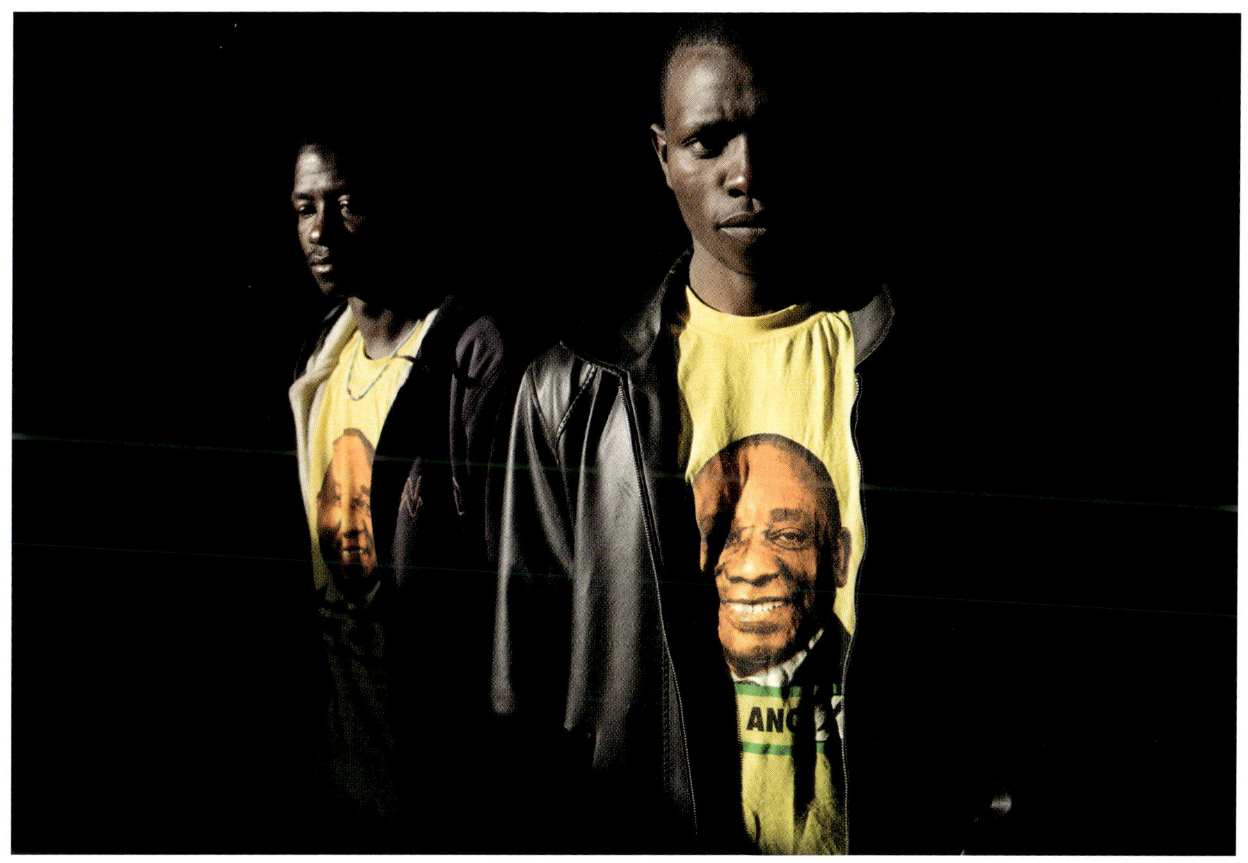

Displaced brothers wear T-shirts bearing the
face of President Cyril Ramaphosa. AS

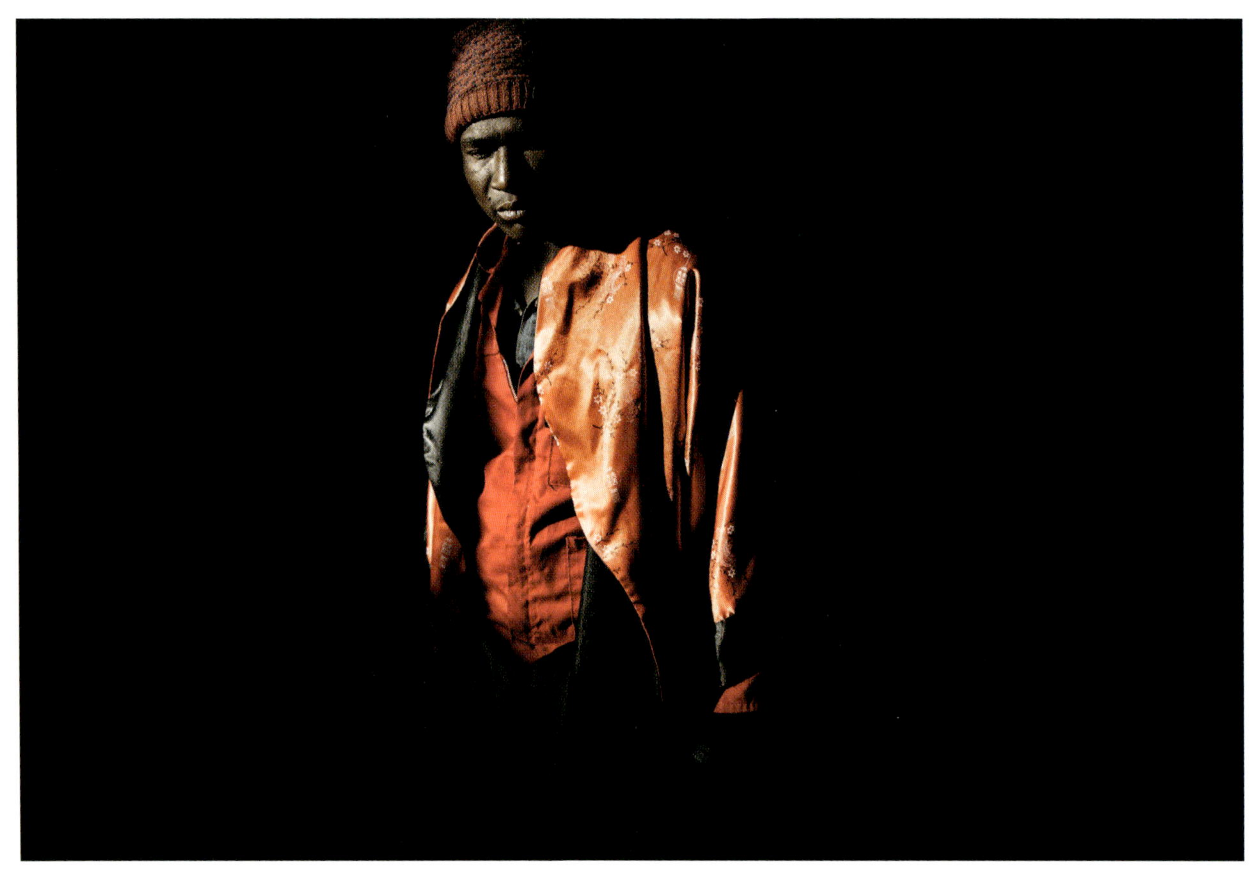

A refugee who was forced to abandon his home with little more
than the clothes on his back as xenophobic violence raged
through his community. AS

'He was running for his life but they got him. They beat him, they poured petrol over him and they burnt him, just because he was a foreigner.'

Lydia Chimbirimbiri
Widow of Isaac Sithole (*Saturday Star*, September 2019)

Bora Riziki was a teenager when she fled her
hometown of Uvira in the Democratic Republic of the
Congo to escape the violence there that saw both
her parents killed. Travelling on foot and by boat and
train, she reached the Western Cape where she met
her husband Rusiga. They settled in Delft on the
outskirts of Cape Town where they had two children,
Ibrahim and Amina. But violence found them again.
Rusiga was murdered in a car-jacking outside
their home; and a year later, her brother, who had
come to live with her, was murdered too. Bora was
referred to the local UNHCR office where her family's
vulnerability criteria qualified them for resettlement,
and France offered them a home. Although she was
apprehensive about the move, and sorry to leave her
friends and her husband's brother Biramba, Bora
was relieved to be leaving Delft.

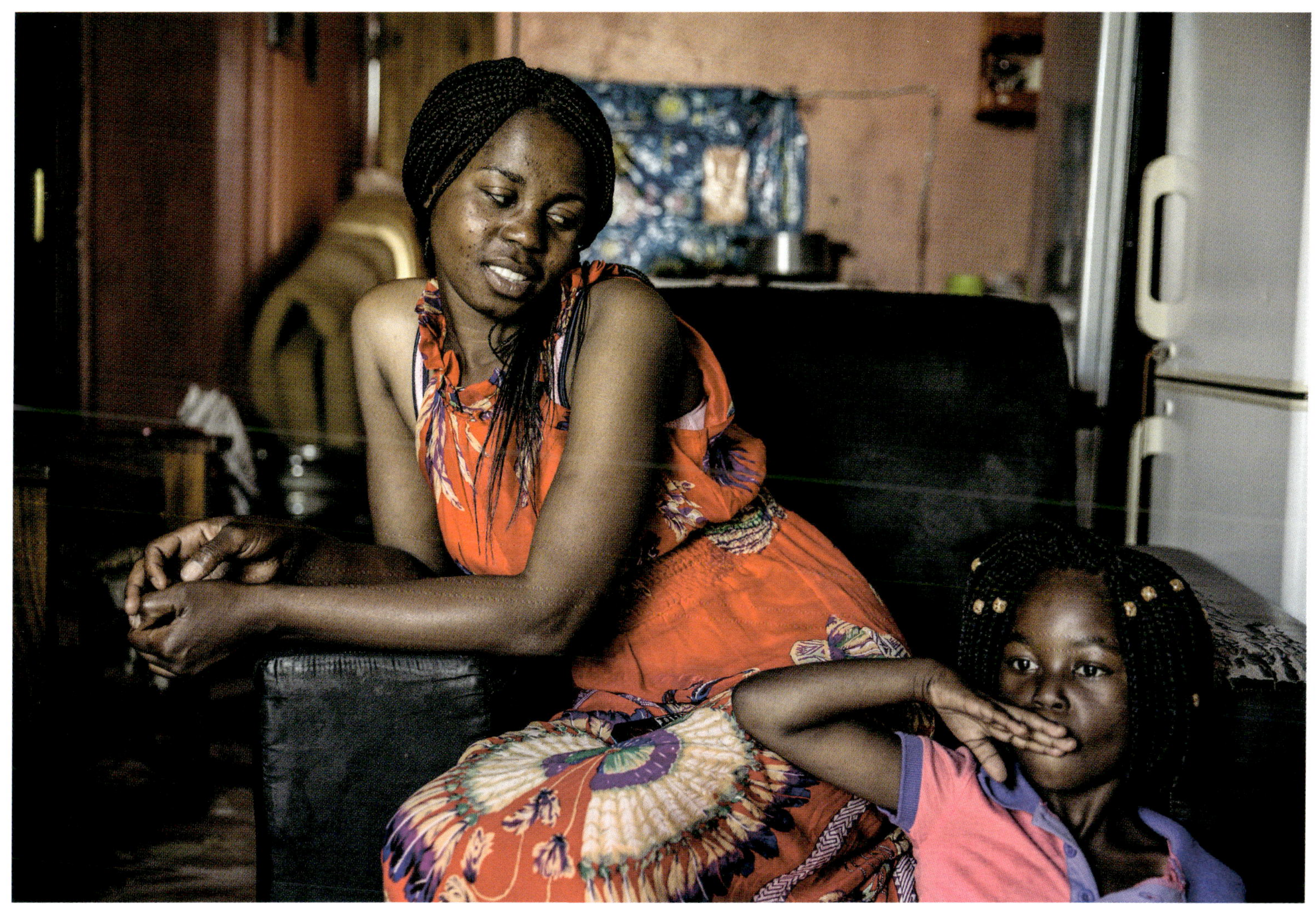

Bora and her daughter, Amina, during
their last days in Delft. JO

It's a big day and Ibrahim gets a haircut
from his Uncle Biramba. JO

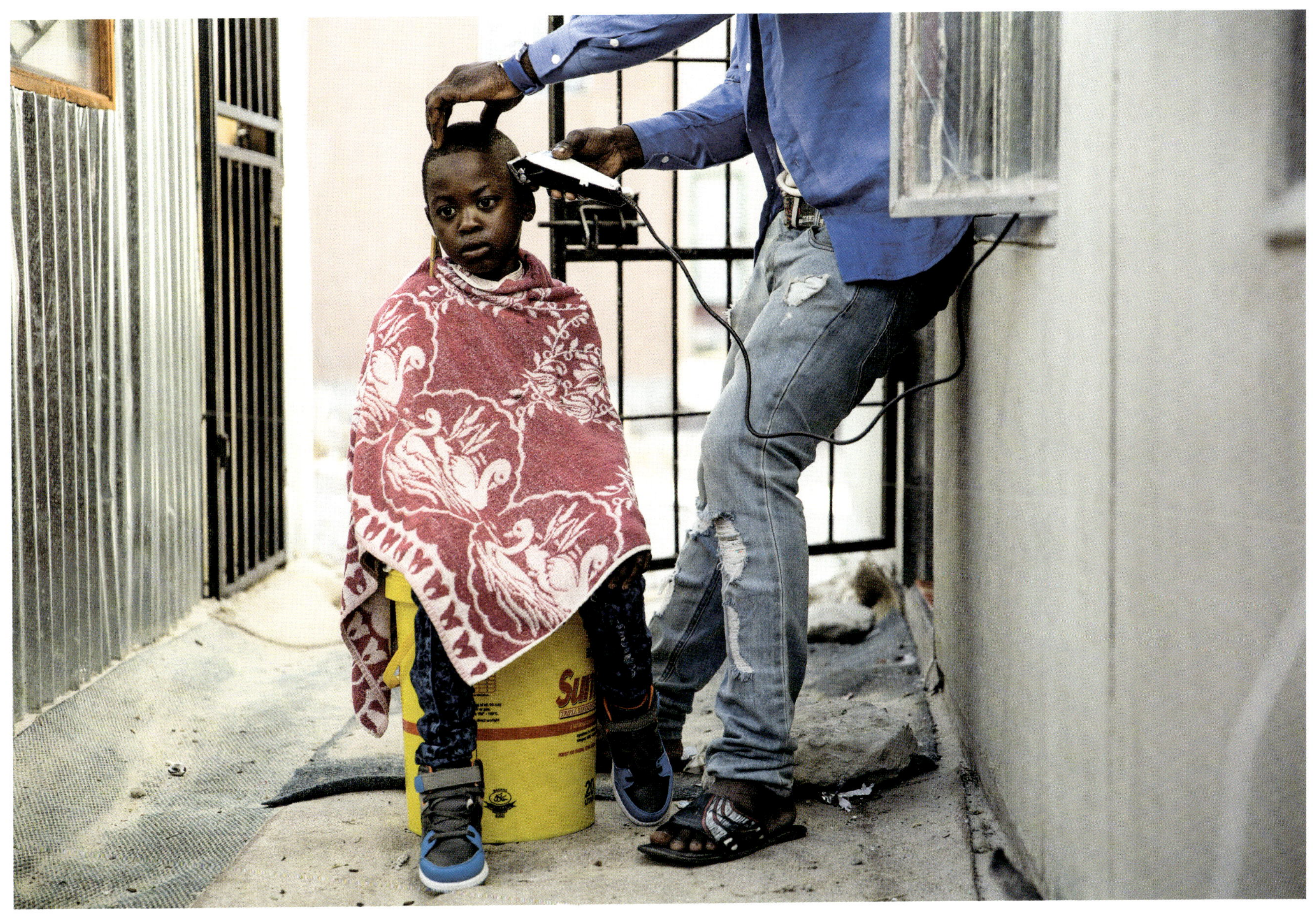

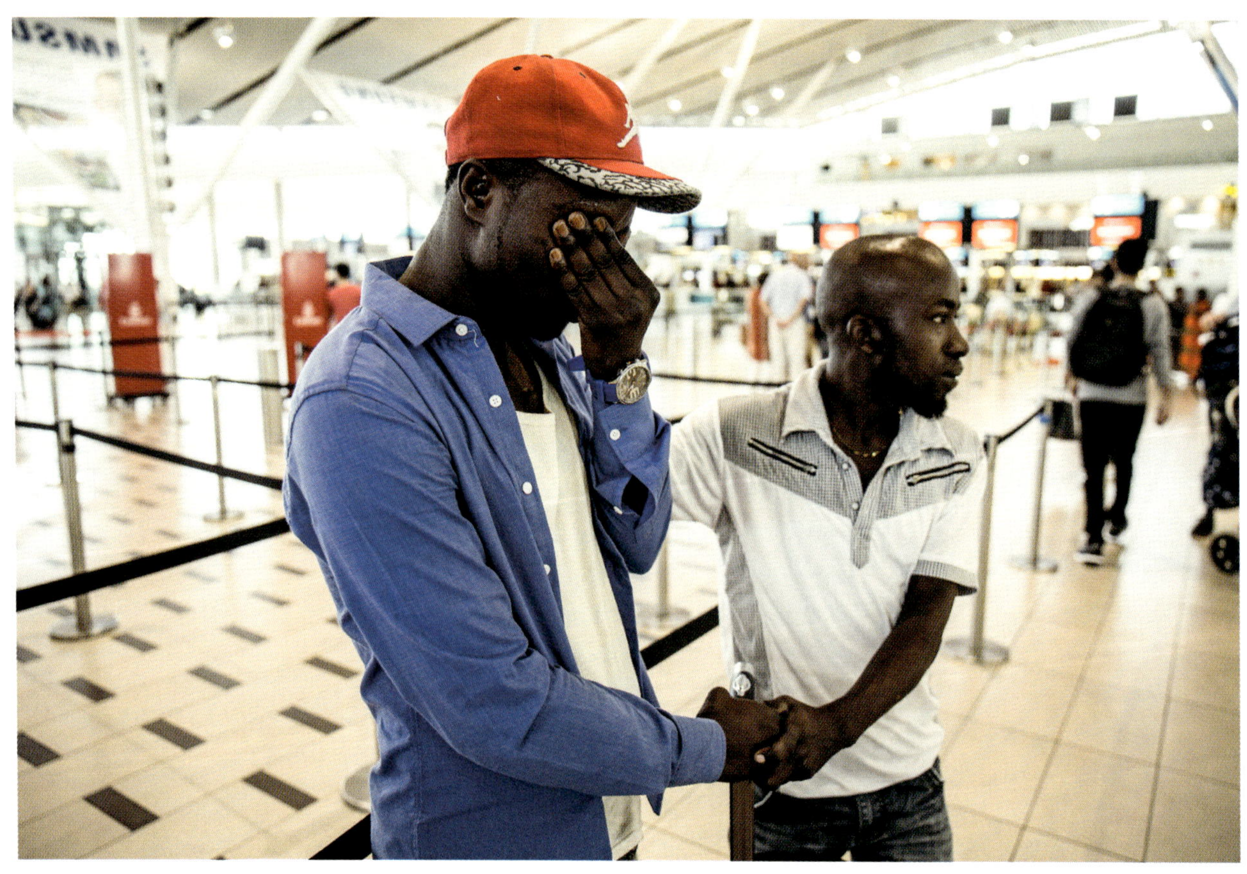

Uncle Biramba wept when Bora went through the
departure gate. He may never see her again. JO

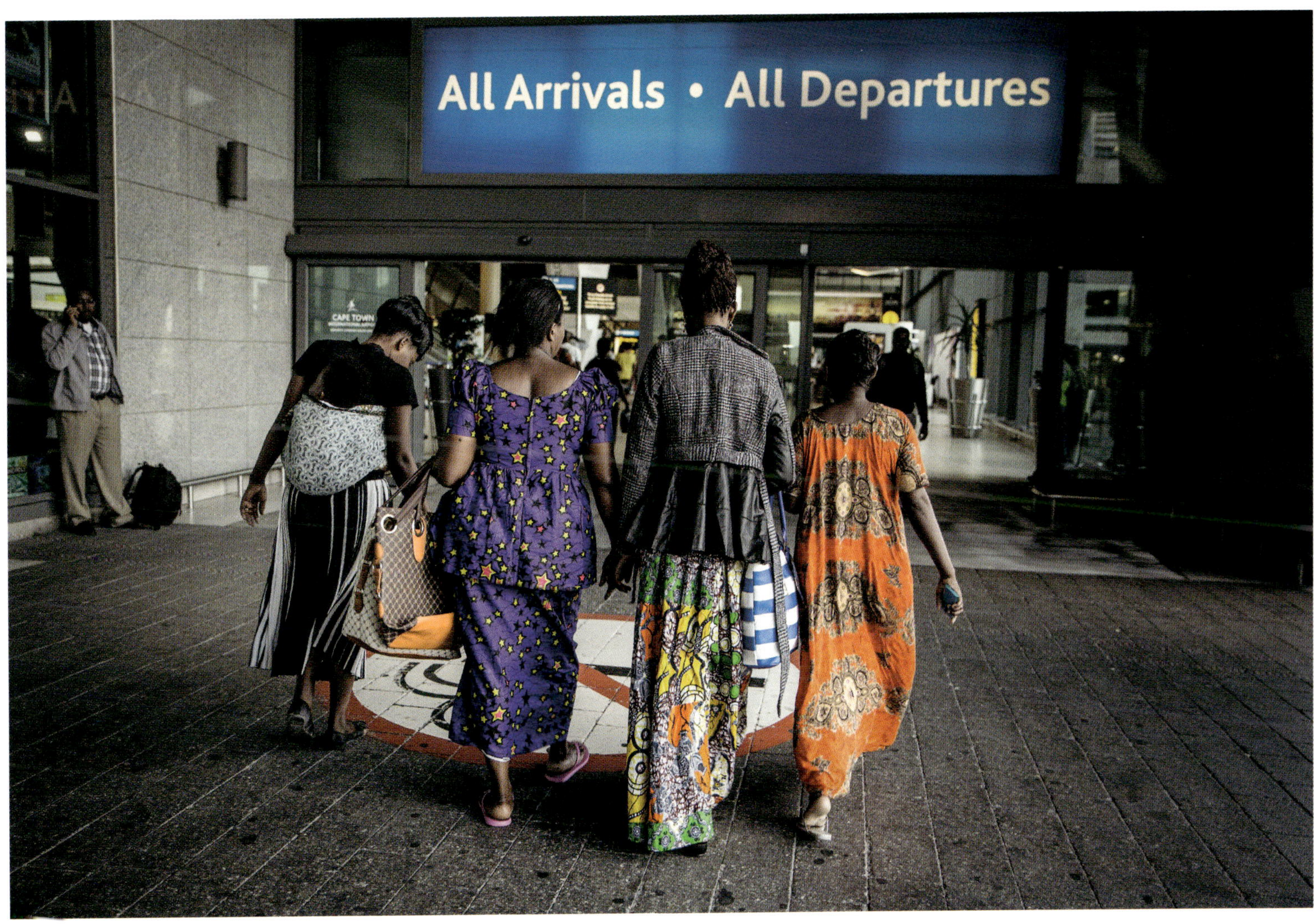

Friends escort Bora, second from right, to the airport to
say goodbye as she leaves to start her new life. JO

'I am a South African. I am Mozambican. I am Zambian, I am Zimbabwean, I am Malawian. I'm Swazi, I'm Sotho, I'm Tswana. I belong to any of the nations, not only all of Africa, but most specially in Southern Africa.'

Graça Machel
Memorial service for Emmanuel Sithole, April 2015

James Oatway is an independent South African photographer. Formerly the chief photographer and picture editor of the *Sunday Times*, he has covered many important stories in South Africa and abroad and has a special interest in telling under-reported stories in Africa. His work centres around themes of political and social inequality and people affected by conflict.

In 2018 his Red Ants project won the prestigious Visa d'or Feature Award at the Visa Pour l'image Photojournalism Festival in Perpignan, France.

On 18 April 2015, he photographed a fatal attack by South African men on Mozambican migrant Emmanuel Sithole. The images sparked outrage and made international headlines.

His work has received various international awards including multiple Pictures of the Year International (POYi) awards. In 2015 Oatway was named the South African Journalist of the Year. His work has been published internationally in *The Guardian*, *Stern*, *Internazionale*, *Le Monde*, *TIME*, *Harper's Magazine*, *Paris-Match*, *The New York Times*, *The Wall Street Journal*, *The LA Times* and others.

Oatway often works with humanitarian organisations such as UNICEF, UNHCR and Médecins Sans Frontières (Doctors Without Borders).

Alon Skuy was born and educated in Johannesburg, and studied photography at The Market Photo Workshop. He began work as a photographer for *The Star*, *Saturday Star* and the *Sunday Independent*, and later moved on to be chief photographer of *The Times* and *Sunday Times*.

Skuy's career has been defined by his depth and range as a news and documentary photographer, notably, his coverage of the 2012 Marikana massacre, the most lethal use of force by South African security forces against civilians since the Soweto riots of 1976.

In 2008, Skuy was awarded the Ruth First Fellowship at the University of the Witwatersrand, for which he produced the photographic essay 'Living Inside a Bridge'. He is the recipient of numerous local and international awards, including, among others, World Press Photo, as well as multiple honours in Pictures of the Year International, in which he was named Photographer of the Year, Local, in 2020.

Skuy has exhibited his work on xenophobia at the historic Constitution Hill, and a selection of his and Oatway's images remain on permanent exhibition at the Johannesburg Holocaust & Genocide Centre.

Acknowledgements

Thanks to the Johannesburg Holocaust & Genocide Centre for supporting our original exhibition, *Killing the Other*, which ultimately led to the production of this book. Thank you Kim and Tali Nates and Jordan Saltzman!

Thanks to Bridget Impey, Megan Mance, Lara Jacob and everyone at Jacana Media for seeing the importance of this work.

We are so thankful to have been able to work with the outstanding Gabrielle Guy on the design of this book. Gabrielle, thank you for your courage in dealing with this difficult material. Your inimitable vision and sensitive touch have resulted in a work of grace and dignity that we feel honours the people who appear on these pages.

Thank you to all the contributors, Professor Achille Mbembe, Dr Jean Pierre Misago, Koketso Moeti, Joao Silva, Justice Malala and Jan Bornman. Your words provide a critical background and much-needed context to this important issue and we value your individual contributions.

Thank you to the survivor on page 25 for bravely telling his story; to Phefumula Nyoni for recording it; to authors Shireen Hassim, Tawana Kupe and Eric Worby, and Veronica Klipp at Wits University Press, for letting us share it with our readers. We withheld the survivor's name for his own safety.

Special thanks to Justice Edwin Cameron for your powerful foreword. You remain a great South African treasure and a critical moral compass for our people.

And to Alexia Katsiginis for her infinite wisdom.

We are privileged to have worked with Robin Comley on this project. Thanks Robin for your invaluable advice, much-needed guidance and for dedicating so much of your time to this book. You are a true legend.

To our journalist colleagues out there covering this story: we are proud to work alongside you, and thank you for choosing not to look away.

To our editors at *The Times* and *Sunday Times*, who have supported us throughout.

Many thanks to Andreas Vlachakis and Lightfarm; and to Darren Jordan and the team at ABC Press.

Very special thanks to the Rosa Luxemburg Stiftung and Graham Pote for their generous support, without which this project would not have happened.

We are eternally thankful to our parents for always being there for us. And more than anyone, to our partners and children. Thank you for your love, patience and support. You are the ones who deal with the fallout. You see us at our worst and often pick us up when we fall. You quietly sacrifice so much. We could not do this without you. Thank you always.

Above all, our gratitude goes to the people that we photograph every day. Often you are at your most vulnerable. You share your most personal and often painful moments with us. We are cognisant of this and take the responsibility seriously. We respect you and we thank you.

— James and Alon

First published by Jacana Media (Pty) Ltd in 2020 in partnership with the Johannesburg Holocaust & Genocide Centre and Rosa Luxemburg Stiftung

10 Orange Street
Sunnyside
Auckland Park 2092
South Africa
+27 11 628 3200
www.jacana.co.za

© James Oatway and Alon Skuy, 2020

All rights reserved.

ISBN 978-1-4314-2978-3

Project consultant Robin Comley
Copy editing Megan Mance
Proof reading Lara Jacob
Design and layout Gabrielle Guy
Image repro Lightfarm

Printed and bound by ABC Press, Cape Town
Job no. 003682

See a complete list of Jacana titles at
www.jacana.co.za

For permission to use any part of this publication, please contact: brothersa2020@gmail.com

Although the names of many people in the images are known, at times it was decided not to identify them for their own safety. Those who are named gave their permission.

Sponsored by the Rosa Luxemburg Stiftung with funds of the Federal Ministry for Economic Cooperation and Development of the Federal Republic of Germany. This publication or parts of it can be used by others for free as long as they provide a proper reference to the original publication.

www.rosalux.co.za

Disclaimer: The views and opinions expressed by the authors or contributors do not necessarily represent those of the Rosa Luxemburg Stiftung.

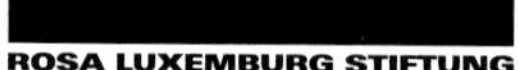

The Johannesburg Holocaust & Genocide Centre serves as a place of memory, education, dialogue and lessons for humanity. It focuses on human rights issues such as prejudice, racism, 'othering', antisemitism, homophobia and xenophobia. Conscious of the dangers of indifference, apathy and silence, the JHGC urges its visitors to be an active voice against instances of hate speech and related human rights violations in their own communities.

www.jhbholocaust.co.za

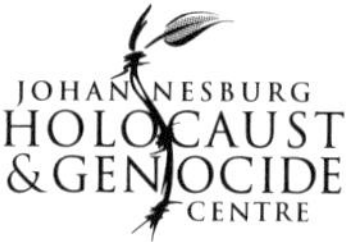

For further information please scan: